3X(7)10) 9110

D0393723

Divided
to the Vein

My parents' wedding, 1949.

Divided
to the Vein

A JOURNEY INTO
RACE AND FAMILY

Scott Minerbrook

Harcourt Brace & Company

NEW YORK / SAN DIEGO / LONDON

Library of Congress Cataloging-in-Publication Data
Minerbrook, Scott.
    Divided to the vein: a journey into race and family/Scott Minerbrook. — 1st ed.
        p.   cm.
    ISBN 0-15-193107-0
        1. Minerbrook, Scott.   2. Racially mixed people—United States—Biography.
3. United States—Race relations.   I. Title.
    E184.A1M538   1996
    973'.0496073'092—dc20   95-25099
    [B]

Text set in Electra
Designed by Kaelin Chappell
Printed in the United States of America
First edition
A B C D E

I who am poisoned with the blood of both,
Where shall I turn, divided to the vein?

—DEREK WALCOTT

Contents

Publisher's Note

This book is a factual account of the author's family and personal history, including descriptions of events in his life, and reports of his conversations and interviews with people described in the book. It also includes the author's personal observations and opinions.

In some cases, fictional names have been used. Each fictional name is designated by an asterisk when it first appears in the text.

Ocieola (right) with her mother and brother.

Ocieola's mother, Nancy Barnette.

ONE / Unacceptable Losses

Man is born to trouble as the sparks fly upward.

—BOOK OF JOB

If someone had asked me what the wind was saying as it whistled through the open window of my car that August afternoon, I would have said it was whispering that I should not be afraid. But I was, deep down in the bone. The very air, so hot and damp as it mingled with the scents of the Mississippi River and the sweet, fertile earth, seemed saturated with the bitter tastes of terror and dread.

I was driving north, past the truck stops, service stations, and one-night motels of West Memphis, Arkansas, to a place I had specifically been warned not to visit. "They carry guns there," my mother had said, and she should have known, since she was from this country. "You might wind up in a ditch." I imagined myself dead—not a comforting thought, but a good preparation. Coming from her, the thought only made me angrier, and the taste of that anger was in the air, too. Anger is the bitter chemical of grievance, and it carried me forward on a rush of adrenaline. But the wind whispered something wise: that this was the land of my ancestors, those Indian and white men and women whose names had echoed in my head for years. It belonged to me more than I'd ever known or cared to admit. As much as I'd ever wanted anything, I wanted to see the place that had haunted me for most of my life.

Mine is the intermingled blood of African ancestors, of Scots-Irish farmers who mixed their blood with the blood of Cherokee survivors of the Trail of Tears dispersal, of Choctaw who mixed their blood with the blood of slaves and traveled north to Chicago. Their lives formed the divided root of my childhood; their notions of race and family coursed through the veins of my expectations, hopes, and dreams. My race and my family were always at odds. Ocieola, whom I was now traveling to see, was my mother's mother, but my grandmother in name only. I had never claimed Ocieola and she had never claimed me. Ocieola was part of my family but not my race. My father is black. My mother is white. And the meaning of the word "family" fell into the rushing waters between the two. Blood was not thicker than these racialized waters. I grew up well aware that if all my relatives were brought together in one room, there would be a race riot. Somebody would call someone else a name, and there would be blood on the walls. The violence of race hate has shaped the divided ground of my soul. Too dark to be white, too light to be black, I've always known that my family's racial quarrels have done me little good.

And now I was on my way to see the white woman who had excluded me from her life simply because my skin wasn't the same color as hers, because my father's skin wasn't the right color. Or so it had always seemed to me as a child. But now I wanted to understand all this in a way that was different from my childhood understanding. I believed that if I saw Ocieola face to face, things would make sense. In some part of myself, I knew that this would be a departure as much for her as for me. It felt wrong to be going to see her. This visit violated the cardinal rules of my racial upbringing: stay away; keep your distance; do not feel the loss. And yet the loss of family *had* haunted me. It felt familiar, and so did the anger I had stored up over the years. Anger and rage were my old friends, surging in my blood as I drove and protecting me from what felt like a violent, warring, foreign land. I passed West Memphis's greyhound racetrack, entered a countryside of low open fields, and sped along the filthy highway going north to where my grandmother lived, in a tiny town called Caruthersville, Missouri.

The distance between us was as palpable as the earth. For that reason, among others, this trip had never seemed possible to me before. I measured it in years and decades, in the thousands of miles between my home in the East and her home here in the South. Everything I'd ever learned confirmed this distance. But now something had changed. Over the years, my rage had become a wall. It was the sweet substance of my defense. But I had to allow that it had clouded my sight. It had limited my possibilities as a human being. I'd never faced up to this before. If the ground was divided, it was partly because of my acceptance of the idea of "family" as something that could be sacrificed to my racial bitterness. Family became an acceptable loss. Racial experience caused deep separations and disjunctions. Mom's family seemed to justify its abandonment of us on racial grounds: race was its own justification. "Family" was cut off from blood ties, from kinship, and certainly from any possibility of love.

If the word "family" meant anything to me, its meaning came from the stories my mother told of her people. They were wonderful stories, even if over time their meaning turned bitter. This was how they began: More than a century ago, some Scots-Irish and French immigrants traveled in covered wagons from the western Tennessee lake and hill country and crossed the Mississippi to settle in southeast Missouri. They were farmers named Hinchy, Smith, Darnell, Barnette. After the death of his first wife, my great-grandfather Charles Smith had married an Indian woman named Lilah Luthenia

Darnell, a full-blooded Cherokee. On Ocieola's side, her mother, Nancy Barnette, was also a Cherokee, and pictures of them all have burned their faces into my mind. They were people who gave their lives to the earth, and under their care this whole region of the northern Mississippi delta, once mostly swamplands, became a cotton-farming center. They also became immersed in the racial customs of the area, and at length they disavowed their part in the pioneer mixing of blood. I wondered if Ocieola would have anything to say about her own mixed heritage. Aware of hers, how could she reject mine?

Soon the family's fates were bound up with the land. They cleared it of all trees so they could plant the fields in long, unbroken rows, and in summer the land blazed forth, white and potent, and possessed them down to the bone. Harvest meant money. It meant that the cash registers in Caruthersville and Hayti and Cooter and Brasher and Shade and Braggadocio and Shake Rag and Cotton Plant rang like music. The stores in Caruthersville remained open at night until the last customer had left the streets and gone into one of the gaming houses, where gamblers like my grandfather Clarence took their money and came out either rich or broke. The cotton gins thrummed and the Memphis-bound cotton wagons squealed, and the land boosted men's fortunes with more cotton, and more money. Harry Truman liked to gamble in Caruthersville. He liked the summer horse races and the life "behind the seawall," as the rough part of Caruthersville was called. He would stay in the town's main hotel and slip out to gamble all night long.

I knew all this from my mother's stories, and I tried to forget them but out of bitterness, they had already claimed part of my imagination. My mother said her relatives had founded a town called Hinchy Switch. Maybe it had never happened. But I, a boy longing to know her people, believed it did.

There were also stories of her childhood, of how she and her brother would scramble up the levee built to keep the river from flooding the fields and paint pictures of the forests on the river-banks beyond. Some of my earliest memories, growing up in Chicago, were of looking at these watercolors of the forests across the

Mississippi and watching my mother's face soften when she showed them to me.

These were the boundaries of my childhood. I know now that her stories kindled in me the simple need for acceptance. This sense of acceptance is the core that binds the past to the future. Lacking this acceptance from Mom's family meant that I was missing the part of myself that identified with those simple Mississippi River folk. No amount of accomplishment or pride had ever been enough to fill the void that this lack of half a family had created. I had tried to reason it out this way: Why should I expect anything different? But I wasn't satisfied. Their distance was something I could not shake. I couldn't pray it away. I couldn't run away from it, though I tried. I was reminded of it daily in my mother herself. Somehow she belonged to them, and my relationship to her was tainted by her family's racial distance.

As a boy, I wondered if the distance of years was something I was personally responsible for. Surely, I thought, it was. I never told my mother this. She had sorrows enough of her own. I felt guilty in a way I couldn't name. I wanted to love these white people, but their rejection turned that childhood dream into hate.

Their lives and mine were separated also by words. Words that said everything I needed to know.

The first time I heard the word "nigger" was during a visit with my mother's family. As a child, I was taken to see Ocieola and my mother's father, Clarence, in St. Louis, where they had moved temporarily. I would see Ocieola only two times that I can remember, and this first time I was five. My mother, then somewhat of an innocent in racial matters, had brought my brother Mark and me to stay with her people while she worked out an alternative to remaining with my father, Alan. They'd had several scrapes in their life together in Chicago, but this one was so serious that she had left him, it looked like, for good.

My memory of that trip is of a family of angry-looking white women who didn't seem to be anything other than angry. There was no joy in them when they looked at me. Mark and I were routinely pushed outside to play, which was fine with us. We played for hours on the trolley tracks, placing pennies on the steel rails and watching from a foot or two away as the trolleys ran them over. I loved it when the wheels rolled over and flattened the coins, distorting the faces and letters and squashing "*e pluribus unum*" out of shape. Finally a conductor hopped off the car and walked us to the door of the house. Ocieola was in the middle of watching "Queen for a Day" when she answered the door.

"Are these your children?" the conductor asked.

"No. But I'm taking care of them," she said. I remember the startled expression on her face.

During the same visit, Clarence got angry with us for some mischief and chased us around the house with a belt, calling us "little niggers." We just laughed and thought it was a fun game. Many years later, I learned that on this trip Clarence had demanded that Mom put both of us up for adoption. She couldn't raise Negro children, he said. Face facts, he told her. We weren't white, and she couldn't raise us as white children. Having Negro children would only slow her down. She returned to Chicago after that. That's what her life was about: scrambling for safety in an abusive and deeply racist family whose feelings for her had changed beyond anything she had thought was possible.

But even on that trip there were small acts of kindness. One day I must have said something that vexed Mark, because he began chasing me around with a sharp stick. He finally hit me with it and opened a small hole in my scalp. I remember how Ocieola dabbed my wound, and how the white towel came away red.

Later, my mother's brother, Huddie,* sat me on his lap while someone told the story of how Clarence learned about his daughter's marriage to my father. It seemed that Clarence and a friend of the family were sitting in the bleachers at a baseball game in Caruthersville when Clarence was asked if he'd heard the news about his daughter LaVerne. No, Clarence replied, he hadn't heard any news.

"Well," the man said, "she's been married."

"That right?" Clarence said. "Who to?"

"To a nigger."

Hearing this, Clarence threw up.

Everyone laughed at this story, and, seeing that everyone else was laughing, I laughed, too.

Many years later, I was to hear this story again from Betty Lou,* my mother's youngest sister, who was then living in a suburb of St. Louis. Betty Lou would claim that she, too, had known nothing of my mother's marriage to my father. My mother has always insisted this was just a pose, one of many her family had used to cover up their embarrassment at her leaving home and venturing out into a world that none of them could fathom.

I don't know exactly when I realized that my mother's memories made me uncomfortable. One day she told me that her first name wasn't really LaVerne. Back home, she said, her name was Audilee. I can't remember exactly why, but I had the feeling that something I couldn't put into words had been snatched away.

Something claimed her. It was love. Her family loved her, but they could not love me. I was a nigger to them. They could not love my older brother, Mark, or my younger brother, Michael, who was still an infant. They were niggers, too. Audilee belonged to the fields where those people of hers lived, people who felt less than nothing for me. She was divided from herself, and remembering those stories was her way of clinging to her loss. Even though I truly loved the stories she told, they were fragments of her past, and they didn't fit in with my life. I was a city boy, and I knew nothing about flooded cotton fields. The stories began to seem more and more quaint, more and more distant from my reality. My being part of her family felt like dying. Some part of me was already dead, rageful, afraid.

I used to have trouble in school because I didn't like the white people who taught me. They reminded me of everything I felt about my mother's family. I hated the principals because they reminded me of Ocieola and Clarence. By then, my inner sentences were coming together violently around words of my own: her people had already become "those white people," "crackers," "those peckerwoods," "those sons of bitches." I was ashamed of any trace of them in my face, in my thoughts. But they were in both places, and I knew I would never lose them. So I tried to forget. Increasingly, whenever Mom got lonely for her people "out there," she would play Ray Charles records, loud. She would listen to him singing about the "old cotton fields at home . . . down in Lou'siana just about a mile from Texarkana," and, Jesus, it burned me! Dad would get burned also. He'd tell her to turn the music off. He'd tell her that her family wasn't anything but a bunch of hicks and Okies. It made me glad to hear him say such things. If they rejected me, I was learning to reject them, too.

The Reverend Martin Luther King, Jr., in accepting the Nobel Peace Prize, said that despair was no answer to the ambiguities of history. It was a long time before I understood that for me race was a channel of despair that began with the obliteration of my mother's family. I was meeting that despair by reversing all those racial stereotypes that people seemed to believe in like fragments of the Holy Rood. I thought my white kin, mired in the Missouri earth, with their faith and beliefs hanging steadfast to the hopes their white skin had seeded in them, were weak, unworthy, and afraid.

I poured all the love and longing I'd ever had for Mom's people into my father's family instead. If her people were dead to me, his were vibrantly alive. Just as those others had cast me out because of the color of my skin, Dad's people brought me in. I felt as though I belonged to them. They were Chicagoans. They were proud of their race. Their boundaries did not exclude me even though my mother was white. Much later I saw just how far I truly was outside their kingdom of race, too, but as a boy I didn't want to see that. It made me feel less like an orphan to believe that just when my mother's people were becoming more and more deeply rooted in the farmlands of Caruthersville, Dad's folk were trying to lift themselves above the mean streets of Chicago. If Mom's people prided themselves on their fears, Dad's folk prided themselves on their courage. If a child must choose its identity—and in America everything depends on this choice—I chose the example of my father and his people gladly. I wasn't a stranger to *them*. They didn't hate me because of the color of my skin.

All this came back to me as I looked off to the side of the north-ward-coiling highway and saw the narrow back roads, now overgrown with weeds. The old highway paralleled the interstate, and I thought about how, in my mother's day, these roads had cut her people off from the future and bound them to their dream kingdom of racial supremacy. She had escaped from this place. It made me feel better to think so. Her escape, though never complete, at least distinguished her as a person who knew how to fight her family's bigotry and fears.

But it was my father's family, whose experience of racial exclusion ran so deep, that I took heart from now. I knew that if I was to be free I would have to embrace these others I'd come to hate; I couldn't love myself if I hated my own flesh and blood. And the only way I could ever be whole was to try to bind my broken past. My father's people had taught me that to choose hate was to choose despair—a mistake I'd made my whole life. I wanted so badly to be rid of that hate now. Ahead of me was an unresolved love, and I didn't know if I was strong enough to let it enter my life.

I remembered that I hadn't seen Ocieola since she paid a short visit to our family twenty-three years ago. I'd lost touch with her as she moved from St. Louis back to Caruthersville and then to the nursing home I was on my way to visit now.

The truth is that I wouldn't be going to see her if it weren't for an exchange of letters with her which had been initiated by my brother Mark a few weeks earlier.

Mark was now a physician, and a gentleman with a life as rooted as my own. At the time, he was shifting from the practice of oncology to specialize in heart and thoracic care. I had always figured that facing his own ghosts of racial self-mortification probably had a lot to do with his becoming a healer.

I found out from my mother, after the fact, that Mark had written to Ocieola to ask if the two of them could visit her. Mark and I had never discussed our feelings about Mom's family, so his effort to contact this woman who had been so deeply separated from us caught me by surprise. Why did he need her permission for a visit? It was a polite thing to do, but I didn't feel Ocieola deserved any such courtesy. But Mark is far more careful than I am in such matters—political nuance is essential to the work of a cancer specialist. My younger brothers, Mike and John, agreed that it was odd for Mark to be offering an olive branch that undoubtedly would only be returned with bitterness.

I also learned that Mom had sent Ocieola some pictures of me and my family. All were returned in Ocieola's letter of reply. My mother had sent the pictures without telling me, and I was incensed not only by this but by Ocieola's reply. After mentioning briefly how unhappy she was in the nursing home, she wrote, "Please don't come and see us. We're too prejudist [sic]. And besides, you wouldn't like us anyway. I want to keep things as they are."

I was almost forty. Ocieola's letter made me feel that there was no time to waste in making a journey to Caruthersville. She might die before I ever got the chance to speak with her or to understand her point of view.

Mark gave up his idea of a trip. But for me, the letter only tore open old wounds. There were no words to explain why she had returned the pictures. Mom was just as puzzled by Ocieola's gesture as I was, and just as angered. In the most secret part of myself, the part that could hardly admit how much I'd missed Ocieola's presence in my life, the part that knew that no amount of denial or accusation or anger could ever fill the well of sorrow her absence had created, I was deeply hurt. This was confirmation of the racial prejudice that had segregated us all out of her life. It took me two days to calm down enough to decide whether or not I should respond. Somehow this destructive family drama had to end. Mark, in his sage way, articulated against my excess of passion. He reminded me of what the philosopher Aristotle noted about anger: anyone can be angry. But "to be angry with the right person, to the right degree, at the right time, for the right reason, and in the right way" is not easy.

Here, in a single letter, written so casually by a woman who was probably only a few years away from death, was the echo of all the words and all the crushing silence from my mother's family. This, to me, was living proof of the divided emotional ground of my childhood.

There are many kinds of ghosts in the world: haints, sprites, spooks and specters, phantasms, shades, apparitions, wraiths, bogeymen, bugaboos, and bêtes noires. I'd become a ghost to Ocieola. And she'd become demonic to me, too. It was not a role I would have chosen for myself, but one that my family's experience of racial division had chosen for me. This was what I'd lost across the dividing line of decades: we'd become far more than strangers to one another, and because I'd never been able to develop the part of my personality that might have blossomed by knowing my white relatives, I'd become something less to myself. There was still some part of myself I didn't even know. None of us had learned what to call this except racial disorientation. But, in fact, it had no name. Race was only its illusory name. Something much more complex was always at work in the flow of emotions, and we didn't have the language to describe it. Not yet.

I recognized that I'd lost much of the tenderness in myself in resentment toward my own flesh and blood, justifying my anger on the grounds of a racial hallucination that had shaped my life. This had to change. I was as much to blame as they were for nurturing it for so long. Hating Ocieola for what she'd never been, I'd learned to construct a defensive self-image that sealed off the possibilities of sympathy and love. I knew as an adult what I hadn't known as a child: that anger obscures more than it clarifies. There was so much about Ocieola I simply didn't know.

After a week of confusion about what to do, I decided to contact Ocieola by phone, to see if I could feel my way through this tight knot of pain. I would ask her why she'd contented herself with such a small world when the world could have been so much bigger if we had only been able to reconcile our visions. I think I underestimated her will. I got her telephone number from my mother and called her at the nursing home.

"Ocieola?" There was a long pause.

"Yes," said a voice that seemed heavy with sleep. "Who is this?" Her voice was suddenly clearer now, almost afraid.

"This is Scott. Your grandson Scott." The words felt brittle and terribly misplaced in my mouth. It was as though by speaking this simple truth I was exposing myself, naked, for the first time in my life. It made me suck in my breath.

"Who?" she said. "I don't know no . . . Who?"

I told her again who I was. I added, "Your daughter LaVerne's son."

"Oh," she said, offhanded and disappointed. "What do *you* want?"

The voice that only a moment before had sounded drowsy was crackling awake now, almost indignant, the voice of a southern white lady. That voice said I'd done something wrong, something indecent and shameful, by calling her.

I told her I wanted to know why she'd sent back the pictures of my children.

"Well," she said, "you know how it is." She let her voice drip into the void.

Actually, I didn't. I thought I did at one time. But now it all seemed part of a tired drama called "race." I badly wanted to be finished with all the posturing, all the false etiquette of racial conduct, in favor of simple human contact.

"I just want to leave things as they are," she said. "Besides, I don't think you'd like us anyway."

"What does that mean?" I was surprised at the anger in my voice. I think that in that moment I just wanted her to say the rest of it: because you are black.

"I think you know exactly what I mean," she said.

There was no love, no caring, no remorse, not even a feeling of consequence—of another opportunity missed. There was only a mounting irritation. Why was I confusing her with the real solution to my needs, which had nothing to do with her? Why couldn't I face the simple reality that at no point had her life touched mine? I felt like a child again. But beneath the anger, all the child wants is a simple acknowledgment as a human being. For me, the absence of this was the central injury of race. The indignity of what was happening, which summarized much of my life as well as hers, should have made me hang up the phone. But I couldn't. I felt I'd already given up too much ground, had given up too easily before.

"I have to go now," she said, and hung up.

I called right back. There was something hot rising in my stomach, something I was feeling in spite of my urge to suppress it.

"Hello?"

"It's me, Ocie. We seem to have been disconnected."

"No, Scotty."

Her use of this familiar name brought back warm memories of her brief visit with us in 1968. But just as suddenly as she spoke my name, her memories seemed to chill into a rebuke that threw me off center. She laid on a thick Caruthersville accent, the kind I'd heard my mother ridicule when she wanted to show us her anger toward her family.

"You cain't come heyah. I want to leave things just the way they orh."

When I said something to the effect that she couldn't possibly be serious, she simply repeated herself.

"Your visit would be just impossible. It would be just too much trouble. I have to go now," she said, and hung up the phone again.

I felt very tired after this conversation with Ocie, but I suddenly had the feeling that if I gave up now I would never be free of that haunted past.

I decided to try one of my mother's siblings, hoping to get a more decent response. It couldn't be her younger brother, because nobody knew where he was. Nor did I try her sister, who now lived in a St. Louis suburb, because I didn't know her last name and Mom said she'd lost touch with her. I did know that Mom's sister Raebeth* lived in Caruthersville. I had no trouble getting her telephone number from information, and I dialed it right away.

A voice I didn't remember answered in a thick southern drawl. "Hellaw?"

I introduced myself. Raebeth was silent for a long time. I explained my desire to see Ocieola, in light of the letter Mark had written and the reply my mother had received. I told Raebeth I felt that Mark's instincts were exactly right: now would be a good time to put a stop to all the madness of the past.

"But Scott, your trip would serve no purpose whatsoever."

Before I could say another word, Raebeth was explaining all the reasons I shouldn't come. She was making cooing sounds, as if to console me. It was lucky for her that I couldn't reach through the wire and grab her by the throat.

"I never liked either of my grandfathers," she said. "And I didn't feel anything at all when they died. I don't see why it should be any different for you." Because *I* am not *you*, said a voice in my head.

That was when I definitely decided not to put off the trip. As I remembered now, nearing Caruthersville, that was the instant when it occurred to me for the first time that Ocieola would probably prefer to die rather than see me. She would die one day, and I would never have the chance to stop the racial war that had been going on in my heart since childhood. One day, my bitterness over this war might infect my own children.

"Let me put it this way," Raebeth said crisply. "I wouldn't want you to come here and be embarrassed. I don't think a visit would be wise. I don't know you. I've never met you. To be frank about it, I've got to live here. I've lived here all my life. I'm not embarrassed by the fact that you're black or anything, but I've got to live here. I don't want to jeopardize my life, and being your aunt would leave me in a hell of a shape.

"We're in business here," she continued, as I held on to the receiver with my mouth open. "We have to make a living. I'm not a racist of any type, but I think that we have a right to be here, and if it was known that my nephew was black it would hurt my business. I want to tell you how proud I am of you. I admire you. I'm proud that you've done so well with your life, and I know you're smart and intelligent and a good person. But I've lived here all my life, and there's a lot of white people here who equate black with trash."

This was the racial wall, each word a brick intended to console and to defend and to shun, each word saying, "Nigger, don't you let the sun set on your ass." This was racial apartheid, so well spoken, so smooth, so sane, so full of hurt. And so close.

"You see, Scotty, not knowing us isn't really a matter to be upset about. Families are dying. They've become less important. Maybe you don't feel this way, but I just don't care about relatives."

I remembered from Mom's stories of how anxious and concerned Raebeth always was about her children and grandchildren, and her white nephews and nieces. I thought about Raebeth's own son who died when I was a teenager, and I couldn't have cared less. This was the way race had reduced me.

"And, anyway," she said, "why did you wait so long?"

The question caught me under the ribs. Here I was, armed with accusations, equipped with intellectual assumptions, padded with righteousness, and this question stopped me dead in my tracks. She was absolutely right. Why had I waited so long? Here was part of the racial chasm that separated me from Raebeth and Mom's other relatives. Both sides were responsible for the missed opportunities. I'd always assumed that if anyone had used racial boundaries to justify human indifference, they had. If anyone was to blame, they were. But now it seemed plain enough that I bore some of the responsibility. I had painted Ocieola as a villain all these years, but she was no more a villain for refusing to see me than I was for wanting to see her. There wasn't anything really complicated about it. These were simple human desires. But they'd always been filtered through a racial prism, which made any possibility of connecting with blood relatives seem unbearably painful. I now realized that by not challenging the source of this pain I'd been doing my part to "keep things as they are."

Before now, I had only guessed that this was the reason I had to go to this land of shadows. Booking a flight to Memphis, renting a car at the airport—these were simply the opening steps on the journey. To me, the South has always been a place of secrets. But we all have part of ourselves locked in the metaphor of geography. My secret—that I had a relative like Ocieola—had once seemed so terrible I kept it to myself. Now it seemed a blessing to be able to disclose this secret and all the weight of it, opening up a new sense of the possible in myself.

Although my parents had separated when I was a young man, their dreams were more alive in me than I knew. I believe one of their dreams was that I should never hate anyone for having ideas that weren't the same as mine. I don't think they dreamed I would turn the beacon of hatred on their own families, on either side. Now I felt I had failed to live their dream, when in that dream was my own. It had become so clouded by my own struggle with racial divisions, which they could never really predict or help me fight, that I'd lost sight of the possibility of my own freedom. I wanted to be worthy of their dream. I wanted to overcome that dead weight of hate.

One way race was defined was by the notion that you couldn't have a white family if you were black or a black family if you were white. You had to make a choice. But not every such choice is a true choice. There is a pit in false dichotomies, and there is no pit deeper than race. I badly wanted to reclaim the part of me that loved the land-scape, that loved the stories about my mother's people, that was not discouraged and not worn out by all the accusations, false and true, simple and complex, that lay at the heart of my racial experience. I wanted to reclaim the part of myself that had been choked off in despair. I wanted forgiveness. I wanted a future as a human being. Maybe I didn't love Ocieola at all. Maybe I'd given up too soon. If I wanted justice—and I did—I would have to work harder at it.

As the landscape whizzed by, I thought about what I wanted to tell Ocieola: that I believed in decency, simple gestures of love and longing, an inclusive definition of family. We'd both lost out because of the racial obsessions of the past. Ocieola was an old woman now, nearing the end of her life. Perhaps we could both calm the racial waters. I realized now that if anyone in Mom's family had ever tried to bridge the racial gap, it had been Ocieola. She'd had the courage once. This wasn't a story my mother kept in some trove of sorrows, but one I had witnessed myself. And I'd all but forgotten about it until now.

This second and last time I had seen Ocieola came back to me as I drove past endless fields of soybeans and watched a vintage double-wing airplane painted yellow make low passes over the fields. The pilot crossed and recrossed the highway ahead of me, efficiently spraying the crops, never losing control of his machine. That was how I wanted to behave, I thought, never losing control despite the turmoil I was feeling.

It was 1968, the year after the U.S. Supreme Court had banned all state laws that made interracial marriage a crime. I had always admired Ocieola for making that trip. It had seemed to me that it must have taken great courage for her to finally come to see her daughter, and maybe it would end the great silence and deep sorrow in my life brought about by the family's racial division. We were living in Connecticut then, in a town called Norwalk. My parents owned a nice two-story house, which my father had fixed up inside and out almost entirely by himself. We all took pride in the place. We pulled the crabgrass in the lawn, trimmed the hedges, erected a split-rail fence and light posts, and laid brick paths all around it.

Ocieola showed up there, unannounced, on a hot August afternoon just like this one. She seemed to materialize out of blue sky and moonbeams. I was playing high school football at the time and had just come home from an early varsity practice, at which we'd all had to chew salt tablets to stanch our dehydration. Oddly, all the doors to the house stood open, and a pleasant breeze was wafting through. At the end of the hall, I saw Mom sitting at the kitchen table with someone. This was also unusual, because normally she would have been at work. But there she was, sitting with a woman whose voice sounded familiar. More than a dozen years had passed between this meeting and the previous one, but I knew instantly that it was Ocieola. Her voice had a lovely lilting quality, the soft southern air of a woman who knows how to behave around company and was doing so. She was small, like my mother, but rounder. She hunched over slightly as she brought a cup of tea to her lips. When she saw me she put the teacup down and smiled, washing away a whole childhood of neglect. In that moment I was ready to forgive her for all the pain her

absence had caused. As I shook her hand, I looked into her face
and saw that her eyes were just like my mother's. Their smiles were
identical. The gentle manner was the same. I think it was one of the
few times in my childhood or youth that I felt truly happy in the
company of family.

It turned out to be a brief visit. For reasons that were never explained to me, and that I never asked about, Ocieola left the next day,
as suddenly as she'd appeared. It was just one more of the disappoint-
ments that I'd learned to ascribe to the old racial quarrel which nobody seemed to have the strength to overcome.

It was now a sweltering midmorning. I rolled up the car windows
and turned on the air conditioner, just as I saw a sign indicating the
turnoff for Braggadocio and Caruthersville. I wondered if Ocieola
would look the same as she had all those years ago, and if she would
remember me.

And then I remembered again my mother warning me not to make
this trip. "You're going to be in for a world of hurt," she said. She
added that Raebeth's husband owned a gun and just might use it.
This news impressed me, but not for the obvious reason. It seemed,
almost, that she was defending her family against me. I saw that her
stake in keeping things as they were was no less powerful than theirs.
What I was afraid of wasn't a gun or a bullet or even the prospect that
I could meet with harm. The feeling of being too late was what I was
afraid of, and it was urgent in my blood as I approached Caruthersville.

There was a sign at the edge of the town, which was planted amid
sweetly ripening cornfields, that said, "Caruthersville: Pop. 5,467." I
drove, slower now, along a rural road with ditches on either side.
These were the ditches my mother had meant when she said I could
be found dead in one. (In fact, just a year after I began this journey,
a black family of four disappeared without a trace in this part of the
country.) I was urged along by the memories I'd come here to test. I
believed that the pain of separation had made my mother's stories
incomplete. They belonged only to her. They were her sorrow songs.
I wanted to claim the part of myself that had languished, unclaimed

and incomplete, because I stood outside those stories. The danger of not claiming these people seemed far more lethal to me than any act of physical violence. I wasn't looking for approval. I simply wanted to see the people and the places that, until now, had made me feel that some vital part of myself was missing. Moving at this slower pace, other words came to me: Where do you go from here? Anywhere that's away from fear.

Ocieola with her daughters, 1928.

Clarence with his daughters, 1928.

TWO / Elaborate Habits of Doubt

What thou lov'st well is thy true heritage.

—EZRA POUND

Just outside Caruthersville was a second sign. It said, "Welcome." Ahead lay the town, and in a few minutes I was driving its streets. Caruthersville was bathed in sunlight. A scent of the river hung in the air, and it mixed with the aroma of the fields. It was like stepping into another world.

I'm a northerner, and the first prejudice I had to confront was a feeling of being hemmed in as I drove up Ward Avenue, the main street. Until now, Caruthersville had existed for me only in my imagination. I had expected a far larger place. Instead, I found a little cow town. From my mother's descriptions, I had expected something far more prosperous looking. Instead, there was a certain desolation along the sidewalks, the feeling of dust everywhere that you get sometimes in small towns—I'd seen many of them in my travels as a news reporter. Caruthersville had the look of a place that was on its way to becoming a ghost town. Its energy seemed to have drained away. It looked like an old pair of shoes worn down at the heel. There was a sense of proud poverty here that reminded me of the little towns I'd seen in Mississippi and Georgia. It felt as if time had sped past the shops, the streets, the city hall, and had bathed everything in the same kind of dust and silence that settle into the corners of church doors.

I watched a handful of tired-looking old folks cross the avenue, and saw groups of kids here and there: at a Dairy Queen, in front of the ruin of what looked to be an old hotel, walking past a couple of vacant stores. The sidewalks were broken. Just ahead was the concrete levee, built to protect the fields of cotton and corn from floodwaters. As Mark Twain wrote in *Life on the Mississippi*, these waters could be as devastating as any conflagration. I rolled the car windows down again and shut off the air-conditioning so I could hear any sounds that might give me a feel for the place. There were none. Everywhere there was a crushing silence.

Although race was surely one reason the people in my mother's family didn't want to see me, I sensed that there were other reasons that had nothing to do with race. In a place like this, where people were so proud and so deeply loyal to the past, and where the environment changed so little, leaving home wasn't something a person did lightly. There was a price for leaving: the risk of being labeled forever as an outsider. My mother's decision to cross the racial divide had only added another kind of weight to her exile. I think she had always hoped for a way back. If you left a place like this, you certainly had the obligation to stay in touch with the people you left behind. You did not shame them by putting yourself above them or beyond their reach. But crossing the racial boundary did just that. It put you far beyond redemption.

I remembered some of the things my mother had told me about Caruthersville when I was a boy. She said that she went to the white high school and the blacks went to theirs. Black people walked on one side of the street, but if a white person suddenly appeared on that side the blacks got out of the way. White people didn't sit with black people on public benches. Caruthersville was the seventh house of hell, I now thought, and it left a scent on you, the scent of death. It was Hades as the ancients described the underworld, from which there was no return except as a shade, a ghost, a shadow of the person you had once been. This was "things as they are."

Driving along, I spotted a large mural on the side of a white building. It measured maybe eight feet by four feet and showed several groups of blacks, all of them black-black and dressed in brightly colored ragamuffin clothes. They were presumably slaves or sharecroppers, working in a green field densely flecked with ripening cotton bolls that almost overwhelmed the picture. One man lay under a tree, apparently asleep. One group was working under the watchful eyes of what looked to be a brown-skinned overseer mounted on a horse. Another group was hauling bags to a wagon piled high with the white fruit of the earth. The picture didn't pretend to be historically accurate. It was simply a statement of what had once been a cherished way of life in this region, which had then been part of the Cotton South.

I got out of my car to look more closely at the crude painting and discovered it was an advertisement for the art store and frame shop around the corner. Next door was the office of the local newspaper, the *Pemiscot Post*. I looked in the large plate-glass window and saw that the office seemed to double as a stationery store.

I got back in the car thinking that this place was far beyond anything in my experience. It was not a part of my past, yet in some way it had shaped my life. I drove past another building and made a left turn, just to get off the main street. Soon I noticed a small group of stores, one of which was a garage. There was a custom-painted mint-green low-slung pickup in the gravel driveway, but no sign of activity anywhere nearby. This was, apparently, Caruthersville at midweek.

Next door to the garage was a bar. There was a bullet hole in the window, which had been covered over with duct tape. Twenty or thirty yards from the bar was a large round whitewashed building. This was Sayre's Round House. I was famished. Seeing Ocieola and Raebeth was very much on my mind, but I didn't want to encounter them on an empty stomach.

I crossed the unpaved parking lot and walked into the restaurant. I was surprised to see three very large clocks in the center of the room,

behind the counter, each of them set to the time in a different city—
New York, Chicago, Paris. I took a seat in a booth with daintily pat-
terned vinyl cushions.

A polite waitress curtsied over and said, "Oh, my. The other girl
didn't set you up." She pulled a large paper placemat from the cum-
merbund of pockets around her waist, and set it down with a fork
and spoon she pulled from another pocket. She left and came back
nervously with a pitcher of ice water, turning my brown plastic tum-
bler over and filling it to the brim. It looked wonderful, and tasted
even better.

At one of the tables near the clocks I spotted a group of farmers,
their caps resting on the tabletop. They spoke in low tones.

Someone laughed, and they looked in my direction. It was a public kind of laugh, and there was much clearing of throats afterward.
A voice came from the group, just loud enough for me to hear.

"Neeger, ain't it?"

The whole table of menfolk began to chuckle.

"Yep," someone echoed. "That's a neeger, all raht."

A hush settled over the room, but it broke when the men began
talking of other things.

It reminded me of the first time I had gone to a Japanese restaurant
a few blocks from my office, which is near Rockefeller Center in
Manhattan. The restaurant was a place that had its own customs.
This first time, I walked directly over to a vacant seat at the counter
and waited for a menu, which didn't arrive. I noticed that the other
customers, all of them Japanese men, waited to be seated, and they
were immediately given menus. I was sure that the waitress was showing preference to the Japanese men because they were Japanese, and
I began to feel a flush of anger. I was wrong, of course. As I watched
the pattern unfold, it became clear that the Japanese men were following the custom of waiting politely to be seated, while I, an outsider, had not. I took the lesson in manners hard, but it didn't have
to be repeated. It had nothing to do with prejudice, except maybe on
my part; cultural barriers are tricky and easily open to misinterpreta-
tion. Now, in Caruthersville, I tried to maintain some degree of equa-
nimity. I'm no good when I'm angry. It makes me pass judgments
that almost always turn out to be wrong.

The waitress brought the menu, and I ordered catfish, hush puppies, and mashed potatoes. The food had no distinctive taste, but was quite filling, and it was a relief to get something into my stomach. As I paid the cashier, I saw two old-style rotary telephones on the countertop and asked if I could make a call.

"Is it local?" she said.

I told her it was, and called Raebeth.

"You're *here*?" she almost shouted into the receiver.

I reminded her that I had called more than once in the past week or so to let her know I would be making this trip—and every time she had told me not to come. So here I was, not a ghost at all, but a real living person.

"But I didn't think you were serious," she said. "You're not supposed to be here." She sounded very upset.

I asked her for directions to Ocieola's place.

"Where are you?"

I told her.

"Have you told anyone there who you are? I mean, you haven't told anyone my name? You haven't used my name, have you?"

I told her I'd been considering it, since it would probably be a good thing for my own protection to let people know I was her kin. Then I said I'd decided against it, because that information might not weigh so well in my favor, us being of different racial groups and all . . .

I told her I hadn't come to embarrass her but to see my grandmother.

"Well," she said, laying on the old accent, "you cain't come here and I cain't see you now. Tonight I have a card game."

I asked her again for Ocieola's address. She seemed to be doing some fast calculating.

"On second thought, I think you'd better come right here." She gave me her address. "Come right here *now*."

Never one for following orders, I decided to try to find Ocieola myself before heading to Raebeth's. I checked the telephone book for Ocieola's address. There it was.

I drove around for ten minutes before locating the nursing home and dialed Ocieola's number from a telephone booth just outside.

I had so much to tell Ocieola, and I hoped that speaking with her would dispel her misgivings. I would tell her that I wanted to stop the quarrel that had damaged us both, that I wanted us to be friends at last, that I'd come because I wanted to make up for all I'd missed, that I was willing to let my guard down and dispense with my own prejudices if it meant we could find some measure of forgiveness for one another. I wanted to tell her what the long years of absence had done to me. I wanted to know why she'd left so suddenly, that time in Norwalk. I wanted to let all my mad anger and rage go. I wanted to explain what it had been like to be unable to forgive her and what a relief it would be to get on with my life without this impediment.

. I also wanted to tell her about my family: my lovely wife, Frances, my older son, Aaron, who was so bright and so beautiful, and my younger son, Terence, who was ebullient and witty and had my mother's eyes and her small, square, able hands. These were my peace offerings, and I truly intended them as gestures of reconciliation, despite the harshness of the conversations we'd recently had. I'd come all this way—through more than two decades and more than a thousand miles—to see her.

So I called Ocieola to let her know that I was in town and to see if I could visit her. An attendant answered the phone and wanted to know who I was. I said I was Ocieola's grandson. The words sounded sweet and strange and forced. But there they were, out of my mouth. Then Ocieola came to the phone. I told her I was just outside and wanted to spend some time with her. I was hoping to show her the pictures of my family she hadn't yet seen, I said.

"I don't want to see you," she said, cutting me short. "I want to leave things as they are. I've got company. You have to go home."

I'd come too far to go home, I told her.

"Sorry. Good-bye." She hung up. She sounded genuinely frightened.

I, on the other hand, was genuinely angry. I slammed the phone into its cradle. I wanted to rage and rush into the nursing home, but something held me back. Maybe it was a feeling that I'd been clumsy in making this approach, or that I'd done enough for one day, or that it had been childish of me to hope I might achieve everything I wanted in a single afternoon.

I stood outside the nursing home and thought about a picture my mother had of Ocieola and Clarence and their four children. Ocieola had such weary eyes then, while Clarence's eyes were gleaming. He had a smirk on his face, a gambler's smirk. Raebeth and my mother were looking at the camera, and Betty Lou wore a fey, almost vacant expression. Frankie was simply a lump in Ocieola's arms. My mother valued that picture. I knew that Ocieola, in her own way, was as much a prisoner of her past and her present as I was. I had come here because my age was still in my favor, and I had a different feeling about my possibilities. For me, there was the possibility of earning my freedom. But I knew that I could never truly be free as long as Ocie was immured behind those walls of the past. I began to think about making another trip here when the dust of this present visit had settled.

It was about one o'clock when I made my way back to the center of Caruthersville, feeling that I was beginning to understand Ocieola a little better and starting to free myself of the past. I stopped in front of the small brick building that housed the local chamber of commerce and went inside. In the office was a small, pale woman with a puffy face and wispy blue-tinted hair whipped into the kind of low bouffant that was popular in the early 1960s. I asked her if she could give me a map of the town. She handed me a community profile and a blue sheet of paper listing the names of stores.

There was one animal hospital in Caruthersville and another hospital, with 125 beds, for humans. The profile listed other facilities and services: doctors' offices, dental clinics, the number of registered nurses and practical nurses in Pemiscot County as a whole. There were four full-time firemen, fourteen city cops, and thirty county cops. The public library held 35,000 books. There was a catfish farm. There were no colleges.

I read on, feeling that a northerner's snobbery—a part of my general attitude toward life—had no place here. The population of Caruthersville was in decline. In 1960, it had 8,643 residents, and 38,095 people lived in the county; two decades later, there were 7,389 people in town and 28,921 in the county. Businesses were struggling—that was surely one reason for the bleakness of the place. I realized my attitude of superiority had been another kind of wall. In some degree, I'd always judged this town and my mother's family by standards that didn't apply to them. The smallness of Caruthersville and the pressures of small-town life, the way a tiny place like this defines its winners and losers, the edifice of memory and its confinements—all this was palpable to me now. I couldn't have known my family before this, certainly not from the terrible distance of what I had taken to be racial animus. And while that was certainly part of it, many other emotions were involved. I did not know these white people. Their feeling of being abandoned by progress, their idea of pride, which took on racial tones partly because of their poor education, the seductions of grievance in a place where the insiders were truly in and the outsiders were truly out—all of this was an inducement to arm themselves with false racial values. That's the only thing they had to separate themselves from their black neighbors, to whom they were not superior at all. I felt for the first time the great blessing my mother had bestowed on me simply by leaving this place.

The heat had made me thirsty, so I pointed my car back toward the bar. It was a Merle Haggard–Hank Williams kind of place. It promised forgetfulness. It was pitch-black inside, except for two lights: one that caught a slice of the bar, and an overhead fluorescent illuminating a worn pool table. I went into the bathroom, and was almost driven out by the overpowering back-alley stench of urine. There were pennies in the urinals.

The bar needed a good airing. Still, I wanted a beer or two to help me cool off and relax, just like anyone else who came through that front door.

The bartender stared at me for a few moments before he came over and asked, "What'll it be?" He slammed a mug under the tap, filled it with foam, and slung it in my direction. I asked him to fill it up all the way. He did. Resentfully. I drank it, and it was wonderful. So much separated me from these folks, I was thinking, not the least of which was my family background. But I was of a different class, too, and this had unconsciously given me a kind of racial snobbery for "poor white trash." I was embarrassed at the thought. Those three words explained why my family had erected a racial barrier against people who looked like me.

Once, when I was riding home on the Long Island Railroad, I had witnessed a confrontation between a white and a black passenger that nearly came to blows, though I had regarded it then as just part of the texture of daily life in New York City. The white passenger had a large black plastic bag over his shoulder; the black passenger was wearing a natty double-breasted business suit to display the class he was swimming in. The black man stepped into the narrow aisle between the padded, benchlike railroad seats, and the white man, with his heavy luggage, suddenly lurched into the same aisle. Neither would give way. The black man tried to excuse himself. The white man, perhaps feeling it was his right to be where he was, did not. A few tense seconds passed. Then the white man exploded: "Do you think you're better than I am?" The question caught the black man by surprise. No, he said, he didn't think he was any better. I thought he should have said yes, he *was* better. By every visible measure, he was of a higher class and therefore, by American standards, he *was* better: better connected, better educated, better looking, better mannered. But he was black, and the white passenger wouldn't let go of this perceived test of privilege. "You think you're better than I am, don't you?" Again the black man backed down. He was trying to act the gentleman. The white man, becoming more and more inflamed, put his bag down and balled up his fists. I noticed that the black man was far better built in the arms and shoulders, and had large hands. I think the white passenger noticed this, too, because he finally backed down.

As I was recalling this incident, I noticed that two white men at the bar were looking at me and my gray pinstripe summer suit. I'd put it on deliberately to protect myself, to stand out rather than try to blend in. It was, I'd thought, a wise defensive move. But here it marked my assumptions of class superiority over these people. It was impossible to determine whose assumptions—mine or theirs—were more at fault. I sat for another minute or so and asked for another beer. I was thirsty and didn't really care whether anyone wanted me here or not. I felt I'd come too far to be trifled with over class or race distinctions. The place was open for drinking, and I was drinking. Shortly the bartender came over and asked me if I wanted another, and I said yes, and he asked if I was from New York, and I laughed and asked him what made him think so, and he laughed and said it was my haircut and my shoes. I told him who I was and why I was here. He nodded his head, and I saw an M-16 behind the bar, which looked real enough to me. There would be no fights here. Someone put on a single—it was Marty Robbins's "El Paso"—and then another, "Hello Walls," an old favorite of mine. Hank Williams, after all, had soul. Maybe even more than I did.

I left the bar with Hank Williams in my head and drove toward Raebeth's house. It was hard to keep out of my mind the thought that at one time Caruthersville had been lynch country. It had been simply a convention of law enforcement then, and it was deadly effective in keeping everyone in place, including my mother's family. In this fertile land, class differences were especially exaggerated. You were in or you were out. If you were a teacher, you were in. If you were a farmer who owned land, you were in. If you were a tenant farmer, or poorer, you were definitely out. During the Depression, because of a system of taxation on the land and on the drainage services that kept the land from flooding, many whites fell into poverty. My mother's people were among them, but they were mostly landed poor, which put them on the outer margin of a poverty that made them proud, mean, and small in spirit. The only thing that separated these whites from poor blacks was the color of their skin, and they made an inglorious religion of it.

To be black was to be forever excommunicated. In the early 1940s, in a town called Sikeston, just north of Caruthersville, a black man named Cleo Wright was accused of harassing a white woman. He was wounded by a local policeman and put in jail. He was then dragged out of jail and shot in the back of a police car. His body was tied to the back of another car and dragged for miles through both the white and the black sections of town. He was finally set on fire. He died asking for the help of God.

In his book of reminiscences, *Roads That Seldom Curve*, the artist Alvin Allen writes about his early memory of seeing the body of a hanged man who "looked dirty and muddy, the color of a tow sack." The man had been dragged along half the dirt roads in the county before he was strung up on a tree in the town of Braggadocio, near where my mother and her family had lived. Allen writes that when he asked his father why the man had met such a fate, the answer was simply that "the man did wrong." It didn't go any further than that.

This attitude of closemouthed cruelty ran as deep in my mother's family as the habit of doubt and suspicion. "Don't complain and don't explain" was one of her favorite expressions. You simply kept silent in the face of grief and hardship. You revealed nothing. To reveal was to admit vulnerability and defeat. Once, when my mother accidentally appeared naked in front of Clarence, he said, "Ocie, that girl has no more shame for her nekkidness than she does for her face."

Theirs was not a happy home life. They moved often, as Clarence sought work, or the prospect of work, in places like Steele, Arkansas, and New Orleans. For a short time the family lived in a place called Midway, on a farm owned by one of Ocie's brothers. He regularly slapped his children silly, Mom said, and they cringed around him, dirty and sneaky and ashamed; it made her sick to her stomach, but there was no escaping it. Ocieola often had to work chopping cotton in the fields, filling hundred-pound sacks and dumping them in wagons that took the fragrant material to market to fill other white people's coffers. There would be wild joy when Clarence came home telling stories about working in roadhouses with names like The Climax, but mostly there was a lot of suffering and hunger.

Mom told me that one time, when they were living in a hamlet called Micola in 1932, they were so poor that they all had to take baths out of the same water. By the time Clarence, Ocieola, and Raebeth had finished, there would be little flowers of filth in the water that she had to step into. Another time, the family moved in with Charles Smith, Clarence's improvident, alcoholic father, who often went off on binges that they called "going to visit Leaping Lena." When he returned, he would keep the family up until all hours of the night reading passages from the Bible. There were frequent quarrels, and Ocie and Clarence would turn on each other. "So what did the old son of a bitch do today?" Ocie would ask Clarence. "What's the matter, Ocie, didn't you get saved today?" he would reply.

Many of the men drank, or gambled, or fought off their despair with various cruel entertainments. Alvin Allen writes of seeing a man from out of town volunteer to be hitched to the back of a car and dragged around and around the local fairgrounds just for the small money.

The women, and some of the men, took their misery to God. Ocieola dragged Raebeth and my mother to many revival meetings run by a fellow named Brother Bradley.

These revivals scarred my mother in ways that fed her later attempts to escape. In the tent meetings, she would sit either terrified or trying to hold in her laughter as the women and men chased each other around when they got the Spirit. And they sang, spirituals like "Beulah Land" or a dirgelike hymn I remembered my mother singing during my own childhood:

> I was sinking deep in sin,
> Far from the peaceful shore,
> Deeply stained within,
> Sinking to rise no more;
> But the Master of the sea
> Heard my despairing cry,
> From the waters lifted me,
> Now safe am I.

And then the people would shout:

> Love lifted me!
> Love lifted me!
> Love lifted me!

These elements of my mother's stories repelled me as a child. That kind of religion seemed far from the dignified Christian Science of my father's family.

The congregation, Mom said, would gather on their knees to pray for the conversion of the sinners, singing, "Why not tonight? Why oh why oh why not tonight?" Mom would almost spit at this. "The brothers and sisters never talked about organizing to fight and struggle," she said. "They never talked about brotherly love. They just talked about self-pity, their degraded status, the bitterness of exploitation. Fighting your way out was for someone else." I loved my mother's anger over social questions, her perceptions about the economic injustices she'd experienced as a girl and that ultimately drove her out of Caruthersville and to Chicago.

Mom hated the poverty that ensnared Ocieola during those terrible years. The poor hate more deeply than anyone, but they hate silently, with their eyes and with their hearts. These poor farmers would see the northerners to whom they had lost their property drive up to the cotton fields in their black limousines, roll down the windows, and watch the people work their way deeper into penury. The two hated each other with a passion. If Mom's people clung to the lonely security of whiteness, it was because whiteness was their salvation, even if it was a false one. They learned to benefit by the racial lie they told themselves. So how did they live up to the truth that race hadn't saved them from being poor? Consider how a lynching might make a man feel better about his own degraded status.

Mom left Caruthersville for the first time in 1942. One of its brightest students, she had fallen in love at fifteen with a young charmer named Corky. He took her to California with him, and she almost died there, of an ectopic pregnancy. She returned home, completed her last two years of high school in a year, and left Caruthersville, first for St. Louis and finally for Chicago, where she met my father. Her experience of returning alone to a town without succor, and without any great joy except in a few personal friendships, made my mother burn for another world. And she eventually found it in the cities of the North, just as a million other young women from all around the country would find it in those cities at the close of World War II. She was part of that wave of the new political and economic order that would enrich the cities and gradually, through massive outmigration, make towns like Caruthersville what they have become today.

I headed now to Raebeth's house. It was after six o'clock and growing dark. I was afraid I wouldn't find the house if I delayed much longer. I found it—a small, neat, ranch-style house set back from the street—and knocked on the door. The woman who answered looked a lot like Ocieola had, that time I saw her in Connecticut. Raebeth had a mixed-up-looking smile on her face, an I'll-have-to-get-this-over-with-as-soon-as-possible look that strained the corners of her eyes. Though I wasn't exactly kindly disposed toward her, I felt I could at least rely on her honesty. I noted that as she invited me in she craned her head out the door and looked up and down the street, like a cartoon image of a burglar about to steal into someone's home.

Raebeth's front room was a profusion of good cheer. It was painted in pastel shades of pink and blue, with many still-life paintings of flowers on the walls. My mother was a part-time artist, in addition to her career in the fashion industry in Manhattan. Her paintings were never of flowers, though; they were mostly landscapes of fields, forests, and rivers, and were filled with a longing for "home." I told Raebeth I liked the paintings, which was true. I asked about her daughter Kay,* a cousin whom I'd never met. Raebeth said she was living in Texas now. I asked Raebeth how old Kay was, and she said Kay was six years older than me. There was a picture of Kay's daughter on the wall. She had a fresh pink face and a nice smile. I didn't ask her name and Raebeth didn't venture it. I told her about my professional life: that I'd been working as a journalist for more than a decade now, but was trying to do more essays and longer reportage. I told her I hoped to write about my mother's family. I said I was working for *U.S. News & World Report*—did she know it? She said she didn't read magazines; she liked "trashy novels." She laughed easily and waited.

Then I said I wanted to know more about Ocieola. "Well." She tensed. "There are so many things I could say. But first you tell me what made you want to make this trip."

I explained how weary I had grown of being angry all the time— at the slights of race, at the misunderstood or poorly understood past that evoked only fear and loathing in me—and how I was ready to challenge that way of thinking and seeing, which had led me into an emotional dead end. After being in Caruthersville just a few hours, I said, nothing seemed as simple as it once had, my conclusions less easy to sustain. I told her I wanted to know more about her family.

"I don't know if families are that important," she ventured. "I have friends who are closer to me than my family."

There followed a conversation full of non sequitur and evasion. We happened on the subject of shame, which I said I'd always felt in connection with her and her attitude about race. There were many kinds of shame, she said, but the worst was the shame of poverty. She said that she well understood how I could resist a racial classification aimed at making me ashamed of having parents of different cultures, but that I knew nothing about the shame of poverty. It had ruined her feelings about her family. She had escaped as best she could by marrying young and having children right away.

"We grew up poor when I was a girl, and you can't imagine what it was like. There were many prejudices against poor people. My classmates would make fun of us because we couldn't afford to put soles on our shoes. We couldn't run around with kids that had things." There was no hint of an accent now. She seemed to be defending herself for acting as she had, for shutting my mother, my brothers, and me out of her life for her own survival. I told her that I'd been ashamed of having a white family when I was a boy, because to me being white meant the absence of courage. It meant the inability to tolerate differences among people. I told her I believed that some people had to make others feel bad so they could feel good about themselves, and that this was moral weakness.

Raebeth didn't blink—I liked this about her. I asked her if her experience of poverty, which in my opinion she had never truly overcome, had affected her attitude toward her sister's marriage.

"Poor people can't give too much away, you know," she said. "When your mother married your father, it was like we had to close the pages of a book."

Easy as that. Raebeth began speaking of what it was like to live in a small town. "There were certain things people would try to use against you."

"Like having black in-laws?" I asked.

She nodded. "I don't know if you'll understand this, but my daddy came from a real trashy family. We had nothing to do with Daddy's people. We don't have any family ties." This was her justification for severing ties with her sister. In fact, all the stories of Caruthersville I'd ever heard had shown that her family was a buffer—though maybe an uncertain one—against the realities of a hostile world. Those whites may have been hard, but they didn't abandon each other. She'd used race to foreclose such a possibility for her sister. I was beginning to feel that maybe it was a piece of luck that I hadn't known this woman, that maybe segregation had its uses, not all of them bad.

"I'm not close to my family," she said, "and my husband's not close to his. You more or less pull yourself into your own little world." I remarked that at least she had the choice; her use of race had deprived me of any such freedom. I said this without malice, not to make her feel guilty but to let her know that she was walking on very shaky ground when she used her family experience to justify her conduct toward my mother and, now, toward me.

Raebeth changed the subject to my mother. She said that LaVerne had left Caruthersville "all stuck up and arrogant and full of ambition." She had abandoned the care of Ocieola to Raebeth and Betty Lou. Raebeth also said that she hadn't known anything about Mom's marriage to my father until I was two years old.

Racial exclusion, then, was the shallow hole in which she had planted the seeds of grief over family wounds of her own, using it to justify the terrible distance between us. As she spoke, I felt what a tragedy it was that I had never realized this, that I hadn't made this journey before now. But maybe I'd had to have children of my own, a family of my own, before I could see just how deeply family mattered to me and how deeply I felt its absence. Maybe that was where this journey had begun: in my love for my wife and children, and my feeling that if they were ever to live free of the dangers of racial division, then this resentment I bore for my mother's people could not continue.

Before my father or my brothers or I ever came into the picture, there was this rift between Raebeth and my mother that neither of them could overcome. The rift took on a racial cast because they chose such different lives; it became more racial by degrees as they drifted further apart, until there was no hope of reconciliation. That hopelessness had touched my life and cast its shadow as a racial one when the issues were always deeper: pride, and love turned away and missed, poverty and its withering effects. I thought of my mother's tearful calls—apparently unsuccessful—to establish common ground. I had been ashamed that she submitted herself repeatedly to rejection, and had given up on Raebeth then. I had given up on Ocieola, too. That had been my way of facing what seemed to be racial pain but in fact went far deeper. I had given up some part of myself.

The whole notion of race I received as a child was that somehow my life was there to prove I could overcome the anguish of the past. I heard over and over that I was of a new generation which didn't have to bear the weight of the past. In fact, the opposite was true. I'd had to bear the weight of what I considered to be the racial hatred of my white relatives, along with the strangely ambivalent embrace of my black relatives, who accepted me, but only so far, as I would learn. I was supposed to be a member of a smarter race of humans who lived "the best of both worlds." To some degree, I suppose that was the promise. At least, I felt I had the option of choosing a racial identity. I ran from a white identity, because it seemed small and dry and helpless against the larger demands of love and hope. My black relatives introduced by their example the idea of dignity. As an act of survival, I chose their world as my own. On a deep level, the two worlds simply did not touch each other. My mother insisted that her people were pioneers. They may have been, but *she* was the real pioneer of her family. She had crossed the racial divide. I had always wanted to trace back to this place of her origin. And now I found that Raebeth's dignity and defensive toughness reflected Ocieola's, and that there was some of it in my mother, and even in me.

Raebeth and I spoke but didn't hear each other. Beneath all the excuses, she lived in a world of exclusion. I lived in a world of inclusion, and this was an intellectual choice, not a genetic one. Who knew where race and family divided, or where they began? Race encompassed so many personal wounds that had found their way into my life that I didn't know any more which was which. My personality carried both the resentments of poor whites and the skills of overcoming great odds that were the heritage of my father's family. Raebeth used race as a way to lose contact with people. I wanted to use it to make contact, so I could taste the best of both worlds. Until now, I felt I hadn't done that at all.

Now Raebeth was allowing that I had been robbed twice—first of a racial identity, and then of a family identity. I asked her how this was possible, since in her case racial identity was utterly incompatible with a family identity—as we Negroes say, a contradiction "from Jump Street." I told her I had chosen to be an African-American simply because it seemed very much the best offense, because her conduct and her family's had always horrified me, and because they had made it clear that I could never belong to them. I said that if it weren't for my father's family I'd have little positive sense of myself. If it weren't for them and the love they tried to show—as much as it was in them to do so—I wouldn't have the strength to be speaking to her now. I'd have "blessed her out." I finished these remarks with a sneer.

Raebeth didn't drop a stitch. "I'm proud of you," she said. "I think you'd be a worthwhile person to know"—to which I wanted to add, *Yeah, if only I was white.* "You're a fine, intelligent person, a good person. But I've lived here all my life, and there's a lot of people around here who equate black with failure." It was becoming increasingly clear to me that it was her version *of whiteness* that was a failure. I told Raebeth she was a bigot.

"I probably am," she said.

Just then Raebeth's husband, Will,* the one my mother said carried a gun, came in the front door. This was turning out to be a regular family reunion. He was a wiry, slight man, and was darker than I am, even when I'm dark. When he saw me, he smiled in an embarrassed way. Was this really the man who carried a gun?

"Well, hallooooo," he said, laughing. He may have been trying to be friendly, but all I could see was the smile of a startled man whose first instinct was obsequiousness. He certainly didn't seem like one of those dangerous people my mother had described, but I knew that it was just this kind of person who would carry a gun for protection, and might even use it.

"You must be Scott. I heard you might be coming," he said. He looked at Raebeth with a serious expression.

"You must be Will," I said, in my finest I-couldn't-give-a-shit style, which I'd learned from my mother long ago. Will went into the kitchen. I watched him.

Changing the subject, Raebeth asked if I liked art. "Only sometimes," I told her. Will picked up the cue. He motioned from the kitchen toward a badly stained Japanese silk screen hanging on the living-room wall. It was a fairly commonplace one, the kind of souvenir a soldier might have brought home at the end of World War II. Will said he'd been in Yokohama and had picked it up there.

Suddenly his face brightened. "You know," he declared, "I have a collection of Indian portraits, pictures of Sitting Bull and Kicking Bird and other great Sioux leaders." I didn't point out that, in fact, the Sioux are now called Lakota, and that Kicking Bird was a Kiowa. "Would you like to see them?"

He led me into his study and showed me the pictures. They were photographs that had been cut out of picture magazines. I told him they were nice. My initial feeling of moral superiority over this man evaporated. Superiority wasn't the point. It was the very thing I abhorred. I felt ashamed. I kept thinking I shouldn't be ashamed, that he was an enemy, but it didn't work. Will was showing me something important to him, something he valued, and I just couldn't find it in myself to look down on him. At the same time, I didn't want to let go of my anger and resentment. I felt terribly on edge because my anger was being replaced by sympathy. Anger was feeling more and more like wasted emotion—which is exactly what it had always been. All that crazy resentment I'd brought with me, along with my dreams of forgiveness, was in *my* head, not in theirs. But it was a habit that made any reconciliation impossible.

"Once when your mother was a child," Will began, "we were coming home from school, and there was this big black guy—uh, uh—" He caught himself. "There was this big black fellow, or black man, rather, named Rufus, who owned a pear orchard in these parts. His land was surrounded by a fence. We all wanted a pear that day, but we were just too skeered to try to climb over the fence. Well, your mother, LaVerne, your mother just went ahead and did it. No fear at all."

"LaVerne always was fearless," Raebeth said.

"And before long she had a whole bunch of pears wrapped up in her skirt, which she held like this—like a basket. We were all scared. Then Mr. Rufus came out. We thought she was going to catch hell for it. We told her to run, but she didn't. She could run very fast, you know, but she just stood there and looked at him. He smiled at her and just gave her a bushel basket and helped her pick some more."

At that moment I completely forgot the way I'd felt about Will in those first few difficult minutes. I now felt I loved him and would always love him for sharing with me this poignant story of my mother as a girl. It seemed to encapsulate the essence of her that I knew, and I could never thank Will enough for that. It was the first human contact I'd experienced with Mom's people. The memory of what he'd just described made Will laugh.

Even Raebeth livened up. "You know," she said, "when we were children, my mother's closest friend was a black woman. They used to talk to each other across the back fence. We lived near black people, you know." I hadn't known. But how shameful that must have been for Raebeth, who hated her poverty.

Why, then, I asked Raebeth, was it so hard for her and her people simply to pick up the telephone and call her black relatives in the East?

"Some people are afraid to change," she said. "We've lived all our lives here." This technically wasn't true. I knew that she and Will had moved to Colorado for a short time to escape Caruthersville. "We have to live here, and you don't understand what it's like living in a small town." The record was apparently on repeat. I looked outside and saw it was dark.

Raebeth asked if I was a reader, like my mother. I told her that I enjoyed books. She said one of her memories of LaVerne was that even when she dried the dishes after supper she always had a book "in the crook of her arm." "She was constantly reading," Raebeth said. "That was one of the big differences between us. I used to get so put out with her. She always had an adventurous side. I've always been more cautious." I smiled.

Then Raebeth began to reiterate her old resentment about being left to care for Ocieola. I thought that she'd been exactly right to ask me why I'd waited so long to make this trip. After so much distance and time, any sympathy I might have had for her present plight regarding Ocieola simply wasn't there. Soon I made my farewells. Raebeth accompanied me to the door, appearing as relieved to see me go as I was eager to leave.

I climbed into the rental car, assuming the porch lights would help me find my way out the driveway. Raebeth flicked them off immediately. I drove away feeling utterly alone, searching for the entrance to the highway that would lead me back to Memphis, to a hotel room and a phone call home.

I don't know exactly how I got out of Caruthersville. The rural roads had no streetlights. I tried to retrace the route I'd taken into town but only got lost. The ditches on either side of the road loomed more ominously now. What if I got stuck in one? Would I be able to find a friendly hand? I tried to imagine someone helping. There was no such possibility here. I drove on until I was completely lost. I stopped in front of a brightly lighted home and knocked on the door. The man who answered politely pointed the way to the highway, and before long I was following the trailer lights of the trucks trundling along ahead of me.

The drive back to Memphis took little more than an hour. I was dazed by all that had happened that day. I was grateful, too, as I entered the city. I don't think I've ever been happier to get back to an empty, funky-smelling hotel room. I opened the window to let in some fresh air and looked out over Memphis at night. The bridge over the Mississippi River was festooned with bright lights, like a Christmas tree, and I thought of the dark waters in the river below flowing past the city toward freedom and the Gulf.

Arvit's father, Arvit Minerbrook, Sr.,
circa 1900.

Katherine's father, John Williams, circa
1900.

THREE / **The Walls of Chicago**

*Before I built a wall, I'd ask to know
what I was walling in or walling out.*

—ROBERT FROST

I f I learned anything from that first visit to Missouri, it was that
accusation, the ability to stand and point a finger at a perceived
enemy, is as sweet a bit of self-deception as there is in life. But ultimately, it is a self-wounding exercise that gives no comfort to the
naked, no safety to those in danger of loss. It is just another way to
build a wall. To accuse others too much is to accuse yourself. To
blame others for your despair is to blame yourself for your own lack
of resourcefulness. Race, which seems such a simple thing on its
surface, is just another brick in the wall of despair. Yielding to that
despair is like getting comfortable in a snowbank after a long, deep
snowfall. You get tired of walking, and so you rest in the snow. You
lie down. You go to sleep. You freeze.

After that journey south, I began to see more deeply how I had
frozen in the bank of my own intolerance. In the months that followed, I began to think in a different way about my father's family,

too. I believe I learned from them some of the limits of my own tolerance. It is one of those strange ironies of racial experience for people of color that no one is innocent in a quarrel, and that those who strive to induce others to be tolerant aren't always tolerant themselves. Historical experience had led Dad's family to have limited use for white people. It was easy for his people to hate whites from behind the walls of the ghetto where they'd been raised. They learned to hate whites without guilt—and with all the justification of the oppressed—from that righteous throne of anger that I knew all too well.

At the same time, one of the ironies of their lives was that they seemed to imitate the very bigotries and hypocrisies that kept them in their place. Blacks in Chicago were marred by their own forms of color prejudice, their own forms of class snobbery. Many of their rituals of passage wounded them even as they bore them up. But slowly, over decades, they were able to build enough momentum to step beyond the limits of their prejudices. They operated on the principle that they could not truly reject others as they had been rejected, could not hate as they had been hated. They cooled the fires of their temper. The complexities of living among whites required practice, patience, discipline, courage, stealth, and coolness. Without studying whites, they would never become different from them. And so they set about watching. They watched over generations. After the 1919 race riots in Chicago, which were some of the bloodiest in American history, the blacks in my family joined hands with others who opted to protect themselves by moving into separate and unequal communities, black and white. They aimed to prepare themselves for the day when they could move out and find greater opportunities, leaving the ghetto behind.

The preparations worked. My father was able to move his family from Chicago to New York to Connecticut. I went to Harvard and became a reporter. My older brother, Mark, went to medical school and became a doctor. Our younger brother Mike went to college, before falling into a pit of despair so deep he couldn't climb out. And John, our youngest brother, went to college and on to a career as a transcriber in Albany, the capital of New York. Two of my father's cousins, Barbara Lawrence and her brother, Robert, Jr., tasted their own successes. She studied history at the University of Chicago and political science at New York University, where she received her doctorate. Robert became a scientist and was chosen in 1967 as the first African-American to participate in the U.S. space program.

The earliest settlers behind the walls knew what they wanted. They wanted to find a place where their lives would be safer than they had been in Mississippi or Tennessee. And they knew what it would take to get there. Far from being an abstraction of history, the movement of my father's family to Chicago was part of my own living history. First came my great-grandparents John Williams and his wife, Elizabeth Moffit, both of them from Jackson, Tennessee. Mama, as she was called in the family, worked as a domestic for a North Side Jewish family. There were stories about her making the trip to work from her home on the South Side through cruel winter winds, hanging onto lampposts for support. When she arrived, her hands would be as stiff as blocks of ice. And after working all day she would return home to wash and clean and cook for her own family.

Her husband was a handsome, hale-fellow-well-met type, a man of refinement. He worked in the post office, a job of great distinction for an African-American man. He was light-skinned, although the single picture I have makes him look darker than he really was. Like many men of his set, John Williams was obsessed with appearances, his own in particular. My picture of him reveals a mixture of Choctaw and African bloodlines, evident in the smooth texture of his skin and in the hair, which is parted down the middle and crests toward the temples in small round waves. At a time when blacks in other parts of the country were experiencing what historians have described as a "black nadir" of lynchings, political disenfranchisement, and loss, John Williams was prospering in a way that gave him a strong sense of himself. He stands before the camera and stares it down. He is dressed in a dark pinstripe suit whose fabric lies perfectly on the angular slant of his shoulders. The coat is thrown open, in a conscious gesture, to reveal a resplendent vest of a lighter fabric—a hint of white linen with gold stripes—and a cravat of a sumptuous material held in place with a golden fob, a miniature statue of a naked woman with her hands folded at her groin. Follow the shoulders down the arms, and you see the right hand tucked into the right pocket, the left hanging loose—a purely masculine "attitude." On the pinky finger is a golden ring that glints. What this outfit cost him, in time or in cash, is hard to imagine, but the lift it gave to his spirits appears to have been well worth the effort.

John Williams was equally obsessive about the appearance of his daughters. One of the stories that came down to me as a boy was his insistence that his wife dress their daughters, Katherine and Gwendolyn (my grandmother and great-aunt), only in the finest linen dresses, which she had to wash and iron herself, winter or summer. My pictures of the girls show them both dressed like little dolls. In one, Gwen is wearing a blue jumper with a large, beautifully woven linen Dutch-boy collar. She sits on a divan, in a pose that bears testimony to her mother's elaborate and exhausting attentions. It's hard to imagine the effort required to keep this up, and the love it must have taken, to work as a domestic by day and then come home and do it all over again. My great-grandfather was clearly determined to challenge the stereotypes of a larger society that saw blacks as inferiors. Whatever the cause of his concern for appearances, it bore fruit in the raising of two young women who tasted at least some measure of self-worth early enough that they were inculcated with it and never lost it.

There are many ways to learn about race. In a story my aunt Gwen tells, she had the fact of color brutally driven home one afternoon when, at the age of five, she was taken to a large Chicago hospital by a close family friend named Emma Higgenbotham, a fair-skinned woman who was helping to raise both Gwendolyn and Katherine. The doctor called out Mrs. Higgenbotham's name—the family knew her as Mama Hick—who stepped forward with the dark child who was as close as kin. The doctor looked at Gwendolyn and her escort and said, "That sure is a cute little nigger girl you have with you, miss," to which Mama Hick responded that the child was not a nigger, she was her daughter. Such demonstrations of the spectral might of racialized experience were bred in the bone of life in Chicago. Strivers as my father's family might be, ambitious as they were to show themselves as such, race always pulled them back to the pit of despair. And so they did not settle, in heart or spirit or mind or body. They swallowed their rage. They climbed above the darker masses as fast as they could. They did so to keep the hellhounds of race at bay. To be black was to never surrender to doubt, or even to entertain doubt. It was to survive at any cost.

Dad's family paid a terrible price for their strivers' identity. When I was a child, I learned that one of the ways some of them answered the question of color prejudice was to pass as whites. My father's other grandfather, Arvit Minerbrook, Sr., came to Chicago from Mobile, Alabama. Arvit was extremely fair-skinned, and made a point of keeping his nappy hair straightened. By the time he was a teenager he was working as a conductor on the Illinois Central railroad, a job open only to white men. Arvit looked white and acted white, but his wife was black, and his sons and daughters were raised as blacks. This was accepted in the Negro world.

Arvit was not well received by the Williamses. As a young man, I remember questioning my father's family in an effort to understand more about just who Dad's father's folks were. But Katherine and Gwen were evasive about Arvit, Sr. Katherine simply called him "the old man." It was only much later that I learned why. As one of those blacks who "passed," he felt he was truly superior to the darker Williamses, although they weren't really very dark at all. Even within black society, I learned, certain blacks valued each other according to color, with the darker ones at the bottom of the scale and the lighter ones at the top. This created rifts even among the Williamses. Katherine was one of the lighter ones; Gwen was not. It was still later before I understood that this didn't mean that lighter blacks wanted to be white or would ever completely welcome whites into their families. These things were simply the bitter fruit of living along the color line.

Cruel ironies compounded along that rift. Some members of the Williams family, including Katherine herself, had passed at various times in their lives, or had tried to. Katherine was said to have been offered a job as an editor at *Cosmopolitan* magazine; she did not tell her employer that she was black. Other members of the family passed as well, including a few who worked downtown in the Loop, Chicago's central business district, at the Palmer House, then an exclusive hotel that never hired black people.

Under certain circumstances, passing was even forgiven. It was all right to pass, for example, if one returned the fruits of one's labor to the South Side. Arvit, Jr., my father's father, could have passed, but he didn't. He worked for a Jewish pawnbroker before opening his own business on the South Side, as a haberdasher to the black mob. When he and Katherine fell in love, his father forbade the marriage because he said Katherine was too dark, even though, in fact, she was just this side of café au lait. Katherine says that when she was fifteen years old and Arvit was sixteen, they crossed the state border and got married in Michigan. To this day, Arvit's family claims that no marriage took place because Arvit's father wouldn't allow it. They say that my father was born out of wedlock, although Arvit allowed Katherine to use the family name to escape social embarrassment. This, too, was part of my racial legacy.

The complexities of the stories about my father's family have always fascinated me. They showed me the strange forms that the strivings of his people took and the lengths to which blacks could go to save themselves from the agony of blackness.

As early as 1957, black scholars like E. Franklin Frazier were bitterly ridiculing the folly of those Negroes who based their self-worth on caste and class status to distinguish themselves from other Negroes and to wrest favorable treatment from less-than-sympathetic whites. By the late 1940s, such Negroes had established a "Negro society" in Chicago, a narrow band of achievement that was limited not only by color and class snobbery but also by the small number of blacks who had actually achieved anything resembling success. Katherine and Gwen knew the most powerful members of this society, those who were most closely connected with white wealth and through their connections were able to deliver vital economic substance to the striving masses of the South Side. Frazier reported, in his *Black Bourgeoisie*, that this Chicago "society" was actually defined by five wives of physicians, three wives of dentists, three women school workers, two wives of morticians, a social worker, the owner of a newspaper, the wife of a lawyer, a banker's daughter, a concert pianist, and the wife of a college president.

One of the rulers of colored society, a physician's wife who works every day, is celebrated for her three big parties each year. The ruler

of society in a southern city has gained fame because she entertains
Negroes who have a national reputation. Another has gained noto-
riety because she is a friend of Lena Horne, and gave a cocktail
party for the famous movie actress.

My cousin Barbara, the daughter of my aunt Gwen, was very
much a part of this world. She was introduced to black society at a
cotillion in 1949, the year my parents were married. Barbara's cotillion was sponsored by a group called the Royal Coteric of Snakes.
The Frogs, the Druids, the Association, the 30 Club, and many others held similar cotillions and other affairs to draw lines of distinction
around their own limited elite. Arvit, Jr., who was by then quite the
man about town because of his successful business on Forty-seventh
Street, black Chicago's commercial spine, had been asked to join the
Snakes, but he refused. He hated the "paper bag test" used to select
the debutantes: the price of admission was that they had to have skin
no darker than the color of a brown paper bag. There were even
churches in Chicago that darker-skinned blacks simply were not encouraged to join.

In 1947, *Ebony Magazine* profiled the cotillion of the Snakes.
The article tells the story in pictures of a young deb and her escort.
Both were very fair in complexion, hers a certain Spanish tint, his
more Latin; both were light enough to pass for white. He wore a
tuxedo and looked terribly elegant in that young, satin-finished,
Duke Ellington way. She, a student at Talladega, was glowing in
pearls and satin. Whether she used any of the various pastes and
creams like the Golden Peacock or Black and White Bleach meant to
"soften" and "help" the complexion—the sort of product advertised
conspicuously in the pages of the magazine—would not have been
an acceptable topic of conversation. It was a given that she did. This
was the kind of society in which Dad's people immersed themselves.

The Snakes' cotillion took place each December. To be a member
of the Snakes or any of the other fraternities meant one didn't sweat
in public. All emotion was tucked neatly into the little purse called
"race pride." The young debutantes and their escorts, drawn from the

ranks of the wealthier "somebodies," practiced and practiced to master elaborate contredanses, waltzes, and reels.

This was the way my cousin Barbara was presented when she was invited to "come out" at the Snakes' cotillion of 1949. When I called her to find out more about the event, she told me a magazine whose name she could not remember had covered the occasion that year. In trying to learn more about the world my father came from, I had been spending long hours at the New York Public Library, and I decided to check into this. I narrowed down the list of magazines that would carry this kind of story to about four, and after weeks of reading, I found the article in question in the January 1950 issue of *Holiday*. Seeing the picture of my cousin's cotillion reminded me of the Delmore Schwartz poem that ends, "The mind possesses and is possessed by all the ruins of every haunted, hunted generation's celebration." Each generation must make its own flawed contribution to the next. I wondered what my generation had done.

The photograph captures both the elegance and the gravity of the event. The cotillion was held in the chrome-and-mahogany-lined Parkway Ballroom, owned, staffed, and run by Negroes "of quality." Especially noticeable is the stiffness of the dancers, who appear to be going through a reel with an almost military precision. From the way the young debutantes and their escorts are dressed to the patterns they are dancing, they strive for a grim perfection. They are all looking down at the floor, as if afraid of making a wrong step, of tripping, of missing a cadence. In the background are ten older men, all members of the Snakes, watching silently with grave expressions on their faces. The debutantes are wrapped in gowns of dazzling white tulle that barely brush the polished maple of the ballroom floor. Look closely, and you can see the wraithlike reflection of one young dancer. On her slender, long arms are elegant thirty-two-button white kid gloves. Around her neck is an eight-inch strand of pearls. The escorts, bronze young men drawn from "the best families," are dashing and trim in black tuxedos with white bow ties, white carnations in their lapels. The picture is saturated with taste and style. The deep concentration on the faces of the debs shows how important it was to get everything just right for the camera, so that the white readers of the magazine would know they held themselves to a higher standard as leaders of their race.

It's not hard to see a certain mirthless pride. These are young people in their late teens, an age that might have been far more care-free had they been white. While I've always felt that such events were probably necessary to inculcate values of discipline and sacrifice, they also display an element of joylessness that speaks of another side of Dad's family. The rituals of social winnowing were extreme. I've never been able to shake the idea that while these rituals taught Bar-bara and her brother, Robert, that success requires concentration and preparation, the very grimness of the occasions stunted their emo-tional growth. The rituals speak to me of a society that was afraid of its emotional power and held it in check with constant, almost Puritanical exercises in self-control. As a result, for all her success, I don't think my cousin Barbara ever thought of herself as beautiful, which she truly was and still is.

When I showed the magazine picture to Barbara, not long after I returned from Caruthersville, it reminded her that one of her friends had torn her gown that evening, during the opening bow just before the debut. The friend had simply wrapped the torn piece around her arm, carrying off the complex moves as though nothing had hap-pened. Such presence of mind, Barbara said, was only to be expected. One was simply not allowed to make a wrong move. Above all, one did not let one's family down by quitting.

I asked my aunt Gwen whether the pressure ever got to anyone. "Oh, no!" she said. "You couldn't let anyone down. It would have been a terrible disgrace." The orchestra had been hired. The ball-room had been rented. Old friends would come to watch and bask in the evening's glow. One had to show himself or herself worthy. Pride of race hung in the balance. At the end, the young ladies received lockets of gold. One was not allowed to fail. "It was a very serious business," Barbara says.

Preparation for success took other forms as well. Barbara and Rob-ert learned to play bridge and chess. They took piano lessons. Barbara liked Mozart and Robert liked Rachmaninoff, whose music he played well. Their religion was Christian Science, whose steely precepts emphasize the theology of mind over matter, of will over doubt, of eternal justice, of the mortification of human desire if not the flesh. "Divine Love always has met and always will meet every human need" was the prayer I myself was raised on.

I once asked Barbara if she had ever hung out in the blues bars on Forty-seventh Street, the heart of black Chicago, where there were famous restaurants like Rum-boogie and others. She was shocked. She said she would never have been allowed into the violent "buckets of blood" in that area. So much self-control must have taught her to force the possibility of uninhibited heathen joy into a corner of her life and let it wait there, with other dreams deferred.

I believe my family was deeply damaged by this schism between desire and denial. To them, low culture, the culture of feeling and emotional release, was shameful. High culture, the complete assimilation into white society—indeed, to be something other than black—was utterly impossible. And their religion, with its rigors, kept them marching, even as it hobbled their ability to feel and to give each other succor for the unescapable racial bind they were in. My father's family lived in emotional stasis, in battered numbness. If you asked them why, they would say it was for the sake of survival in Chicago, which by the 1940s was one of the most segregated cities in America. Emotional displays of any kind were a sign of weakness to them. And so they were hobbled. I've always believed that their emphasis on austere intellectual pleasures drained their ability to enjoy each other. There was no language for anything but frustrated striving.

I cannot help but feel that for all the fancy cotillions and Christian Science meetings, for all the hard striving and social climbing, for all the pride they felt, my father's family were trained never to allow themselves to find emotional peace or rest. And this may be the most damaging effect that race had on them, and on me. Feeling the deep satisfaction that leads to joy is impossible for anyone who cannot feel safe. Being black is the most unsafe thing in the world, and I don't think my father's people made the world much safer for themselves or for the generations to come. In their world, and in mine, a single drop of African blood lays you open to the flail of racial violence, and this puts you at war with the world. Fighting this war creates a personality that is cold beyond telling. It makes you afraid somewhere deep inside that can never be touched.

As impressive and devoted to excellence as my father's family truly was, these very qualities were not enough to save them from being Negroes at odds with their environment. Their achievements could not eliminate the reality of physical danger or damage to the soul that black people encounter simply because they are black. No amount of overachieving could lessen the pain caused by the denial of their basic rights as human beings. Race hate denied them any middle ground. If you were black, you excelled. Otherwise you became just another nigger. Somewhere deep inside each member of my father's family was planted the seeds of profound self-hate and self-love, and these seeds sent strangled roots down into their souls. Love was not entirely possible to them, and yet their ethic did not allow them to fully embrace the ecstasies of hate.

In a trunk where my father kept his old college materials, I came across a poem he wrote about being a Negro. It says all that needs to be said about his feelings on the torment of race:

> Nigger, nigger on the wall
> Ain't you got no brains at all
> Can't you see that wall's been plastered
> Get off that wall you dirty bastard
>
> Nigger, nigger standing there
> Can't you see that no one cares
> When you get old and you get bigger
> You'll just be a bigger nigger.

Whether he realized it or not, my father has always struck me as a man who has a ragged place deep inside himself that could never be made whole. It is a hollow place. After I returned from Caruthersville, I began to see how anger and rage had created that vacancy in him. I recognized it because I've seen it in myself. Some part of my father's capacity to feel was destroyed by his experience of the dangers of simply being a black male. This, too, I've seen in my own life. My father achieved a great deal before he was overtaken by his ghosts. To this day, I fear that his raging ghosts are now my own, and that one day they will also destroy me.

As a child, he was raised in a society of unsatisfied black women. There was never a steady male presence in his life. The women who raised Dad gave him nearly everything he wanted. Everything, that is, except unconditional love, which was what he most needed. The women were utterly incapable of giving this. They were afraid of him. He was Katherine's child, a "perfect child of God," they said, quoting Christian Science scripture. This meant that he was indulged when he misbehaved, instead of being patiently disciplined. If he broke a precious crystal pitcher belonging to one of the women in the family—as he did once—he wasn't punished for it. Another time, when Katherine had visitors, she asked her son to fetch her a glass of water. He went to the toilet, dunked the glass in, and brought the cool water to her. He wasn't corrected for this, either.

Katherine was many things, but she wasn't a warm woman. She had her vanity. She had her positions as a socialite and as the wife to a series of husbands. And she often had to work to help support the family. But she didn't have the time to be bothered with her son. She was only sixteen when she gave birth, and she turned the care of Alan over to women who treated him like a prince, consistent with his mother's status.

Dad says he spent much of his childhood in the streets, in an effort to find his own way. He ran wild as a boy, and none of the women in the family could rein him in. He lost respect for his mother early on, and the others were just interlopers. It wasn't that he was badly treated. For instance, during summers and holidays he would be shipped off to relatives in Indiana, where he could enjoy the open country life. Except for the infrequent times when her caprice allowed her to be affectionate with him, he was mostly on the sidelines of her life. He would tell me, years later, that she simply didn't know him. They talked together now and again, but their conversations were usually competitive verbal jousts in which they would make nasty remarks about each other or people they knew. The game was to see who could top the other in cattiness.

Katherine, meanwhile, was busy running from one marriage to another. After giving birth to Alan, she left Arvit and married a tailor.

Next she married a gambling, politically connected park supervisor, followed by two other men — they were brief flings — and, finally, an army man named Harold.

As a teenager, Dad sometimes got mixed up in defending his mother from one or another of these men. It created an emotional relationship between them that was full of both love and resentment. After the breakup of Katherine's marriage to the park supervisor, she cut the man's clothes in half with a pair of scissors. When he returned for them, he knocked her down a flight of stairs. Dad and Harold went looking for him, intent on "breaking" his bones. I don't know if they completed their mission, but Dad felt it was his duty to take it on — real men didn't allow such things to happen to their mothers.

Dad once told Katherine that he didn't like to be seen with her because people were always mistaking him for one of her suitors. As a boy, he watched the parade come and go. He hated them all and scorned the presents they gave him as clearly being just part of their efforts at seduction. And he would clearly mark out his own territory. "You can't punish me," he would tell them. "You're not my father."

One of Dad's first jobs, at age twelve, was running errands for a pharmacist. Often his deliveries were to the whorehouses on the North Side. The prostitutes would pay with the twenty-dollar bills they got from their johns and would let Dad keep the change, which often was a lot. He learned early on how to keep money in his pocket. Katherine would use her various connections to find him jobs like working as a stock boy at Brooks Brothers. As a young man, he benefited from his family connections with the Williamses, some of whom were members of the Brotherhood of Sleeping Car Porters and worked on the trains running between Chicago and New York City. He worked on the trains for a while, and his stories are peppered with such incidents as witnessing black cooks spit into the food of white passengers. And he learned, as Malcolm X and thousands of other young black men did, that you could make plenty of money buying drugs in one city and selling them along the way or in New York.

Another one of his jobs as a young man brought him into the South Side hotels and brothels on South Ellis that were owned by Al Capone. Dad would keep in his head the results of horse races all around the country, and when the "wise guys" came into the lobby of this or that hotel to find out who had won, he'd tell them. The tips, he says, were large.

My father describes many of these adventures as though they were part of a jolly, frolicking life. But to me, there are echoes of the earlier neglect and of a spirited rebellion against the women in his family.

When World War II came, Dad was just of draft age. He was sent to Germany after spending his months of basic training, ironically, at an army base near Caruthersville. In Germany, he and a handful of black friends skipped off a troop train headed north and spent about two weeks in the occupied territory getting drunk. He later met some Africans there who were selling hashish as an additive to cigarettes. There was also rocket fuel, for a "roaring drunk." And there were all the German women who threw themselves at black soldiers. Dad told me he once had to spank one of them for being too forward. But she, in turn, told the military police about his absence from his unit, and he landed in jail.

Katherine came to the rescue, using her political pull with her congressman, William Dawson, to get Alan admitted to West Point Preparatory School, a training ground for West Point Military Academy. Lacking the necessary academic skills, he soon found himself in trouble, particularly in math. He has always said that he was given "the silent treatment" by the white cadets, but a man I met who knew my father in those years told me that everyone liked him and wanted to help him get ahead.

While at school, he became ill with a bad case of strep throat, he says, and was sent to a hospital at Mitchell Field on Long Island. He and another cadet (now a wealthy doctor in Detroit) would steal white starched sheets out of the hospital's linen rooms—it seems to me that at this point Dad's enjoyment of his early freedom as a "streety niggah" came into play—and travel to Harlem, where they would sell the sheets for cash and use the money to buy marijuana. Then they'd return to the base and peddle the weed there. It was one more lucrative enterprise for him, a return to the security of having money. He says he had gotten to know several jazz musicians, people like Dexter Gordon, from the time he spent in the Chicago club scene. In Harlem, Dexter would sell him heroin, and Alan began using it.

Dad was a regular user by the time the war was over. He would go back to the clubs where marijuana was sold before the war and buy packets of heroin in the men's room. It was a funky, mysterious life. When he speaks of it—in almost the same reverent tones as Barbara speaks of her cotillion debut and the world of Negro society—he describes the cachet of knowing how to test whether the product was any good, how to "tie up," how to spot a police officer. One time the heroin was so powerful that his friends thought he'd overdosed and fled from the uptown hotel room they were in. "I saw them leaving!" Dad recalls. "When I woke up from the nod, I went to the window to see where they'd gone. They were running out of the hotel, fast as hell. They thought I was dead."

Arvit eventually found out about his son's heroin addiction, and tried to get him involved in the haberdashery business. Arvit proposed that Dad take over the original store on Forty-seventh Street, and Arvit would open another one. Dad tried for a little while, but it didn't work out. The two were able to make up for some of the lost time between them, but by then Dad's habit made it impossible for him to put his feet on the ground. All Arvit did as a father, Dad says, was warn him about his drug habit; Dad would allow him to do nothing more.

Bereft of a mother, without a father's presence, Dad, at least in his own estimation, had already raised himself. For him, gangsters were the only invulnerable men, and he imitated them. For a long time, I was certain my father *was* a gangster, and this impression glamorized him in my eyes. But years of watching and listening have taught me that he was not unlike many of the young middle-class black men I've known, who have thirsted for distractions from the hard business of growing up. His childhood, like theirs, was protracted by overindulgent women who feared that his adult life as a black man would be hard enough, so why tax him too early?

Throughout the rest of his life, he hauled this pained and untouchable core around with him. He never learned to measure out his efforts. When he did give, he gave everything he had all at once. He threw himself into his interests, but he never learned to pace his way through to completion. There was a pattern to it. He dropped out of Roosevelt College and the Illinois Institute of Technology, yet he never worked fewer than two jobs at the same time. He had a very clear picture of the world of work, but he rejected as irrelevant any training that didn't bear directly on that world. He didn't believe in the credentialism that Gwen imposed on her kids, nor did he believe in the chaos of Katherine's world, either. It wasn't that he was afraid of school; he simply lacked the measured discipline that Barbara and Robert had learned.

I remember asking Dad once about the cotillions and social whirl of Negro society. He laughed. "That was for the women," he said. "They knew nothing of the world of men except how to get things from them." In his eyes, the cotillions were for phonies. Besides, by the time they became popular, he was a married man with a child, my brother Mark, on the way.

A photo I have of my father at Barbara's cotillion shows a rather ghostly, wanly smiling person. He has the fey look of a very handsome man who isn't entirely "there." Mom *is* there. She looks rather dainty in her sequins, which match those of the dress she helped Barbara make for her coming out. There's even a picture of all three of them standing together and smiling broadly. There's no hint of the internal strains beneath the surface, or of the very different directions in which the three were already headed. Dad says that as he and Mom were driving home in his new car after the cotillion, another car crashed into them. I don't know if he was using drugs that night, but I can't exclude the possibility.

I see that picture in a very different way now than I did as a naive young boy. Then I saw the romance between my parents as perfectly invincible, because that's what I needed to see to sustain my own belief in a coherent, well-defended world. They had a lot in common: a damaged sense of self caused by a home environment that was bitterly fragmented and emotionally chaotic. Each had an extraordinary need to be accepted and loved but didn't know how to receive love or acceptance. Both came to love material possessions as compensation for emotional loss and grievance. And each had experienced despair. There was something in both of them that could not be touched.

I remember once, as a child, watching a western movie and seeing a uniform that reminded me of something I'd seen before. Almost instinctively, I went to the closet in our little apartment in Chicago and pulled the string attached to the bare lightbulb. It snapped on, and the bright light revealed a well-kept scarlet-colored dress uniform with gold braid on the arms, massive epaulettes over each shoulder, gold buttons down the chest, and dark pants with military stripes down either leg. In a box on an upper shelf was a cadet's pillbox hat. I put the hat on my head. It sat rigidly, too large for me. Fearing I might get caught with one of my father's precious belongings, I quickly packed it back in the box.

These are the images I had of my father when I was a child, and they now seem as strong as all I was to learn later about his struggles as a boy, as a teenager, and even as a man. Racial pride contributed to my sense of him as someone who soared over any of my white relatives. But there was only so far he could love me, and I came to suspect that the reason he couldn't go further was partly because I didn't belong to him. I wasn't black enough.

Today, as then, I think of my father as an unfinished man. He was a man who brushed aside many chances to accomplish what others wanted of him in favor of following his own course. He was a tireless worker who taught me how to strive hard and to find a sense of myself in the world of action that he had learned about as a child. His careless waste of opportunities, as self-destructive as it was, has also come down to me as part of my emotional heritage. I've learned to fight it, maybe as he learned to fight the limitations of his environment. That part of Chicago is in me, even as Caruthersville is in me. No one ever escapes his or her past. But unlike those people in Caruthersville, who seemed completely absorbed and lost in their past, my father's family taught me to name my experiences and to look toward the future. This pointed me to a larger sense of myself, to a world of greater possibility, and, finally, to that trip to Caruthersville and back again, to a place where I feel there are no walls to fill me with despair.

My grandmother, Katherine Vivian Williams.

My grandfather, Arvit Minerbrook, Jr.

My father, Alan, at 16 with his mother, Katherine.

FOUR / **The Limits
of the Possible**

*Words lead to deeds. . . . They prepare the soul, make
it ready and move it to tenderness.*

—SAINT THERESA

On a lovely autumn evening, my parents were strolling outside a theater on the North Side of Chicago. They had just
seen some foreign film; neither recalls the title. But it apparently had
made them forget for a rare moment that they represented something
new and astonishing: a handsome black man and a beautiful white
woman together in a crowd, unaware of anything but each other,
unself-consciously enjoying themselves. They let down their guard.
There was a crowd of people around them as the movie let out, but
as the crowd thinned they found themselves alone. Someone walked
up behind my mother and punched her in the middle of the back,
giving her a blow hard enough to knock the breath out of her. She is
a petite woman, so she thought that maybe someone had accidentally
knocked into her, and that's what she told my father. When he turned
around, a group of white men—Italians, he says—jumped him
without a word and beat him severely.

Mom says Dad fought back, but of course my father, who interprets life with a certain calm detachment, insists it was no big deal. What concerned him the most wasn't the odds against him or the cowardice of four men beating up one, but the fact that in the brawl he tore the lining of his new Donegal tweed jacket. It was one he'd had custom-made after meeting my mother. It just didn't fit him right afterward, he said, so he gave it away to a friend.

It was 1948, and my parents were both students at Roosevelt University in Chicago. They hung out with an arty crowd—white people who went to the clubs on the South Side every now and then, and blacks who were mostly war veterans putting themselves through school on the GI Bill like my father was. Both my parents were in their mid-twenties. Dad, having met African soldiers during the war, had returned to Chicago with a profound interest in the art, culture, and freedom struggles of Africa. Mom was already in business for herself as owner of a couture shop.

I don't imagine for a minute that race wasn't important to them when they met, or that they believed it would simply disappear or cease to matter to the rest of the world. They were trying to create a different world, and their idealism certainly played a part in their plans. When two people of different races decide to turn their backs on a social code, as my parents did, it sometimes seems an extraordinary thing to say that they were willing to face the troubles ahead simply because they were in love. Surely, the conventional wisdom says, there must be other reasons behind their determination to live their lives together. And there must have been. But if they stood for anything to each other or to their children, it was the fact that theirs was no different from the attraction of any human being to another. That's what they were to me. It was impossible for me to see the racial elements of their complex marriage until much later. While the incident outside the theater probably reminded them of the ferocious opposition they would have to face from the outside world, it also showed them they were strong. They had survived. They could stand together and overcome.

My mother likes to tell other stories about their early years together and about how they faced the subtle and often not-so-subtle problems of racial etiquette. I think that proving the impossible was indeed possible excited her more than it did my father because she was more given to the dreams in her head. Dad was already driven by the harsh reality of being a black male. But I think her dreams helped to inspire his. And when she would sit by the window and fret that maybe they had no future together after all, that the world wouldn't let them simply *be*, he would return from his classes and write out her favorite Carl Sandburg poem, which began:

> *It's going to come out all right—do you know?*
> *The sun, the birds, the grass—they know.*
> *They get along—and we'll get along.*

And Dad introduced her to the poems of the Harlem Renaissance writer Countee Cullen, the son-in-law of the historian W. E. B. Du Bois. She loved e. e. cummings's work, too. When she was particularly worn down by all the opposition she saw ahead of them, Dad shared with her a Cullen poem called "Any Human to Another."

> *The ills I sorrow at*
> *Not me alone*
> *Like an arrow*
> *Pierce to the marrow*
> *Through the fat*
> *And past the bone.*

Dad wrote the words out for her. This was their courtship, and stories of it have shaped my own dreams of the world's possibilities. I met a man many years later who told me he had introduced them, at a party of the art crowd in Chicago—an interracial set who all knew each other. Accompanied by someone at the piano, my mother was singing, or was trying to sing, like Ella Fitzgerald, the man said. It didn't quite go over, but he admired her attempt; anyway, it was all in fun. He knew both my mother and my father, and when he introduced them, he said, it was like watching two rare birds meeting for the first time. "They flew off together, and after that you never saw them apart," he said. When I asked Mom about this romantic story, she said she had never tried to sing like Ella Fitzgerald at any party.

My father says the first time he saw her he recognized instantly that they were meant for each other.

They were married in 1949, in a small private ceremony attended by members of his family and, of course, none of hers. Her best friend, a white woman named Kay, was there for support. In the picture I have of the wedding, they are the only two whites in a sea of tense brown and black and cinnamon faces. The minister who married them was the Reverend Archibald Cox, a well-known and highly respected member of the black community. He was also a friend of Katherine's, and very pale-skinned.

My parents knew that the color of their skin placed them in a new and dangerous category that would test them for life. The fierce pride instilled in LaVerne by her upbringing and the charmed life Alan had led made them both feel they'd found something special and different in each other. As long as they had each other, she would say later, they had a world. They had the language, the charm, the pizzazz. He was bright and handsome; she was beautiful and was skilled at a craft she cared about intensely. They were both gifted and, in a sense, self-made. They were brave. They asked for little from the world but an honest chance. They didn't ask for sympathy. They were too busy with each other's magic for that. Maybe LaVerne wouldn't be able to live on the North Side, where the other whites lived, where the fine houses and opportunities were. She would give that up. It was more than worth it to her because she was showing what was in her heart, as well as the distance she'd traveled from her hometown, where something like this was utterly impossible. Marriage to a Negro was a test of her convictions, of her courage and grit, of the very things her childhood had instilled in her, even if those qualities were never meant to be tested in such an enterprise as an interracial marriage. Alan's sense of style gave her courage.

But the relationship was read quite differently by Dad's family. To Katherine, it was clear that this ignorant white girl was out to get her beautiful boy killed. She was livid at LaVerne for putting her son at such risk. And because of her opposition, the marriage didn't play well among the other women in Dad's family. Not in the least. They never admitted my mother inside the golden circle of their esteem.

They attacked her shamefully, not physically but emotionally and spiritually, and she resisted them even as she wanted to be accepted. But any such acceptance was impossible, and this caught her quite by surprise. It was one thing for her to break down the walls of prejudice in herself, it seemed, but quite another to expect Katherine to breach the walls of her own prejudice and fear and accept her daughter-in-law as a human being. I don't think my mother fully appreciated this, or fully acknowledged the weighty meaning of the fact that, in black society, having a white wife was no virtue. If Mom expected the Negroes of Dad's family to be more tolerant than the whites of her own, she was sorely disappointed. For the most part, Dad's family considered the marriage a fearsome disaster. Only Gwendolyn's daughter, Barbara, who was then a student, showed Mom any degree of affection.

Katherine interpreted the marriage as a personal insult and an encroachment on her ability to maintain power over her son. It didn't matter to her now that she'd once loosened her claims on Alan by letting him be reared by others. A white girl had strayed into her personal territory. She would never regard Mom as her daughter-in-law, and referred to the marriage as "a long-term affair." Katherine's psychological assaults on my mother would be unceasing over the next three decades.

An early meeting between the two resulted in an immediate collision of cultural values and laid out the terms of engagement. Mom tried to be polite, as any daughter-in-law would. Her courtesy was a miscalculation. She should have shown strength and supreme indifference instead—even a touch of cruelty would have been sufficient to get through Katherine's defenses. Katherine read Mom's attitude of respect as a form of racial condescension: the white girl thought she had to be nice to her enemy. Katherine lived in a no-holds-barred world: she construed any sign of respect, any show of *politesse*, as proof of Mom's unworthiness. Being nice to Katherine, who lived by her wits and gave no quarter, was a show of weakness, even a gesture of defeat. In her terms, for this white girl to be nice to her assumed that Mom lacked nerve or, worse, that she was declaring a contest of wit and will over possession of Katherine's son. It assumed that the two women had agreed to something, and that Katherine would give up without a fight. Katherine was determined to disprove any such assumptions. These misunderstandings were born of racial and cultural dimensions of which my mother was as yet unaware. If there was to be a war of wills, Katherine would put everything she had into winning.

When my parents were first married, Katherine was living at the Pershing Hotel, a place where Charlie Parker often played. She invited the young couple to her apartment one evening, and when they arrived Alan called up from the lobby to let Katherine know they were there. She summoned him. Alone. This was her opening move.

For the next hour Mom stoically cooled her heels, like an errand girl awaiting a meeting with the queen. Finally, after he'd displayed his own humility, Dad called Mom up to Katherine's rooms. Mom shouldn't have waited, trapped and vulnerable, but it was too late. My father had done nothing to intervene on her behalf, but instead had deferred to Katherine's will. She had won another advantage. Mom should have walked out and never returned. Instead, she swallowed her pride and went upstairs.

She was summoned into Katherine's boudoir, now very much on the defensive and doubtless showing her anger and hurt. Katherine was wearing a beautiful and seductive coffee colored chemise nightgown that outlined the contours of her body. Basking in all her glory, she lounged on the bed, cool and detached, with the gown spread out regally around her.

Dad was sitting in a chair on the other side of the room waiting for the confrontation of wits to begin. He was by now quite accustomed to Katherine's gamesmanship, but he hadn't warned Mom about it. Katherine was playing that game as old as racial oppression—the game of slowly humiliating one's opponents before destroying them. Now it was the white girl's turn to learn.

"So tell me, LaVerne," Katherine began. "Have you decided what race your children will be?"

In describing this episode, Mom has always tried to make it seem that the question left her unfazed. I know better. Still, she didn't dare give Katherine the satisfaction of seeing the mark it left on her sense of honor, of "face." The old Caruthersville instincts took over in an instant.

"Well, I guess we'll have to let the children decide for themselves."

Wrong answer.

What Katherine has always said she wanted to hear was that, given the realities of race and the need for LaVerne to prepare her children for the battles that lay ahead, she understood that any children she had would, of course, be black. This, to Katherine, would only have shown good judgment. America hated mulattoes almost as much as it hated black people, and LaVerne should have been prepared to defend the children that were sure to come along. But was Alan's white wife willing to subsume her own racial identity for the sake of protecting their children? LaVerne was in revolt against her people, but not that deeply. I don't think she understood yet how completely vulnerable her marriage to a Negro made her—even to the point of requiring her to strip off all traces of her own unacknowledged racial pride. This wasn't possible for her—she was never a guilty rich white girl. LaVerne felt she'd already crossed one river, and she wasn't about to admit she carried any negative racial baggage with her. Katherine, however, knew otherwise.

Mom hadn't come all the way from Caruthersville with her well-honed sense of pride to be tested like this. She was aiming for a world in which color would no longer matter, but here she was finding out it still did. Color had always been the only thing that mattered in the world of Negroes. On another level, Katherine also wanted Mom to show herself up as nothing but a common Missouri white girl. Mom's answer showed both how innocent of the world she really was and how prideful and obstinate she could be. What mattered was to demonstrate moral superiority, and Mom wouldn't give that up to anyone. Katherine was practical down to the bone, and Mom was idealistic and naive in this deeply challenging world of negritude.

The two women were at loggerheads from this time forth. Each insisted on standing on the reality of her own racial experience, which was connected to deeply held emotions. Neither would give in to any alternative. Brave though it was, Mom's response was exactly the kind of answer that Katherine had expected. Mom had failed

Katherine's test. It drew the line between them. What Katherine knew, and Mom could never have known, was a brutal reality: white America feared and hated black men with a special killing rage, and it would hate LaVerne Smith for having innocently crossed into black territory. Mom would have to examine her experience as a white woman and decide how much of it might be dangerous to her children. To Katherine, passing along "whiteness" to any children would disable them from fighting the racial wars ahead. I think Katherine's question might also have shown Mom how she, too, could be harmed by holding on to her racial values. But that message was lost in the rudeness of the question.

On another level, I think something even more basic separated my mother from Katherine. Mom was in love with Katherine's son. Love was not something Katherine could feel for anyone but herself. It was not possible in her world; it was too dangerous an emotion. Where Katherine came from, a woman had to keep love at a distance to survive in one piece. To Katherine, love wasn't something you gave but something you took. She was too afraid and too alone to love. Who, then, was the more disadvantaged of these two women? Who bore the deeper wounds? And who had more to offer the spoiled child who was LaVerne's husband and Katherine's son?

My mother missed something else, too. Harsh though it was for Katherine to ask such a question, it was a brutal form of affection, and as close to any form of human acknowledgment as Katherine, in her vanity, could ever give. What Mom heard in the question was a demand that Katherine be allowed to teach her, and this was something I think Mom would not allow because of her own distrust of the world. I think the question so frightened her that she drew up the drawbridge and lost any sympathy she might ever have had for Katherine. In the long run this lack of sympathy caused both women to build up the wall of fierce resistance between them. The argument became racial when it was actually freighted with a deeper emotional meaning that they might someday have tried to understand.

What they both missed that day was a chance to help each other. I suppose, in a way, it was never possible. They each spoke a different language because of their cultural experiences—the confused subtext of race. And it cheated them both. For after this, Katherine would never be allowed to teach her grandchildren the close allegiances that black people have always created for their own survival. And Mom lost, too. By insisting that she could raise her children according to interracial ideals for which there were no blueprints, she lost the experience of a woman who could have helped her make us less divided and tangled in finding our personal identities. Each of us might have known far earlier that because we existed in the black world we could never completely exist in the white one, a world in which we would always be seen as pariahs because of the color of our father's skin. I have always heard Katherine's question as a door to mutual understanding. But neither of them walked through it, and the opportunity did not come again.

Race is such a weak vessel for human emotion. I believe that the fear of loss was too much of a challenge to Katherine's pride, and blinded her to larger human possibilities. Who could separate that pride from one's racial experience? Katherine clung to her dislike of white people, and that was her limit. Mom didn't know—and perhaps couldn't know—the defensive language of blackness. But fear of loss, fear of failing, the need to cling to personal vanity, to be acknowledged as powerful, these are human frailties, and race is a leaky bowl to hold them. Fearing loss, Katherine backed herself into a defensive position of intolerance. It has always seemed a bitter irony that she wasn't willing to live up to the same ideals of tolerance and idealism that she and other Negroes demanded of the rest of the world.

Despite his efforts to stay out of it, Dad was ultimately enmeshed in the racial net as well. He'd started to break away from his unhappy past with Katherine, but he was never able to do so completely. I think he was bound to his mother by her emotional poverty—by what she could not or would not give him: nurturance, acceptance, understanding, unconditional love. In what turned out to be the major irony of his life, he found exactly these things in his wife, but he couldn't accept them from her because he wanted them from his mother. He used the very nurturance he found to punish Katherine for what she could not give. As a consequence, he spent most of his married life shuttling between these two powerful women, in a divided allegiance that in the end went far deeper than the divisions of race. Human emotions, when mixed with racial issues, are prone to shatter like glass. This volatile emotional triangle took on a racial dimension that only deepened private wounds and kept them from ever mending.

Once, when my mother asked outright for Katherine's love as a mother-in-law, Katherine addressed her directly: "I'm sorry, but you've got the wrong guy." I think Mom kept hoping Katherine's attitude would change, but it never did. Part of Katherine's rage came from the fact that she'd never found a man as strong as she was, able to give her the emotional sustenance she needed. She'd had to make it on her own resources her whole life, as many black women do. She would never let a white woman inside her most intimate circle. For his part, Dad could never step outside the circle of his mother's rage, and it marked him his whole life.

When I think of the three of them, I often think about the faith in the possibility of love that is required of any lover, the terrible exertion of will it takes to give oneself completely to another person. This will was absent in my father. Having a mother like Katherine, who only knew how to survive, not how to surrender herself to love, how could my father know how to give love? A human being has the power to choose the kind of person he or she wants to be. But no one can claim that power through rage or hate, which are at the heart of racialized thinking. Seeing herself as a Race Woman, Katherine was bound completely by the limitations of that game, and in the end she was imprisoned by it because she could never conceive of a world without blinding rage.

In the course of their relationship over the next three decades, Katherine would vacillate between trying to reclaim her son by teasing him with gifts, and trying to keep her distance from him. Even after my parents were married, Dad acted as though he couldn't make up his mind which he wanted more—his mother or his wife. Mom kept the faith, as women tend to do, and never gave up. When Dad showed his divided loyalty, she tried to carry on without him. What all women seem to know about marriage is something that men tend to ignore: a man must choose to put his mother behind him and make his wife the center of his life. If he fails in this, the marriage usually won't last. A man must choose between his past and his future, and I think my father was so divided in himself—as many men are, regardless of their race—that he could not choose between the two.

When my mother asked for proof of my father's faith and commitment, he heard her pleas as challenges to mend his divided soul. Like Katherine, he learned to substitute needless acts of mental cruelty and the withholding of affection in place of love.

Among her stories of this time, Mom says that at one of their get-togethers she asked Katherine—a bit too longingly, perhaps—whether she would ever be part of her mother in-law's "golden circle."

Dad leaped up, angry enough to strike her, but something stopped him. Hitting her was a thing he did in private. He wouldn't give Katherine the satisfaction of knowing he mistreated the woman he'd interposed between them. He *would*, however, display a sanctimonious black rage.

"What are you?" he shouted at Mom, in front of his mother. "Some kind of dyke?" Katherine did nothing to intervene; this white girl had to be kept in line.

It went on endlessly like this over the years. Most often, Mom was left to fend for herself. There were no other external challenges like the assault outside the theater that had occurred at the beginning of my parents' relationship. Instead, the challenges sprang from their own ghosts and demons, woven out of the patterns of their individual temperaments. Compared to these kinds of troubles, the beating they'd received was child's play.

Early in my parents' marriage, Katherine said to Mom, point-blank: "You know, LaVerne, you're such a *white* white girl."

Another time, at one of Katherine's parties, Mom couldn't find her pocketbook when she was ready to leave. Katherine pounced. "Has anyone seen LaVerne's pocketbook?" she called out to the guests. "It seems she thinks someone has stolen it. Let's all stop what we're doing and help LaVerne find it."

At times like these, Katherine was in all her glory. What should have been a simple, normal rivalry between mother-in-law and daughter-in-law was freighted with the complexities of an ages-old racial quarrel. Race should have played a minor role, but instead it exerted a spectral power to frame all those questions about human nature that are hard to answer.

Interracial relationships are regarded with the same cynicism today as then. Conventional wisdom goes something like this: Whites date blacks for the thrill of the forbidden, for the dangerous lark, but the relationship can never be serious. When the excitement is gone or is challenged by the real dangers of racial prejudice, both partners return to their own kind with a certain chastised awareness, never to stray again. They have learned that the excitement of a racial adventure is not the same thing as love. My father's family apparently believed that a white girl like Mom would just go back to dating white men and would use her experience of dating a black man as a symbol of personal freedom. Or, if she was more sensible, she would simply keep it a sweet secret of her private quest to step beyond the narrow boundary of conformity. She would never reveal her secret to the white man she would eventually marry: it was common knowledge that white men didn't like their women "tainted" by experience with a black man. It brought down the value of the merchandise, as if it were goods at a fire sale.

This traditional belief was rooted in the black experience of loss. To my father's family, the greatest danger in his marriage to my mother was that the family might lose him across the color line. Marriage to a white woman might open up certain opportunities for improvement in his social status, but at a tremendous cost to his family. Crossing the color line in this way meant that Dad might have the chance to "opt out" of the social contract that kept Chicago's Negro masses bound to one another within the walls of the South Side. "Marrying white" meant he might abandon that narrow, defensive circle of Negro life in favor of a life where he would benefit from exposure to the flow of opportunities available in the white world. Crossing the color line was considered too risky, a kind of death in the family. Losing someone "across the line" brought secret shame on the family whose member had "crossed."

Despite her strong instinct for survival, Mom was in completely over her head in black Chicago. She had strayed into a hornet's nest in which the commonplaces of decency were largely impossible because she was the wrong color. She did not know that race—whether practiced by blacks or by whites—is, finally, a crutch for deeper human frailties and failings, a bad excuse for bad manners, a false elevation, a confession of every kind of human weakness.

At length, my mother found herself alone and unprotected among my father's people. When she tried to hire a housekeeper, she always seemed to end up with a black woman who treated her with contempt and cheated her. But she could not protest without having Katherine or my father accuse her of being a racist.

A year after they were married, my blond haired and blue-eyed brother Mark was born. Dad's people lavished Mark with gifts while neglecting Mom. All Katherine could say was that LaVerne was a good mother. I was born a year later (without the blond hair or the blue eyes), leading Katherine to complain that Mom was having too many babies too quickly and putting too much pressure on Katherine's son.

My own memories of Chicago date from the age of three or four. I think that one side effect of all the conflicts swirling around my parents was to make my father nervous about having children who could not be readily identified as his. We were fair-skinned boys, my brother and I. In the pictures I have from those years, it would be hard to claim either of us as Negro children at all. This is ironic, because light skin was still accorded great honor in the black community. But I think Dad's own chestnut-brown complexion distracted him somehow. I've always felt that if we'd been darker, he might have embraced us more willingly.

I remember mostly that my mother always seemed overwhelmed. She hired one housekeeper who was very dark and refused to work, and they were constantly at odds. I feared and disliked this woman, who treated Mark and me brutally. If she wanted me to go somewhere, she would pinch my arm with fingernails that were like talons on my skin. She would talk for hours on the phone, but when Mom confronted her she would deny it and complain to Dad. She was not dismissed; she simply stopped coming, and that caused further

trouble for my mother. Dad never reprimanded the woman or de-
fended my mother against her.

Actually, my father didn't spend much time at home, and when
he was there he always seemed just out of reach. He slept a lot, because he was tired from the long hours he worked—usually two,
sometimes three jobs at a time to support the family. I remember him
from this time as a tall, slim, handsome man, who could swim far
out into Lake Michigan on a summer day—out beyond the safety
buoys, until his body was just a dot on the water. I remember one
time he stepped on a tack and opened up a small tear in his foot, an
incident that scared me. But he made a game of it by jumping up and
down on one foot and holding the other. Once in a while he would
take Mark and me with him on a night job of making deliveries on a
juice truck.

When we did get to spend time with Dad, he could be funny and
gentle. One Christmas, when we were living in an apartment on
Drexel Boulevard, he helped Mark and me make a wonderful snowman, complete with coal eyes and a carrot nose. Another time, he
took us out to get a Christmas tree. He had played a lot of basketball,
and had strong arms and legs. With Mark and me in the back of the
car, he drove home holding that tree against the outside of the car. I
thought it was the greatest display of strength ever

Sometimes he would take me in his lap and read me the Sunday
comics. I loved the safety of being there with his arms on either side
of me like two solid walls, the smell of tobacco on his breath, while
he read "Joe Palooka."

But such moments were rare. Mostly I remember a withdrawn,
troubled man who always seemed distracted. He would do things that
I thought were funny but in fact were quite careless. Once he left
Mark and me in his Ford while he went to shop for a Christmas tree.
He had parked the car on a steep hill, and Mark and I, thinking it
would be a great game, released the parking brake. We began drifting
downhill at some speed. Dad returned in time to leap into the car
and slam on the brake, but Mark and I got a good scolding.

Another time, I was out walking with him and saw a dog I wanted
to pet. I had a dog, too, whose name was Scuppers. Thinking the dog
in the street would be as gentle as Scuppers, I reached out to pet it.

My father didn't stop me, and the dog bit me. It left a deep hole in my hand, and I had to be taken to the hospital. I remember feeling very unsafe after that. I wondered if my father hadn't warned me because he wasn't paying attention or because he wanted to teach me a lesson.

He seemed terribly careless in other ways, too. Often, he brought his drug-addicted friends to our apartment while Mom was at work. They would play records too loud and would laugh or argue in disturbingly loud voices. Mom would come home to find the place upside down, and she and Dad would get into a fistfight about it. She fought back, but he always won. Once, when she came home and complained about the strangers in the house, he threw a tricycle at her and broke her arm.

A turning point in my relationship with my father came when I was about four years old, although I buried the memory so deeply that it was years before I could recall the incident and place it among my earliest recollections.

One afternoon, Dad and a friend of his took Mark and me to a beach on Lake Michigan to swim. Dad was laughing with his buddy as we drove. At the lake, I remember the blue of the water and the terrible heat of the yellow sand, which burned my feet. I walked into the water up to my calves. Dad lifted me up on his shoulders and walked out into deeper water. I remember looking down from his shoulders, and the drop seemed frightening. The blue lake stretched out before us into the huge blue horizon. It was breezy and I was getting cold. Mark was with the other man.

"Do you know how to swim?" Dad was teasing.

"Sure," I said.

"You sure you know how to swim?"

"Sure I do," I said. I was terribly excited about swimming, even though I didn't have the faintest idea of what it entailed.

Did I know how to swim? Yes. Did I know how to swim? Yes. Yes. Yes. I'm sure I *did* know how to swim in that moment, if only he would please put me down.

The next instant, he was holding me over the water by my wrists. My legs were kicking wildly, as if I were riding a bike or trying to run.

Then he dropped me. I remember the sudden, riveting punch in my stomach as I plunged into the cold lake. It must have knocked the wind out of me. I involuntarily inhaled, and the blue, blue water bit into my lungs. I remember the feeling of panic that seized me. I began gulping and inhaling more water. Water was gushing painfully into my stomach. I was gasping for air. I opened my eyes wide and saw my father's long legs, which looked like tree trunks, drifting up, up, up, magically, just beyond my reach. I grabbed for them. They seemed to be floating away. Rays of light shimmered down into the azure blue liquid. I realized I couldn't breathe. I tried to take in deeper breaths. My nostrils were stinging inside, as if someone had poured hot wax into them, as though they'd been turned inside out.

Suddenly I was snatched up through the water and into the air, and I was choking and crying, water gushing out of my stomach and lungs and snot coming out of my nose. I could hear Dad telling me not to be upset. Dad hated it when we got emotional. It wasn't allowed. He was a black man, as we would soon be, and black men had to be tough. I should be tough and stop crying, he said.

But I wasn't tough. My head was splitting. I must have cried too much, because Dad said we had to go home. I cried in the backseat all the way. I cried when we got home, and Katherine was there and told me not to cry. Boys weren't supposed to cry. I remember her saying that. But I couldn't stop.

Many years later, I have come to realize that this incident planted a seed of doubt about my father's love for me, a doubt so deep that I could never again think of him as someone I could trust. He died for me that day, in a way I felt deeply but didn't understand. It was such a painful feeling of abandonment that I was stunned into silence. No words could describe such a thing.

When I was five or six years old, Mom decided we should move to a new housing complex being built in a suburb of Chicago called Harvey. Dad didn't want to go, so she left him and moved us there herself, although he joined us later. Mom was trying to put as much distance as she could between herself and Katherine and all the troubles associated with her presence in Mom's life.

But other problems were weighing her and my father down. Dad was taking drugs on and off. He says it was cocaine, but Mom insists it was heroin. I remember that a black woman carrying a bag was always hovering around the house. Cars would drive up in front and then leave. One afternoon, Dad bought a whole truckload of slate and piled it in the middle of the living room, where it lay, untouched, for months.

All I know is that I couldn't stand to be around my father after that experience at the lake. Being with him made me feel sick. One day, when Mark and I were playing outside in the construction debris from all the homes still going up, I fell and slashed my leg open. Dad took me into the bathroom, but he couldn't find any suitable bandages in the medicine cabinet. The only ones we had were for finger cuts: they wrapped around the finger and were tied in place by white strings. Dad tried to use some of them on my leg, but they didn't work. The cut just bled and bled. He seemed to lose interest then, and handed me a table napkin to hold on the slash until my mother got home from work. The scar is still visible on my leg today. My mother says it was around this time that she found a gun in the closet. She drove out on a deserted road and threw it away.

Not long ago I asked my father what he remembered about this time. He says he was striving to make a better world for his family. He'd bought the house in Harvey with his veteran's benefits. It was a tract home, a lot like those in Levittown on Long Island. It was part of his dream to own such a place, he said. My mother had picked out the one she liked, and if anyone was messing things up, it was she. She just pushed him too hard. She always wanted things to happen fast. She was a white girl who didn't understand what it meant to be black. "Your mother didn't like that place at all, and here I was," he says, "slaving to make a go of it."

But the cocaine is harder to explain away, as is the gun and the general feeling I've had that being with him at that time was almost like being with someone who wasn't there. These things had been part of his life before he met my mother, and he couldn't readily give them up after he had children. Maybe the indulgence that he had been raised on was another thing he couldn't give up. In the end, these habits created an emotional vacancy. He was a man in a trance.

When I told my father once how I remembered the incident at Lake Michigan, he denied that I could remember it at all. "You were so young," he said.

But there are some things I haven't told my father, certain feelings about how he behaved when I was a young child. I had the feeling then that his neglect simply showed he didn't care about me. He would literally lose himself in whatever he was doing, and this became just another way of hiding from the terrible pull of responsibility. At one time, it was far easier to call his struggle by a racial name. Now, his faults seem merely human ones. For my part, I learned to keep my distance from my father. This was a habit of self-protection that he taught me, and along with it a profound lack of trust for other people. Such habits have no racial names. I've never been able to lose them.

We didn't last long in the suburbs. My mother left my father again, taking Mark and me to live in an apartment on the North Side of Chicago. Dad accused her of hiding out there among people of her own color, when she was simply desperate for her safety. One afternoon, dead drunk, he came looking for her, and crashed through a window of her apartment. Even now, he says he believed she was using her race against him by escaping to the North Side, where black men were not tolerated.

They had a brief reconciliation, but Dad refused to act like an adult, and soon she left again, this time for New York City, where she'd taken a job as a designer in the fashion industry. My parents seemed to be testing the limits of their partnership, which was mixed up with race in ways that I may never understand. There are some regions where a person's racial experience can't be separated from human experience, and if Dad saw Mom's attempts to be free of him as racially tinged, Mom saw them as a simple expression of her will to survive. Dad followed us to New York eventually, where at least he was away from his mother and could begin again under his own steam.

The city would allow each of them to grow in a way that Chicago never could. For my father, it was a place where he could explore his strengths and his weaknesses, and fail or succeed. For my mother, it was a place where her career could take off. But we all carried with us the baggage of a race-haunted past, and it has taken a lifetime for any of us in my family to disentangle ourselves from it. It is a weight each of us bears alone. For myself, the stories of the buffeting my parents withstood from each other and from others gives me pride in their endurance and determination. But perhaps the most secure part of their legacy is the way they tested their limits and showed me that the value of my own life would also lie in the ability to stretch the limits of the possible.

Me (left) and my brother Mark, 1954.

A portrait of me (left), Mike, and Mark, painted by my mother.

FIVE / **The Legacy
of Dreams**

In dreams begins responsibilities.

—WILLIAM BUTLER YEATS

Our first home in New York was the ground floor of a pink stucco apartment building. Very soon after we moved in, I began to wet my bed. I was utterly helpless to control myself. Most often, these episodes of waking up in the middle of the night in an icy wetness came after I had dreamed my mother was being murdered and I could do nothing to stop it.

She would be attacked in the most horrible ways, one more violent than the last. Always the murder involved her head being cut off. Her beautiful face would be asleep in those dreams, with her hair arrayed beautifully around it. In one horrible dream, I saw her head separated from her neck as though twisted off like a bottle cap. *Pop!* In another, the head came off and the neck along with it, ragged with gore, like the head of a nobleman displayed for the masses during the Reign of Terror of the French Revolution. Or so it seems to me now. In another dream, her head flew off like that of a Charlie McCarthy doll—

revealing the long stick that held it on. In yet another, it was sliced off in a car crash—maybe because I'd recently heard on the radio about a car accident in which a famous Hollywood actress's head had landed on a tree branch many feet above where her body lay bleeding. Once, I saw my father stabbing her to death with a knife.

I would try to intercede in the drama that preceded her inevitable fate, always a very real moment of terror, but I could never prevent it. I soon began to feel that *I* was killing her in my dreams. I grew even more ashamed, but I couldn't tell anyone about the dreams. I could only pray never to have them again—the most useless effort of all.

What bothered me wasn't the bed-wetting itself but that the macabre dreams seemed inescapable. Sometimes I'd lose control of myself even before a dream started. I was terrified to go to sleep, but sleep would always steal into my eyes. Then I would wake up in a cold puddle, always surprised that it was there. Afterward, I would scamper over the cold tile floor to my parent's room, and get into bed next to my mother, always on her side. Each time she would wake up and tell me in an irritated way—for she was tired from her work and would remind me she had to get up in the morning—that I should be ashamed of myself. This didn't do much good. I didn't like being wet, but I couldn't help myself. I didn't like being shamed, either, and soon I learned to go to the closet, get a fresh sheet, and silently remake the bed myself.

Our home was beginning to feel again the presence of the danger that would engulf it in the coming years, when my parents fought noisily in a way that seemed to bind them closer to each other than any form of love. They clashed increasingly over trivial things, like whether the dishes were washed or the floors swept when Dad got home. I forced myself to stop hearing them, to literally block the sounds before they reached my ears. It was a kind of self-hypnosis that would begin after Dad slapped her—I always remembered that first slap very well—and made her cry, or tore her clothing, as he liked to do. It happened often enough that it was clear she was in trouble and so was he.

My younger brother Mike, born in Chicago in 1955, was two years old now. He was a stout, round-faced baby with a mirthful expression. I loved to watch him run around roughshod, in a diaper that was never fastened securely enough to his body. He would pull pots and pans from the cupboards, slam doors, and demand attention from the part-time maid. She, in turn, refused to have anything to do with him.

Maybe it was my perception of my mother's vulnerability that worried me the most. I felt that she was close to exhaustion all the time. My dreams of her murder seemed to be a way of expressing what I thought was happening to her, or maybe even what I wanted to happen, because she rarely acted like the warm, caring mother she'd been in Chicago. This feeling was also connected to a sense of impending danger that surrounded my father.

These memories are mixed up with others of those early years when we lived less than five hundred feet from Central Park, a vast and wonderful green escape where Mark and I spent a great deal of time playing. Its huge granite boulders were whales, and we were bold seafaring men. The horse trails were mysterious paths threading into dreamlands under the stone bridges, and these dark places were the dwellings of trolls like the ones in the books Mom used to read to us. For me, the park was where I felt safe. Another favorite escape was the vast labyrinth of the Museum of Natural History where Mark and I would spend countless hours after school, on weekends, and on holidays. We always visited the dinosaur skeleton room, where the forms of all those predatory beasts were assembled, heavy boned, skyscraping, awesome. But we loved most of all the giant blue whale—all pitted and scarred, strung from wires, and surrounded by a wide circular walkway—on one of the museum's upper floors.

Occasionally we were reminded of our still-powerful connections with Dad's relatives in Chicago. One afternoon a surprise visitor, Sadie Higgenbotham, arrived. She was the daughter of Mama Hick, who had cared for Katherine and Gwen. Dad called her Sister, and, though not a blood relative, she was one of those women who had helped raise him. She was a small, rail-thin woman who wore delicate spectacles, had skin as dry as silk flowers, and was very pale— almost as light-skinned as Mom. Sister wore old ladies' black lace-up shoes, very severe looking, which seemed to announce what she was

about: all business, no pleasure. Mom would discuss passages out of
the Bible with her. She was constantly telling my mother that Dad
was a child of God and we shouldn't judge him too harshly; that he
was a man and had men's failings; that, like Hagar in the wilderness
with her child, maybe Mom in her despair over him was overlooking
the well with its pure, sweet drinking water. This kind of talk confused
me. Sister seemed such a gentle, kind soul, but her hands scared me.
They were very rough and worn, like the bottoms of old shoes, and
they reminded me of claws. And yet I remember that when she patted
my hand I felt at home, calmer than I ever felt around my parents.
For the short time she stayed, I sought out her lap and would linger
there, resisting my parents when they tried to take me away and put
me to bed.

What I liked most about Sister was that she never raised her voice.
Whenever Dad started to get mad at Mom, or at Mark or me, Sister,
who was a Christian Scientist, would say, "You have to live more
truth, Alan." These were magic words. Some kind of spell would fall
over my father then, and his whole body would relax. Sister's visit
was like one of those flashes of light during a storm, when things that
were invisible in the night are suddenly thrown into bright relief. It
was one of the few times in my entire childhood when I remember
Dad being so calm, assured, and unafraid.

I never learned exactly why Sister came. The impressions that remain of that period are of my father and mother as very young people,
terribly unsure of themselves, trying to work out the human dimensions of a complex interracial marriage. I think my father was enjoying his freedom away from his Chicago family, but he also felt
guilty about it. My mother seemed relieved, but burdened, too, and
this was a part of their uncertainty and conflict. Mom had been the
one who made the decision to move to New York. She knew that the
marriage wouldn't survive a year longer in Chicago, or anywhere else
that Katherine and her entourage held sway. In later years, she would
tell me that the move was a desperate attempt to make my father
bear some of the responsibility for his new family. My most lasting
memory of Sister's visit was that somehow my parents didn't fight at
all while she was there, or for a long time afterward, and that our
home felt safer than it ever had before. If I tried to do something I

knew would displease my parents—like staying out too long in Central Park, or inviting other kids in and eating up all the butter and white bread, or leaving sugar spread all over the countertop in the tiny kitchen—Sister would take a look at my mother and say, "You must teach your children *truth*." Mom would visibly bridle, but she listened, and it made her seem less frazzled. I think both my parents longed for and needed some kind of guidance, but could trust no one to give it, least of all their respective families.

For a while my nightmares disappeared, but the calm didn't last. Not long after Sister's stay, I began to act out more often, and my nightmares returned. I was unhappy about seeing my father so seldom. He'd taken a job as an insurance adjuster for a company in the city, and it seemed to keep him away from home for long hours. When he was home, he would continually criticize Mom for housework that wasn't done—which she couldn't keep up with while trying to gain a foothold in the fashion industry, a brutally demanding profession, and perhaps doubly so for a white woman with a Negro husband and three young children. I began looking for things to do that would keep me out of the apartment, and often those things seemed to get me into trouble. I would stay outside way past dark. It was a thrill to me to get into trouble; I loved to see the expressions on adults' faces when I did something surprising or provocative. My mother didn't like physical punishments. But my father seemed to relish them. His favorite method of discipline was the hairbrush. From the time I was six until I was too big to be hit anymore, it was his main way of showing he cared. I think I actually enjoyed his punishments in a way, because outright affection seemed so hard for him to give.

One of the few times my father showed us any affection came as a complete surprise. One afternoon he decided it would be fun to take us boys to the horse-riding stable on the corner of Amsterdam Avenue and Eighty-eighth Street. For what seemed a long time, Mark and I were allowed to walk around inside and look at the horses. Then we got to ride bareback, under the close supervision of an attendant. Afterward my father made up a song:

> *Just give your horse a carrot*
> *And we'll all take a ride!*

As he sang he leaped up, clicked his heels, and laughed. I was so astonished by this performance that I hardly dared watch him. And yet this rare instance of his unburdened happiness is one of the enduring memories of my childhood.

It was around this time that my mother began to attend regular Sunday-morning services at the Second Church of Christ Scientist, at Sixty-eighth Street and Central Park West. It was her idea that if she could teach us "truth" through the words of the church, which seemed to remind her of Sister and her kindnesses, I would begin to settle down. She wasn't so concerned about Mark, who was my opposite in most ways. Where I was unruly, he was calm. Where I acted out, he was firmly under control. I admired this in him and hated the lack of confidence in myself. I was becoming a problem child, and Mom felt Christian Science might help me.

It did no such thing. Christian Science teaches that a person can overcome pain, hate, fear, anxiety, envy, depression, stress, or illness by meditating on the power of God's love and surrendering to it. God's love is an act of displacement: in the void of godlessness, faith in God makes one whole. This may have been the lofty objective, but to me it seemed an uninspired and humorless farce, an artifact of Chicago. Maybe Mom thought it would help her gain control of a situation that was veering out of control, but to me it was a waste of time. For a while Mom was very hopeful. Every Sunday for several months, she would dress Mark, Mike, and me in dark, serious-looking suits, white shirts, and handsome ties—the worst kind of torment for any child—and haul us off to that huge stone building with the words "Second Church of Christ Scientist" in large letters above the doorway. For hours and hours, it seemed, people would sit in an enormous airy room listening to loud organ music and saying prayers that were too tiresome to pay attention to. I was fidgety and so was Mark. There wasn't much singing, and not much of anything else that held my interest. I would look up at the plain, white, high vaulted ceilings painted white and yawn. Dad was never with us, and that automatically gave me an excuse not to pay attention to Mom's frequent hard glances. To break up the dreary routine, I would step out to go to the bathroom.

Soon we were placed in a Sunday-morning Bible class, where a nice, smiling woman would tell us stories about Jesus and John and Paul and the other Apostles. When she asked us questions about the stories, I would reply that her questions were silly, making her smile disappear as though she'd been slapped. Right on cue, Mark would join in, laughing. I remember how horrified the other children were at our not responding to the usual commands from the teacher. We became expert at disrupting her authority over the class.

There was a girl named Naomi in the class, and it was such a different-sounding name to us that we targeted her right away for special torment. We repeated her name again and again, in different ways, until she began to cry.

"Naomi," I chanted. "What kind of name is that? Naooooo-mmmiiii. NaomiiiiiNaomiNayomeee."

We broke up, laughing hard. Once we began, we couldn't stop. I remember looking out the window, seeing what a bright, warm day it was, and longing to be anywhere but here, listening to stories that didn't seem to concern me at all: old-timey stories about David and Solomon that I knew would soon put me to sleep. I was angry at having to be here. I wanted to be with my father, not my mother.

Naomi sat with her hands folded in front of her, but she was turning red and tears were streaming down her cheeks.

I started laughing so hard that I fell off my chair and that my nose ran. Naomi continued to cry big wet tears. I knew by instinct that I could tear into her then. I felt a great deal of satisfaction at knowing I could make someone cry.

My satisfaction didn't last long. We were taken together, Mark and I, back into the huge, airy, well-lit church hall, where Mom was sitting alone.

"You have to teach your children truth," the man holding us said to her. She was shocked, then angry, then ashamed. She gathered us up and we left the church, and I don't remember ever going back, which was just fine with me. The misbehavior produced no punishment for us: punishment would have been most un-Christian Science-like. Thereafter, we were left to fend for ourselves at home on Sundays while Mom went to church by herself. I slipped out regularly, and began the habit of straying around the streets that came to characterize my behavior while we lived in the city.

When I think of New York City's Upper West Side at this time— in the late 1950s—I think of the great luck I had in being there then, when the streets were far safer for young children to grow up in than they are now. It was possible for children to roam the streets freely, without being molested. It was possible to stay in Central Park until well after nightfall and not worry about being in danger. I had no sense of fear, of peril, or even of limitation in those years. The Upper West Side was, simply, a pleasant area of brownstones that had been well maintained but were not much changed from what they'd always been. There were stores of every description up and down Columbus and Amsterdam avenues: candy stores like Domsky's, which was owned and run by an elderly Hasidic Jew; clothing stores and toy stores in abundance; restaurants, and smaller places that served spit-roasted chickens. It always made me hungry to watch the chickens turning a bright cinnamon color that wafted its flavor straight into my mouth. It was possible then to go into a toy store and buy cap guns and holsters and cowboy paraphernalia—this was the current rage— on what was called the "layaway plan." For me and Mark, that consisted of paying twenty-five cents a week, which we got from Mom, until the total amount was paid. We knew something important was happening when Fidel Castro was on the cover of *Time* magazine during the revolution in Cuba because we saw the magazines on every newstand within miles of our house.

Over the next few years, we moved three times, to various apartments in the West Eighties, and everywhere it was the same. There was no great matter to racial tolerance. No one welcomed other groups wholeheartedly, and yet, with everyone thrown together, everyone made room for each other. In a building we lived in on West Eighty-eighth Street, there were Muslims on the first floor, who held prayer services day and night, and a homosexual couple on the second floor, a dancer and his crazy lover. We lived on the top floor. I had no sense whatsoever of being any different from our neighbors. There were blacks and whites and Hispanics, Jews and Catholics, rich and poor, all living in close proximity. We were completely free to mix with children of other cultures and classes, and it was one of the blessings of our early education to learn that if there were limits to people's tolerance toward one another, we could test those limits without much fear.

The desire to spend as much time as possible away from home seized Mark and Mike and me early on. Mike would spend long hours in the company of a Hispanic family named Hernandez. Mark's schoolmates then were mostly Jews and other whites. I used to laugh at their names: Corky Lieberbaum and Stanley Horowitz. My friends were mostly black and Hispanic, along with some Irish kids who blasphemed the church and said horrible things about Jews, which I swallowed without question.

I remember once, when I was eight or nine, seeing two young men whom I knew to be Jewish because of the yarmulkes they were wearing. They were waiting for a bus at Eighty-second Street and Columbus Avenue. I was curious to see what they would do if I called them the name that my Hispanic and Irish friends used, so I walked boldly up to the older one and said he was a "dirty kike." Before I could blink, he hit me hard on the chin. I walked away holding my jaw, amazed that anyone could have hit me so quickly. That was one way we learned our manners, and it was quite effective, since I never called anyone that name again.

Our delightfully ungentrified area was full of what could undisparagingly be called "character." On mild evenings, bums would collect on the front stoops of the old brownstones and have their evening meals of white rice or any other dish that could be had on the cheap. While they ate, slopping rice and gravy all over the stoop, they talked and shouted at each other. Sometimes there were fights over money. But the clashes were brief, often ending with someone getting knocked down the stairs or finished off with a black eye. The cops would be called, but they would show up late, long after the dispute was settled, and simply roust the army of poverty off to another part of the block. The bums would then alight like a flock of pigeons on the front steps of another brownstone.

There were also many artists and general nonconformists in the area. My friend Sophia Henry's* mother was a prime example.

She was a devotee of the persecuted Austrian psychotherapist Wilhelm Reich, who believed he'd discovered a new form of physical-biological energy he called orgone. He built and sold orgone boxes, in which his patients were supposed to sit for hours to absorb life-enhancing rays. Woody Allen poked fun at a Reichian chamber in one of his movies, calling it the "orgasmatron." Reich died in jail in 1957 for defying a federal government order to stop selling the boxes. To Mrs. Henry, that only confirmed his sainthood. She owned an orgone box—a sort of metal tube the size of an electric boiler with a seat welded to the inside and a door cut into it—and when I visited Sophia her mother would often be sitting in the box freeing her sexual energy.

Mrs. Henry was not shy about letting go of her feelings in public, either. At any hour of the morning or night, she would throw open the upper-story windows of her apartment and howl to the world. While I knew that she was a bit odd, in my eyes she was admirably brave and bold. So was her daughter. The first time I ever saw a girl's anatomy, it was Sophia's, and she was quite aggressive in showing it to me and demanding to see mine.

Against the freedom of this environment, so different from the segregated world we'd left behind in Chicago, were the narrow rages my father brought into our home. He was rarely happy, and seemed haunted by inner shadows. I would later learn that he had been treating his pain and grievances with heroin and other drugs during these years, but all I could see at the time was his lack of sympathy for Mom and his children. There were a few brief periods of peace, but strife was the dominant mood. When I returned home from school in the afternoon, there would be signs all over the apartment of a battle my parents had just had: splattered beans from a pot hurled against a wall, the pot left at the bottom of the stairs. It confused me even more that when they weren't fighting, they made love.

I attracted friends who, like me, had hated school from the start. We deeply and shamelessly hated our teachers, the principal, and the building itself. Public School 166 seemed like a prison. The stairwells were narrow and dark, and the wire mesh in them made them feel like cages. Whenever we had the chance, my friends and I left class on the excuse of being sick. I'd act listless and moan, and tell the teacher my throat hurt. When she tried to feel it, I'd puff it out by pushing my tongue down hard so the glands underneath would look swollen. Once, I skipped school for three weeks before a teacher called home and put an end to it. I received a spanking from my father for that.

This didn't stop me from raising hell as much as I could. I'd meet my friends Juan* and Eusebio,* who agreed that school was the worst place in the world to be when right nearby there was Central Park. I liked to sit by the well-lined cinder tracks and watch the handsome brown horses and their riders—usually women dressed in black jackets and hats and white shirts with ruffles and beautiful black boots. My favorite activity was to sit on a bench and shoot paper clips at these fine-mouthed horses. When a horse was hit, I enjoyed watching it dance suddenly and gallop away, digging up huge clots of cinder as the rider tried to control it. I liked to hear the thud of the hooves as the horse veered onto the grass.

My friends came from many different ethnic groups and economic classes, and we learned from each other both ethnic tolerance and the usual slurs of intolerance. I don't think that at this time I ever considered skin color as something that defined my friends or myself in a limited way. There were certain glaring exceptions, however. Once, I developed a crush on a white girl with blonde hair like my mother's, but when I walked with her out of school to where her mother was waiting, the woman snatched her daughter away and pushed her into a cab. She avoided me so pointedly after that that I knew there was no way I could be her friend. When I asked her why, she said it was because I was a Negro, but that meant nothing to me. Though it hurt that she didn't like me because I was a Negro, I had no sense that being a Negro was anything to be ashamed of. I brushed the incident aside.

Being a Negro certainly didn't mean I had to be careful in selecting my friends because of any prejudices their parents may have had. I was curious about all kinds of people. My best friends were Eusebio and Juan, and no one in their neighborhood ever made me feel that I didn't belong. With them, I could walk farther uptown, to where most of the Spanish-speaking kids lived, and their parents would feed us as soon as we walked in the door. "You look hungry, boy," the mothers would say. They would tie their aprons tighter around their wide hips, and cook up rice and beans, or sometimes spaghetti with red sauce, and I would eat, and they would push us outside to play again. Often I would go with them to the movies. One time, during *The Magnificent Seven*, just at the point where James Coburn was demonstrating his skill with a knife, Juan and Eusebio got into a fist-fight with some kids from another block. I stood back and watched as their arms flailed like windmills in the dark theater, blurring the images on the screen. I relished their violence and pride. Far from being afraid of this attitude, I admired the way it made people afraid of them.

The wildest of my friends were the Cohans,* Gil* and Billy,* two Irish kids. I loved their daring and their desperation. The Cohans and I, and sometimes my brother Mark, would wander through grocery stores stealing food. The Cohans were poor, but I didn't realize that that was why they were stealing food. I thought it was an act of bravado, and I became good at it, too.

The Cohans didn't try to hide their poverty. They lived in a small apartment on Columbus Avenue, in an area where many other poor people resided. Like many city apartments, theirs was dim because it faced a dusty air shaft that natural light couldn't filter down into. Their teeth were bad, and they were always ravenously hungry. I was surprised at how much Gil and Billy could eat. The Cohans' place was always upside down. Gil and Billy seemed a little ashamed of it, but their eyes would catch mine and I knew not to say anything. The kitchen was lit by a single naked lightbulb that was never turned off. Pots and pans and dishes were piled up not only in the sink but on the floor beside it as well, and on the aluminum kitchen table. An old-fashioned toaster—the kind where you inserted the bread by lowering the side of the toaster itself—was plugged into the wall with a frayed cord.

Mrs. Cohan was a tiny wraith of a woman. Occasionally she would come into the room wearing little more than a cotton shift hanging from her emaciated shoulders. Her hair was matted on the sides and never combed. I never asked Gil or Billy anything about her, and I never inquired about their father. Likewise, they never asked about my parents. That was what friendship meant: knowing when to ask questions and when to keep quiet. I didn't talk about how their hallways were strewn with dirty laundry, because I knew that if I did it would hurt their feelings. The whole apartment reeked of filth in a way that I have never experienced since, but I didn't talk about that, either. I also knew that in many ways they were no different from me, because I needed and wanted things I couldn't have, too. This taught me to think about them as I would my own family. In a way, they were just as important as my family was. In fact, through these close ties to friends I was creating my own sense of family, to make up for the one into which I had been born and which seemed to be splitting apart.

By contrast, the homes of my black friends, Paul West* and Bart Williams,* were the very picture of neatness and order. They lived closer to the Hudson River, over past West End Avenue, where a number of Negro families lived. Their parents were always smiling, glad to see their children playing so happily with other children in the neighborhood. There were statues and pictures of Jesus all around the West's apartment, and a piano in a corner, which everyone, even Paul and Bart, played. Mrs. West* was often home when I visited Paul, and she would make us wonderful tuna-fish and lemon sandwiches and iced tea.

At the other end of the spectrum, I fell into a friendship with Burleigh Martell,* who came from a family of German Jews. Burleigh lived in a large brownstone down the block, on Eighty-eighth Street closer to Columbus Avenue. He was a child of privilege. Every other morning, his mother, a short, stout, watchful woman, would have bottles of seltzer and Hires soda delivered to their basement door. The bottles were taller than the ones sold at the local supermarket and came in large green trays, with each bottle in its own square.

I always visited Burleigh's home alone. My other friends, Gil and Billy and Paul and Juan and Eusebio, weren't allowed there, Burleigh said, and I never questioned why. I assumed it was because Burleigh had his own set of friends, and I was happy to be one of them. He had toys of every description: a Hi Ho train set, cowboy boots and hats, even six-shooter cap pistols. Mark and I, who had to buy our toys on layaway, often found that by the time we got them, they seemed less interesting than they had at first. My toys never seemed as valuable to me as Miles's, which were always the best.

Everything was easy at Burleigh's home. His mother always served lunch for us. If he wanted to hear music, she would take the record out of its jacket and play it as long as he wanted. The two of them were more like business partners than anything else. "Thank you, Mother," he'd say when he finished eating or playing. "It's quite all right, Burleigh," Mrs. Martell would say. But Burleigh didn't participate in the rougher kinds of play that my other friends did, play that I preferred even more than my visits to Burleigh's home.

With Gil or Billy or Juan or Eusebio, there was always the joy of ducking under a subway turnstile and catching a train to wherever it was going. We traveled all over the city sometimes, not getting off until the end of the line. There were some subways going way up into the Bronx, and others that went out to Coney Island, in Brooklyn, and these we'd take as if we were going to a foreign country. I loved to watch the different kinds of people getting on and off the trains, going their private ways, and often I skipped whole days from school to do so.

The riskiest means of travel was considered the most desirable; we preferred it because it earned a boy respect. It was called "hitching," and it involved hopping on the back fender of a city bus, grabbing on as best you could—either to the metal lip of the engine doors or to the metal frames in which advertisements were inserted—and hanging on for dear life as the bus sped on its dangerous way, over potholes and bumps. When you had your fill you'd simply hop off.

There was an art to this. The bus drivers were specifically instructed not to let kids hitch rides, and they would often stop short, jump out, and chase us away. When this happened, we'd simply wait for them to give up and would hop back on again. My friends and I traveled up to Harlem and into Spanish Harlem this way. Despite our youth, there was hardly a thought of danger. Once, on our way back from a jaunt uptown, just as it was getting dark enough for the cars behind us to turn on their headlamps, Gil fell off, but nobody missed him until the bus stopped. We all clambered off the fender and began to search for our friend, who came limping along with a huge tear in the knee of his pants. We thought at first he'd been run over.

When I was nine, we moved to an apartment on the top floor of a brownstone walk-up. It had a skylight that flooded the dark hallway from afternoon until late evening. Winters, Mark and I would take our ice skates, go to the Wollman rink, and skate from morning until night. Or we'd make snowballs filled with rocks, which we took over to Amsterdam or Columbus Avenue and threw at the trucks speeding by. I liked to hear the booming sound when a rock hit a truck. The driver always pulled over and stopped to see if he'd hit something; then he'd see us and curse, as we ran frantically and happily away.

I began to curse, too. Motherfucker. Son of a bitch. Bastard. Cocksucker. These words made me feel powerful, and soon I was able to toss them off casually and with conviction. By the time I reached the fourth grade I was becoming harder to handle. I cursed constantly at my teachers, or at anyone else who presumed to order me around. Although I was reasonably bright, I found it hard to do well in class when I was assigned a teacher with a foul temper whom I didn't like. I had also come to hate the caged-in feeling I got in school.

Most of the students in my class were whites from parts of the city I didn't go to but Mark, increasingly, did. The white kids would invite Mark to play in their homes farther uptown, and he began to spend more time with them. As these friendships deepened, Mark's interests became more intellectual. We were both members of a Cub Scout troop at a local church, but instead of the knots and wood carving that interested me, Mark immersed himself in scientific experiments. He won second prize in a school science fair that year, for a large battery whose terminals were hooked up to wire that was wrapped around a nail to make a magnet. I remember seeing it displayed in the principal's office when I was called in for disciplinary problems one day. Mark hadn't mentioned a word about it to me, and my parents were equally surprised when they found out that he'd entered and won.

Mark was becoming more distant from me as he found satisfaction in being praised for his achievements. He made friends with one kid named Bob Wunder,* the son of a famous acting couple who lived at the Dakota, a huge luxury apartment building near the park. It had enormous iron gates and a doorman who allowed people in and out. I was not allowed in.

If Mark was becoming part of another clan, so was I. I was spending more time with Juan and Eusebio. We had in common an aversion to authority and acted out against it as much as we could. At school, I would invite myself into classes where I didn't belong. When my class was at an assembly or was outside playing, I would simply wander off. One time I wandered into the art shop, where a teacher was demonstrating how to emboss copper and rub it with dark felt to make the embossed places stand out. I sat down and created a face with a stencil tool I took from another student. Then I walked over to the teacher, who was busy helping someone else, and asked if I could have a wire pad like the other students had. I didn't know what to call it.

"Can I have a shiner?" I asked.

"A what?" the teacher said.

"A shiner," I repeated.

"Yeah, you can have a shiner," he said, and cuffed me on the side of the head. "You know what a shiner is?"

"No," I said.

"It's a black eye."

Why did the teacher want to give me a black eye? I didn't know what a black eye was, but it didn't sound very friendly. So I left that class and returned to my own, which was in the assembly hall watching a play that was supposed to be about the Founding Fathers. My brother was in the play, which was being staged by the brightest students in several grade levels. Each student had made a large painting of one of the fifty states and was to walk out on the stage and shout its name.

Mark was very good. He did Ohio, and shouted out its name. Then his class sang a song about America:

Misto Christo Christopher Columbo
He sailed the ocean one fine day
And on that trip he took so far awayo
He found the U.S.A.

Later they performed a skit about Anne Boleyn, Henry VIII's second wife, and sang another song:

With her head tucked underneath her arm
She walks the bloody tower.
With her head tucked underneath her arm
At the midnight hour.

I thought this skit relating the unfortunate tale of the poor queen who was now a ghost was truly wonderful. My class never did anything fun like that. In my class, where we were constantly being told by the teacher to sit down, be quiet, and not shout, there were regular outbreaks of chaos. Stealing someone else's stuff was always cause for a riot. And when the teacher told me to do one thing I would always do the opposite. I was trying to get her attention, but I always got the opposite kind of attention from what I wanted.

Around this time, I was beginning to have trouble seeing objects and letters clearly. Things would blur uncontrollably if I looked at them closely. Mom took me to an eye doctor, who said that my left eye was nearsighted. A weakness in the muscle also caused the eye to wander. To correct these conditions, I was fitted with a pair of brown tortoiseshell glasses. They helped me to see better, but I thought they looked awful. I associated glasses with Jerry Lewis's idiot characters. I felt very stupid in them, and feeling stupid filled me with shame and anger. I refused to wear them, and managed to lose several pairs.

I didn't connect my eye problem or my contrary behavior with my failing grades. I was sure I got bad grades because my teacher, Mrs. Daniloff,* didn't like me. She was a white woman, just like my mother, but I knew she didn't like me. She made me feel timid and afraid, the way I had in the presence of my mother's people as a small child. It wasn't a conscious reaction, of course, but one that was buried deep in the bone of memory.

Mrs. Daniloff smiled at me a lot but seemed to give the other students more attention. She began giving out tiny stick-on stars for our achievements—one star for each grade above 80 in arithmetic, reading, spelling, and science. It was just like the stock market. At the end of the day, you could tell who was up and who was down according to how many stars each student had next to his or her name. I was sure that the only way anyone got those good grades was by smiling back at the teacher, who would then give that student the attention he or she wanted.

Not so, it seemed. After further observation, I realized that it was always the quieter students who did well. I wasn't one of them. I couldn't sit still. Mrs. Daniloff would try to explain something to me, but I wouldn't understand her explanation, and she wouldn't take the extra time to explain it twice. I grew increasingly angry and impatient. Often I literally couldn't see what she wrote on the blackboard, and even if I could, I wasn't able to concentrate well enough to learn something that might earn me a star. I didn't listen very well, either, and didn't take directions well at all. Simple instructions sounded to me like harsh orders. I could usually figure out what I was supposed to do by reading the student exercise book later, on my own. But in class I was too nervous, too frightened of being thought stupid.

After several months of trying to get a few stars placed next to my name, I gave up even trying to be nice to the teacher. I had by this time discovered a companion-in-arms named Pablo,* who had been transferred into my fourth-grade class from what were called the lower tracks. At lunchtime we sided with the lower-track students against our upper-track classmates, deliberately instigating fights between students from poor backgrounds and those who definitely were not poor.

During art class one day, Pablo and I made a drawing of Mrs. Daniloff's body showing large breasts (which she didn't have) and excrement falling between her legs. When she walked behind us and saw the drawing, she shouted at us, at the top of her voice, "That's the most disgusting thing I've ever seen in my life." I wasn't embarrassed at all. In fact, I was rather proud of myself. She was finally paying attention to me. Pablo, however, started to cry, attracting the attention of the entire class. I sat rigidly still with a smirk on my face.

The following week, Pablo and I were placed in a lower-track class taught by a woman named Mrs. Rosen.* It was a class of black and Puerto Rican students, with a few white kids mixed in. I hated Mrs. Rosen instantly because of the brutish way she bullied the students. She was a sturdy woman with a hard, no-nonsense look in her eyes. Her hair was dyed blonde, and she wore a pair of reading glasses strapped around her neck like the reins of a horse, or perched on top of her head. Mrs. Rosen never stopped shouting. That was how she controlled us. But it seemed to me that she spoke differently when she talked to the white students, and this made me dislike her even more than I disliked Mrs. Daniloff

One day, as we were going out for afternoon recess, Mrs. Rosen lined us all up at attention at the classroom door and asked to look at our hands, saying that clean hands were terribly important. I didn't care much what Mrs. Rosen thought about my hands. Something angry must have registered in my face, because when I looked up she was turning beet red.

"Don't look at me like that," she said.

She slapped me. It was a hard, fiercely stinging blow that burned my cheek. Humiliating as it was, I wouldn't give her the satisfaction of seeing me wince. I continued staring at her. She was stunned. She moved her glasses from her head to her nose. Then she put them back on top of her head. Then she took them off altogether and marched over to her desk. Then she forgot what she wanted to do there and marched back to the classroom door. Nobody said a word. I was in my glory, full of malicious glee. The room was silent, leaden, like the inside of a Roman Catholic church.

Soon we were walking down the steps of the building and spilling into the courtyard for recess. I felt I had won a game of nerves. I hadn't given in to this adult. On the way out, some of the class pets asked me if the slap had hurt. Lying, I told them with a keen mixture of pride and contempt that it had not. But it had been so loud, they said. I smiled and said I hadn't felt anything. Physically, I was uninjured. But my stomach told me something terrible had happened.

I never told anyone at home about the incident. I was certain I would be blamed. I felt guilty, but complaining would do no good. Mom and Dad were having their own troubles, and I didn't want them to get involved in mine.

There were brief weeks when my parents got along, but mostly they seemed locked in a mutual and exclusive sadness that made me feel like an outsider. Dad was losing weight and was all skin and bones now. He drank constantly. He was like a ghost in his own home.

Many years later, my father told me that he'd been using heroin again at this time. He'd gotten to know a heroin dealer in Harlem who was about to go to jail on a drug-possession charge, and Dad helped him and his friends enjoy the dealer's last score before he went off to prison.

We knew none of this then, of course, but the signatures of addiction were all over him. He rarely ate and was on edge all the time. He had a desk in the living room where he kept his papers from work, but he'd let weeks pass before he touched them. Then, in a single weekend, he would get rid of the enormous pile that had accumulated. At night he and Mom would fight. She would come home from her job of designing children's clothing and women's dresses and find that she now had to cook dinner, or clean, or do something else that Dad refused to do. They battled over large things and small, and Mom always seemed to get the worst of it.

At this stage, Katherine began anew her efforts to "help" her son out of his hardships. She knew he loved lobster, and one week she sent him a whole barrel of them. Mom had to cook them, of course. Dad gorged himself, and then he stopped eating any regular meals with us. It was as though he couldn't stand the sight of us. At other times Katherine would send steaks, and the same routine would apply. She even invited us to visit her where she and her husband were now living, near a military base in Madison, Wisconsin.

In 1957, Mom was pregnant again, but this didn't make my father treat her any more kindly. In one of their fights he kicked her in the stomach. Early the next year my youngest brother, John, was born. I remember Mom telling me some time later that one doctor had told her not to have any more children because black blood and white blood were incompatible. John was born with glaucoma, which runs in Dad's family, and had to have a series of operations to drain the fluid from his eyes. It was this fluid, Mom said, that was blocking his vision. For months, while Mom waited to see whether the operations were successful, she was terribly low and always seemed tired. She didn't eat; she didn't cook. Things at home fell apart even worse than before. The apartment was filled with her sadness. She would fix herself drinks, smoke cigarettes one after another, go to work in the morning, and afterward visit John in the hospital.

One afternoon I went with her to the hospital. I remember the cab speeding through Central Park, which was alight with spring, and the taxi driver's utter silence. At the hospital, Mom had me stay in the waiting room while she went in to speak to the doctor. In the end, the surgeons found that the pressure from the glaucoma had destroyed the optic nerves in both of John's eyes. My brother's blindness was irreversible.

For many months, Mom seemed wild with unspeakable grief. When she finally brought John home, I remember looking at his face and thinking it was a face of perfect beauty, the kind that took your breath away. I fell in love. He was small and thin and quite pale, and had jet black hair, like an American Indian's, and fine, high cheeks. When I watched my mother change him, I saw a dark plug in his navel and noticed that he had a large penis with large balls. I wondered why they were so big.

But it was the eyes that caught me. I would look into them, fluttering open and shut; they didn't focus on anything. They were the blue color of waterfalls, of rainy summer evenings. Mom took a few weeks off from work to take care of him. It seemed to keep her going in the months that followed. I spent many hours watching him while she was away at work. I was mystified. He did most things quietly. He slept quietly; he ate quietly; he burped quietly after he ate. He even cried quietly.

After Mom went back to work, Dad stayed at home to take care of us. He began bringing home a haggard young woman named Starr,* who had long, beautiful legs and wore high-heeled shoes and shorts. Her legs seemed to start from somewhere under her arms and continue endlessly down to her shoes. Starr's hair was short and her skin was the color of honey in a jar. She was the most stunning woman I'd ever seen—or she would have been, if she hadn't lost most of her front teeth.

Sometimes I would come home from school and find Dad with Starr in his bed, buck naked. Dad had her around for weeks during the day, while Mom was at the hospital or shuttling from there to work and then home. He told us not to tell Mom about Starr, and we didn't. Thinking back on it now, I know this was his way of acting out his own grief and the loneliness that seemed to overtake him after John's birth. But whatever it was that brought Starr into our home, it only made things much worse. Instead of helping Mom come through this difficult time, Dad created still more distance between them.

Maybe a month after John's birth, Mom came home from the hospital earlier than usual. Starr was prancing around the kitchen merrily washing dishes wearing her shorts and one of Dad's T-shirts. I had just gotten home from school, and from an upstairs window I saw Mom coming into the building. I ran downstairs and warned her about Starr. She remembers me putting it this way: "Mom, there's a woman in our apartment."

She began screaming at Starr and shouting for her to get out. I'd never seen her so mad. Starr, scared, did as she was told. I was relieved to see her scamper away.

Then Mom marched toward the back of the apartment. It was a sunny day, and light was streaming into the bedroom through the rear windows and spilling onto the large bed, where Dad was lying with only a sheet covering his stomach and private parts. One of his feet was propped up against the wall. There was a vial and a needle beside him. He was snoring.

Mom stomped over and slapped him dead in the middle of his chest, shouting that he was a son of a bitch. She brought her weight down harder and hit him again, with a heavy thud. He didn't respond. She hit him harder still, and Dad finally woke up, slowly, almost dreamily, as though coming out of a heavy fog. At first he smiled.

"Hello?" he said, looking around. But when he saw Mom, he suddenly became very angry and alert. He closed the door, and then he slapped her and knocked her down. They started rumbling. She screamed for me to go and get help. "Call the police," she cried. I rushed from the room and was out the door, running down the stairs two at a time.

Then I heard a thumping sound behind me. It was Dad. He was shouting at me to stop. I kept running, afraid that he was going to hurt me, too. I heard his footfalls as he leaped down the stairs. I ran as fast as I could and made it to the first-floor hall. As I grasped the knob of the huge oak-and-glass front door, I heard him hit the floor behind me. He bellowed at me to stop. I opened the door a little wider and had almost made it to the outside foyer when something crashed and the world suddenly went black.

When I woke up, my father was carrying me back upstairs. I passed out again. Then I was in the apartment. Three of my fingernails had been sheared off, my face was bruised, and Mom was holding a rag over my forehead. I felt proud of myself, like a good warrior. Then I slipped back into unconsciousness. For days Dad was nowhere to be seen.

He was talking more often now about going to see his mother in Wisconsin. But he was acting wildly. His eyes were always ablaze, and though he never stopped working—in fact, he worked more feverishly than ever—he was also drinking more, and settling into a pattern of overwork that would escalate in the years to come.

One day during that hot summer of 1958, with the sun pouring into the front room, he commanded Mark and me to strip down to our underwear. While we did that, he got a box of Brillo pads from under the kitchen sink and placed half a dozen pots of hot water at different points around the living room. Then he told us to get to work and scrub the old wax off the whole floor, which was laid out in black linoleum tile.

For the whole day we scrubbed and scrubbed. We tried to turn it into a game, sliding on our bare hands and feet and using the pink soap from the Brillo pads to make huge drawings all over the black floor. Every now and again Dad would come in or would send Mike in to see how we were doing. Mike would come sliding across the slick floor, laughing gleefully. Finally we dumped all the pots of water on the floor at once, creating a flood. Dad had to mop up the mess before Mom got home and saw what we'd done.

Not long after John's birth, Mom's and Dad's fights took on a more overtly racial tone. When he beat her, she would scream that he was a nigger—trying to hurt him with this word as one might break the skin with a stone—and he would counter that she was nothing more than a white tramp from cotton country.

I began to act out even more, in my own way. Instead of stealing furtively, as an act of bravado, I began taking things from right under the noses of shopkeepers, trying to get caught.

I would go alone, usually, though sometimes my friends would come to watch and take bets. We would go into a store and see if I could get away with something big. There were a few rules to the game: You never stole from your parents, because if they caught you, you got beat. You never stole from a place where there were a lot of people. You simply went into a store and selected certain items that you could hide easily. You acted quickly. Then you walked out calmly. You never ran. Anyone who ran attracted attention, and the first rule of successful stealing was never to attract attention. You never stayed too long in a store, or rushed through it. I never got caught. The key was to look innocent.

This was my routine: After school I'd head for one of the large grocery chain stores. I'd steal things I knew I didn't need, and sometimes things I did. I liked to take large boxes of paper clips and rubber bands; I'd break the paper clips in half at the top bend, hook the longish clips on double rubber bands, and have an instant slingshot. I liked the process of walking through a store as though looking for something, then snatching whatever I wanted off a shelf—a box of cereal or a can of peaches—and, as I walked to another aisle, slipping it quickly under my shirt or in my pants under the belt buckle, sucking in my stomach to make room. Approaching the door, I would pretend to have lost my money, feverishly patting down my pants legs. I stole relentlessly and almost professionally: lunch meat, fruit, bags of potato chips, toothpaste, mouthwash, gloves, socks, underwear. I stole a coat once from a clothing store, simply sliding it over my shoulders and slipping my arms into the sleeves. When I brought the things home, I hid them. I never opened the packages or wore the overcoat. Eventually the socks, underwear, and other things wound up in the garbage. I wasn't afraid of being caught with them—I could lie that someone had given them to me. I simply lost interest in them after the thrill of stealing was over.

I saw kids my age who did get caught, though I don't think I realized then that most of them were black or Hispanic. They always put up a fuss, and I loved to watch them perform the ritualized loss-of-nerve act. They'd claim they'd lost their money, and if the store clerks threatened to call their parents the kids would blubber in earnest. I vowed to myself that I would never lose control. I always carried enough money to pay for the things, so that if I were caught I could just say I'd forgotten to pay.

Fighting was all Mom and Dad did now. They quarreled about music, about money, about Katherine's constant gift giving, and about Dad's drinking and drug taking. During one quarrel when Mom was holding John, Dad snatched him away and then threw him back at Mom so that their heads cracked together, loudly. John got a black eye and Mom's face was badly bruised.

Mom would tell me many years later about the sound advice she got from her female friends, both black and white: no man was worth as much trouble as Dad was giving her. But she felt at the time that she was in too deep, was committed to the teeth. She had no faith that any other man would accept her after having married a black man, having his children, and having remained with him for so long. Caruthersville had taught her that much. For Dad's part, he knew he had her where he wanted her. Race became the prison they had made for each other.

Something deeper was happening, too. I think my mother was so tired and so desperately unhappy that she couldn't see any other options. She left my father several times, dragging Mark and Mike and John and me off to the homes of one or another friend. But somehow Dad always found out where we were, and he'd get Mom to come back home, either with threats or with promises to change his ways. Loving my father as she did, believing in him despite his faults, my mother did what millions of women of every race do all the time: she went back home and hoped for the best, hoped she could reform the man to whom she'd given so much of herself.

Just as suddenly as Dad became nasty and hateful toward us, he would turn around and become the friendliest man alive, establishing a pattern that would repeat itself over and over in the coming years. He would take us to the circus or the movies. He took Mom to see *West Side Story* on Broadway. We would go for walks in the park, and I would see people staring at us as we passed boldly along.

I started to see Mom in a different light. In calling Dad a nigger, I thought she was trying to describe his behavior and had forgotten that he was a human being. I felt she couldn't see him anymore. I also thought that maybe John's blindness had infected her with a deeper pessimism. But I knew Dad was my father, and I feared and loved him with the burning fear and love and reverence that most young boys have for their fathers. I thought of myself as being exactly like him, only younger. I was really being asked to choose sides over who to love, and I couldn't choose either side without splitting myself in half. I couldn't choose his side, because he was acting like a bully, the same as Mrs. Rosen and the other teachers were. I couldn't take Mom's side, either, even though I wanted to defend her. Their love and their hate divided me, and no matter how far I ran there was no escape.

The word "nigger" explained nothing, certainly not why Dad was losing control of himself. It was just a word Mom used when she was so hurt that it was the only way she knew to hurt him back. And it did. It hurt so much that it would make him chuckle in that incongruous Chicago way he had—the way he did when he was trying to show he hadn't been hurt at all. Race was one weapon they used with deadly accuracy. It was hard at these times to understand why they hurt each other so much. It seemed that Dad beat Mom because that was the only way he had of communicating his emotions to her: his fear of losing her because he was black and the world was against him. But there was something else. I think my father knew that she was stronger than he was, and he was cowed by that strength. It made him lash out at her courage with his fists, even though it was her courage that kept them together. And part of her simply took satisfaction in her strength, and in knowing that no matter how badly he beat her or humiliated her, she was still the only woman who would stick with him. In a fundamental way, they couldn't get around their personal histories, and it didn't matter what color they were: the world of their sadness closed in on them as their differences destroyed any hope that they might find a way to talk to each other.

Later that summer we received still more gifts from Kathcrine. More live lobsters arrived, in a large barrel filled with ice. Dad was now the only person who would eat them. Mom refused. Then, a little later, Mom told Mark and me that we were all going to drive to Madison, Wisconsin, to see Katherine.

And so we did. Dad popped NoDoz tablets and drove straight for three days and nights. He couldn't wait to get there. When we arrived, Katherine and Mom started arguing almost immediately. Katherine said things about John's blindness that made Mom so angry she started throwing things. They all drank heavily, Katherine and her fifth and last husband, Harold, Dad and Mom. Soon Mom returned to New York with Dad, John, and Mike, leaving Mark and me behind.

Those two weeks at Katherine's were perhaps the strangest and most racially tinged period of my entire life. Every morning when the sky was clear and the hot sun was beating down on the Wisconsin countryside, we followed the same unerring routine. Mark and I were given our breakfast by Harold at about eight o'clock, and then we were instructed to put on our bathing suits and were marched out to the backyard, where Katherine had set out two lounge chairs and a small table holding a pitcher of lemonade and a bottle of baby oil.

All day long Mark and I were made to lie there in the hot sun. When we went numb from boredom and started to throw the chairs at each other and run around the lawn, Katherine would allow us to bathe in an inflatable pool until the sun went down. Within a week, we had both turned a shade of brown even darker than Dad.

Katherine delighted in the transformation, and so did I. I admired my color because it seemed to please Katherine. The darker we grew, the more she smiled. One Sunday afternoon we were dressed up in our best clothes and made to participate in a fashion show at a local Baptist church. "How delightful your children are!" someone said to Katherine. I wondered what difference it made whether Mark and I were light or dark, but obviously it mattered immensely to Katherine. As we grew darker still, she began introducing us to her social circle. She had us play with the sons and daughters of people from the base who knew Katherine and Harold. Mark and I tried hard to pick fights with these stiff, joyless children, but Katherine always intervened in time to avoid a breach of etiquette.

At the end of the summer, when Mark and I were to return to New York, Katherine mounted a strong lobbying campaign with Dad to keep us with her, so we could be raised as proper Negroes. Was this what it meant to have relatives? Mark said he didn't like Katherine very much because she was always giving orders. But I liked her in spite of that. She gave us cool lemonade and sandwiches while we basked in the sun. I liked the way she looked, too, especially her smile and her pretty hands which were always soft and neat. But I didn't much like her temper, and I didn't like the plan to stay in Madison. Neither did Mark. I missed my mother, and became afraid of Katherine after she started telling us we might be staying with her. I didn't like the way she pretended that she was our mother. I had a mother already, and it bothered me that Katherine acted like she was something she wasn't. Toward the end of our visit, I chipped a tooth in the YMCA swimming pool. Katherine searched hysterically for a dentist who could file the tooth down and put a cap on it immediately—as though she felt she had to return me to my parents better than new. Instead, I was all brown and pretty but was missing half a tooth. Katherine said the accident had spoiled her plans entirely, and now she was very angry with me. But at least we were brown, and that was something, she said. Today, I wonder whether she would have let us go so easily if I hadn't had this new imperfection.

Dad was overjoyed at seeing us back home. He was as happy as I'd ever seen him. At first I thought it was because he had missed us. But it gradually dawned on me that Katherine's gift of sending home colored boys was what was making him happy. We were brown now, his color. For weeks, he would smile and chuckle at us, constantly comparing our color to his. How lovely that Katherine's special gift to him worked, briefly, in our favor.

One afternoon Mark, Dad, and I went to the local Woolworth's and crowded into a photo booth. The machine churned out a dozen little snapshots, and Dad laughed when he saw them. I have those pictures still. We do look alike, and he has an expression on his face that is unlike any I've ever seen before or since: an all-embracing delight. For several months he rained attention on us. We were his now, and I never felt as close to him or more accepted by him than during this time.

But our tans faded, slowly, and he began to distance himself again. It was like watching a ship departing from a pier. The old fights with Mom resumed. I went back to roving the city, and about a year later we moved out of New York for good. Dad said the move was because I was becoming a thug. But I know it was because he was losing control of me and Mark and Mike, of his wife, and even of his own life.

Our house on Bettswood Road in Norwalk, Connecticut.

My youngest brother, John, with my father in Norwalk.

Me (left), Mike, and Mark on the fence in Norwalk.

SIX / Ambition

Sanity is madness put to good use.

—GEORGE SANTAYANA

On the long drive from Manhattan to Norwalk, Connecticut, Dad warned us that when we met Benny Schumer,* the real-estate man, we'd better look sharp. "Shake the man's hand," he instructed us, training his eyes on the road ahead. "Be still. Look sharp. And don't cause a ruckus, or I'll knock you into next Sunday."

This colorful phrase he used when he wanted to assert his invincible authority to keep us quiet for a while, which always made me lose my mental footing. I found the expression abstract and slippery and faintly amusing. One could hit a person hard enough that he or she would be moved into another *place*, but how was it possible to move someone forward in *time*? Could one person knock another into next year? Then I remembered that I'd been knocked forward a few minutes myself once or twice, and the lack of clarity vanished. I quieted down. We all did. For all of twenty minutes. But our nervous energy finally overcame our fear. I looked over at Mark, who looked at Mike, who looked at me, and we all exploded in a burst of the giggles.

"You boys sound like a bunch of goddamned pussies back there! You want me to pull this car over?"

"No!" we chimed in unison, and were silent again.

I looked out the window then, that Sunday morning, as the leafy Merritt Parkway pulled us closer and closer to the city of Norwalk. The gravity of the trip was obvious: that morning Mom had made us dress up in our Brooks Brothers, Church of Christ Scientist best. It was important to make a good impression, she said. John had remained at home with her.

I didn't like the idea of moving out of the city, even if I didn't yet understand what this would mean. Making a good impression certainly didn't concern me. But the idea of a new house excited me. In our various city apartments, space was a constant problem. A new house would mean more space. In Manhattan, there was also the problem of roaches. My brothers and I would sometimes wake up in the middle of the night and, armed with wet kitchen towels, would suddenly throw on the kitchen lights. On all the walls and counters, we'd see the creatures swimming and crawling over each other, racing to get back into the cracks and shadows. We would swat at them, knocking as many as we could to the floor and squashing them under our bare feet.

"Will there be roaches in the country?" we asked Dad.

"No!" he said.

"There won't be any roaches."

"Are we really moving?"

"Yes," he said, still focusing on the road ahead. "We're really going to move."

It was hard to believe that we were finally going to get out of the city, since we'd already been through this a few months earlier. Mark and I had accompanied Mom then to a place in Connecticut called Ridgefield, where she had previously selected a house with the help of a real-estate man. But when we arrived, the man's pale, tight smile came apart at the seams. He took one look at Mark and me and glowered. The look made me feel that I should scurry into a shadow. It was a cold accusation of a look. He stared very hard, the way white people in the city sometimes did when they saw us walking with our parents. Mom could sense our discomfort, and seemed confused by the man's suddenly choked and distant tone. He told us to look around the house while he waited outside. Mom did not take the hint.

It was a white-painted house set deep in green woods. It was so very, very clean—I'd never seen such a clean place. Even after Mom had scrubbed the floors and the walls and washed all the dishes and made the bedrooms neat on the weekends, our apartments in Manhattan had never looked as clean as this. The house was brand-new. The whole place smelled of wet cement and linseed oil, and of fresh paint on the naked walls. Every grain of wood on the honey colored floors stood out under the finish. I could hear my shoes clicking as I walked to the windows. Light was streaming in, as sweet as butterscotch candy.

When we came back outside, the real-estate agent seemed in a terrible hurry. His whole demeanor said he wished he were somewhere else. Weeks later, we learned that Dad had showed up with Mom to tour the place one afternoon. The real-estate man had taken one look at him, another at Mom, and declared that the house was unavailable—it had just been taken off the market. Mom said Dad just chuckled. I knew this was a bad sign.

This time, Mom said, things would be different. Mr. Schumer, the new real-estate man, was a Jew, and Jews were different. Dad said that if there was one thing white folks hated more than Negroes, it was Jews. They had come up the long, hard way through the ghettos of Europe, just as Negroes had come up from the South. They had clawed their way to the top, running grocery stores and kosher markets like the ones on the Lower East Side in Manhattan. One time, Dad had taken Mark and me with him to visit some of his insurance clients downtown near Delancey Street, a place I'd never been, even with Gil and Billy Cohan. What a revelation! I saw many tall men wearing long black frock coats with black buttons fastened all the way to the neck. They looked like giant crows. Some wore fantastic huge stiff-brimmed hats trimmed with fur. They went into buildings with

Hebrew writing on them, or into stores whose signs said GLATT KOSHER.

All of this was swimming in my head as we drove. The ribbons of concrete on the parkway narrowed and became grassy roads lined with trees dressed in crisp, clean autumn—gold, pale yellows, and reds—that gave the air a tangy taste, like new apples.

Mr. Schumer, who owned his own business, had an office near what was called the Green, a large grassy area shaped like an egg, with two churches along its periphery. We parked our car in a parking lot at the back of the building. I'd never seen a parking lot like this— in the city, cars were mostly parked on the street. As we stepped into the office, a breeze caught the scent of Dad's Old Spice aftershave, clean and sharp. Inside, I almost tripped. The floors were so thickly carpeted it was like walking on pillows. I looked down at my feet. They sank into the carpet as into the sward of a grassy park. The windows looked out onto dark tree branches, and I could hear them tapping against the glass like busy squirrels. There were several women sitting behind desks, and they didn't look surprised at all when we entered. They smiled. Dad put out the cigar he had just lit and handed his overcoat to one of them. Mark, Mike, and I followed his example. She disappeared with the coats, and another woman led us into Mr. Schumer's office.

Mr. Schumer appeared out of a side-room door, a small, radiant, cannonball-shaped man. I liked him right away. Dad flashed his best smile, a beacon of light in the small room. Mr. Schumer pumped my father's hand rather briskly. His face was shiny and his cheeks were red, like pickled beets.

"Hellooo, Mr. Minnabrook. Glad to see you. Glad to see you. Yes. Yes. Yes." I remember his nervous smile very well. It was not the way people usually looked at my father, especially when they saw him with us or with my mother, but was free and open, almost with a hint of gladness. Dad laughed, too. But it wasn't like Mr. Schumer's laugh. The sound coming out of my father's throat was dry, tight, and coiled. It said something very different than the smile he wore.

"Heh heh heh heh heh. Nice to meet you, too, Mr. Schumer, heh heh heh," he said.

Mr. Schumer's large round face beamed. His wisp of hair was combed neatly over the top of a shining dome. There was pungent cigar smoke in the air, curling from the ashtray where a long panatela was balanced on the edge. He stubbed out the cigar, apologizing to Dad for smoking in such a small room. I noticed that, despite his jovial appearance, Mr. Schumer's face was tightly drawn around the eyes, just like Dad's. Mr. Schumer's eyes said he was being careful, watchful.

He moved to the desk, which was covered with a thick sheet of Lucite, unbuttoned his suit coat, and sat down with great relief. His belly pushed the limits of the belt at his waist. He bent forward slightly and folded his hands together on top of the desk. I could see from the couch where I was sitting that Mr. Schumer liked to wear a good deal of gold on his fingers and wrists. His hands were big, and he had short, stubby fingers with hair on them. They reminded me of the butchers at our local supermarket, who wiped their hands on their blood-soaked white aprons before they shook Mom's hand. Only Mr. Schumer's fingernails were buffed smooth, and he smelled as if he had taken a bath in lemon soap: clean, clean, clean. His shirt sleeves ended in gold cuff links that were like little exclamation points. He was beginning to perspire, tiny beads forming at the top of his forehead.

Dad introduced us quietly, one by one, and Mr. Schumer bellowed our names back. He reached out his hand, and I put mine forward to shake it. My hand disappeared midway up my arm, like a baseball in a catcher's mitt. When Mike got up to shake hands, Mr. Schumer gave his cheeks a pinch. Mike giggled, squirmed out of reach, and ran back to the boatlike couch. Dad stiffened slightly, but just as quickly he seemed to regain his composure. He smiled. Mark was acting bored and sullen, and sat with his head propped in his hand.

Dad drew his chair closer to Mr. Schumer's large desk. There were no papers on it at all. Almost immediately, as he conversed lightly with Dad, Mr. Schumer's feet, strangely, began to dance. They seemed to be tapping out signals, like Morse code. His chair, resting on a thick plastic pad, was jumping up and down. Half his body said it wanted to stay and close a deal, but the other half said it wanted to cut and run.

Mr. Schumer continued in this odd dance of indecision for about five minutes. Then he collected a set of forms from a drawer in his desk and began to fill them out. He asked my father questions and chuckled at Dad's answers, which were peppered with stories about his insurance work, stories he told Mom sometimes. They were rather violent little vignettes that he found amusing. Once, he said, he had investigated the case of a woman who was hurrying to work through Times Square and was sliced in half by a falling sign that blew off its roof mount when a bolt came loose.

"Yes," Mr. Schumer said as he wrote. "Very interesting. You must see some interesting things in your line." Oh, yes, Dad said, there were all kinds of interesting cases, such as the one involving a tenement owned by a Jewish landlord that caught fire because the wiring was frayed and old. Luckily, all the people got out safely before it burned to the ground. He'd settled that case for a very reasonable sum. His bosses were happy with his work. Sometimes there were car accidents involving his clients. The legalities of such cases interested him, Dad said. He would probably get much deeper into the legal end of the job as he gained more experience, and he looked forward to that. Dad smiled again, with a confidence I'd never seen. Mr. Schumer nodded, but his eyes did not light up. He busily completed the forms, and Dad signed them with his gold Cross pen.

Many years later, we learned that the house we bought in Norwalk had been owned by a Jewish family who had not been greeted warmly by their Christian neighbors. Dad said there'd been certain "incidents" involving this family and some of the local residents, and Mr. Schumer had been hired to dispose of the property quickly. The joke was on the neighbors, however, when Mr. Schumer turned around and sold the house to us.

Four months after the meeting with Mr. Schumer, a moving van arrived at our apartment, and the guts of my New York City childhood—furniture, toys, Mom's paintings, Dad's desk and cabinets, boxes upon boxes of books, Dad's records and high-fidelity system, the black steel sling chairs, boxes and bags of clothes—were transported to the house at 7 Bettswood Road. It was February 1961, and we were starting over in a place that would be our home for the next eleven years.

The day we moved in, a heavy snow had fallen. I had never seen anything so white, even in Central Park. It was so white it hurt my eyes. The snow in Connecticut wasn't anything like New York City snow, which blackened quickly with cinders and slush and then turned to rutted ice. But Norwalk wasn't the Upper West Side, and I already missed my old neighborhood a little. I missed the dangerous friendships with Billy and Gil Cohan, and with Juan and Eusebio and Paul, my running partners, and I was sorry I hadn't had a chance to say good-bye to them. Connecticut was so quiet, so clean, so neat-as-a-pin. So safe. So lifeless. There was no sloppiness to it, no "give."

On that first day, Mark and I made snowballs in our huge yard and threw them at the telephone pole in front of the house. Then we went inside and didn't know what to do with ourselves. We decided to go for a walk. Everyone we saw seemed to be in a car. The Green, with its churches, was no more than a quarter mile from our house. But nobody walked on the Green; it had pathways, so people wouldn't step on the grass, and they were plowed now, so no one would walk on the snow. Nobody was having a snowball fight, either, or making a snowman, or building an igloo, as they would have been doing in Central Park. The Green was just a large wasted space with a memorial to war veterans at one end and nothing but useless trees at the other.

Even the food tasted different in this new place. The milk was sweet, and was delivered every day by a man who arrived at 5:00 A.M. and brought two bottles in an aluminum box to the front door. Mom and Dad tried at first to have food delivered to the house, but there was no such service, so we had to go downtown and bring back our dinner—ham sandwiches and waxy potato chips.

Downtown Norwalk seemed terribly scaled down, almost a miniature town, like the make-believe places in fairy-tale books. There were no regular buses with bumpers you could ride on, no subways to carry you to the faraway neighborhoods. There was only one movie theater, and it was closed. There were no huge buildings with elevators, no streets crowded with traffic, no bars or lounges, and no drunks leaving containers of Chinese rice on the stoops of apartment buildings.

Instead, there were solidly built stores and banks, churches and more churches, and a large red-brick building with a sign that read DAUGHTERS OF THE AMERICAN REVOLUTION. It, too, looked like a monument, since it seemed to be closed all the time. I figured that this was what Mom had meant when she talked about the DAR. Dad said the DAR hated Negroes and hated anyone who didn't have "blue blood." Did people in Connecticut really have blue blood?

There was a single grocery store downtown, tended by an evil-smelling man named Mr. Smith, who never changed his clothes. He sat behind the counter and watched as you picked out your groceries. There would be no stealing here. If I wanted to buy something, he said, I didn't need to bring money. He'd just put my name on a list, and I could pay him later. I remember that he wrote my name down in a loose-leaf notebook, using the stub of a pencil, as "Meinerbroke." The wood floors of the store were badly warped. When I asked Mr. Smith about this, he took an hour or so to tell me about a major flood of the Norwalk River, which ran about a hundred feet away, some years ago; the flood had ruined his floors, and damaged many other buildings in the neighborhood. In the coming months I would hear about this flood over and over again. It was the major news event in Norwalk of the last several decades.

Next to Mr. Smith's store was the Greyhound bus station, where the woman who owned the building sold tickets and helped passengers with their baggage. "What's your name, boy?" she said as I wandered by. I was ready to scramble. "Don't just look at me!" she barked. "Answer. Use the language. You do speak English, don't you?"

"Yes."

"Well, then, use it!" She winked and handed me a piece of candy called a Mary Jane. I'd never tasted anything so good. It was better than a jawbreaker, better than a Pez pop-up drop, better than Juicy Fruit. I walked out of her shop floating in heaven.

Next to the bus depot was a cavernous old building, as big as an airplane hangar, where the city buses were parked at night. I'd never

seen anything so huge. I walked in and wandered around. There were
pictures of nude women on locker doors. A mechanic working on a
bus looked up and asked me if there was something I wanted. When
I said there wasn't, he told me it would be best to go home. I did.

Dad said we had moved to Norwalk so I could become a better
student. "You were becoming a little thug in New York, and it worried me," he said. "Now you'll settle down. There's nobody to be a
thug with here. And if I die, you'll be safe here." This sounded
strange. I felt like crying when he said he might die. And did he really
mean it when he said I was becoming a thug? Dad had never voiced
any concern before. I was surprised to hear that he had been paying
attention to me, after all.

Early in the week, Dad took Mark, Mike, and me to Tracey Elementary School, a musty old place that smelled just like P.S. 166.
We entered the main office through a large wooden door that swung
open and shut with a heavy, final-sounding bang. A petite and very
polite woman named T. Barbara Sitwell* introduced herself as the
principal and invited the four of us into her office. She had raven
black hair and reading glasses perched on the tip of her nose, and her
voice was inviting enough, but I couldn't bring myself to meet her
straightforward gaze. Dad introduced himself, and Mrs. Sitwell
shook his hand. She said she was glad to have us as students at her
school, but asked my father why she hadn't received any papers for
us. We had arrived in the middle of the term, she explained, and she
didn't know what classes to put us in. As she spoke, I noted that
she had a close, watchful manner behind that soft voice, and that she
kept rubbing her hands together. I was used to teachers who screamed
and shouted and looked as if they had just awoken bug-eyed from a
nightmare at 2:00 A.M.

Mrs. Sitwell turned to each of us and shook our hands warmly
and firmly.

"And what grade were you in?" she asked Mark.

"Fifth grade," Mark said eagerly—he was such a show-off in
those days.

"And were you a good student or a poor one?" she said, smiling.

"Mark is a very good student," Dad said.

"And you," she said, looking over her glasses at me. "Are you a good student or a poor one?"

"Excellent," I said, lying proudly. I'd been failing nearly every subject in the city. I actually had no idea how far behind or how utterly lost I was.

"And what sorts of things do you like to do?" She was pressing me. Maybe I wasn't that good a liar after all.

"Oh, I love everything," I said. My mouth was engaged, and once I'd started I couldn't stop. "I love art. I love music. I love reading." Those were the worst lies of all. I hated all those subjects, and I'd never read a book for pleasure in my life. What I really liked was exploring museums, hitching rides on the back of buses, and stealing things, not to mention getting into fights and watching other people do the same.

"And do you like arithmetic?" she said.

"Yes. Very much."

"I'm sure you do," Mrs. Sitwell said. I was trembling and squirming in my seat, but Dad stepped in then and introduced Mike. Mike was sucking his thumb, something he did when he was nervous. Mrs. Sitwell looked at him and asked my father what grade he was in. Dad said he would be entering kindergarten.

"Very good," Mrs. Sitwell said, standing up in a way that signified the meeting was over. She took my father's hand and shook it firmly. I looked at him. I don't think Dad was able to accept her forthright manner, judging from the stern expression on his face. We all shook her hand and drove home in silence. She subsequently informed my parents that she would call them when our papers arrived from the city.

While Mom and Dad were away at work, I spent the next week or so exploring and observing the routines of the new neighborhood. Next door to us lived the Kohls,* a family with three children. The Kohls did not introduce themselves to us in those first months. Mom and Dad would say hello to Mr. and Mrs. Kohl, but that was it. In fact, in the eleven years we lived in Norwalk they never once came to our house for a visit. The Kohls had a dog named Rock.* I learned this early on, because Rock liked to chase the milkman. Every time he came to the porch Rock would run him back to his truck, and one of the Kohls would call out, "Rock!" to get the dog back indoors. Rock chuffed as he walked, like a bull who's proud of the inviolability of its territory. One of the first things I did was to make friends with the dog—which proved much easier than getting to know the Kohls.

Though it was never openly discussed, there was a strict color code in Norwalk. "Connecticut etiquette," Mom called it wryly, and there were signs of it all around.

We noticed it when we joined the Congregational Church on the Green, less than half a mile from our house. The women in the church let Mom know right away that she could not be one of them. She might be a high-flying fashion designer, and these women might be wearing some of her designs, but that mattered little, it seemed. They didn't welcome her into their sewing circle or ask her to teach Sunday school. Nevertheless, she enrolled the three of us in the Sunday school. Dad stayed home.

Across the street lived the Ornachevs,* Mrs. Ornachev and her sons, Herbie* and Janos.* There was no Mr. Ornachev. He had divorced his wife, and the boys were spoiled and angry because of it. One day just after we moved in, when I was on my way downtown, Herbie came up to me and called me a nigger. The word was like a rock that had hit me beneath the eye. I can't remember many times in my life when a word has had such a physical impact. I'd heard it many times before, of course, and had seen the damage it could bring, like when my parents quarreled and Mom would let it slip out to hurt my father's feelings. I found my fists hardening, and before I knew it I was attacking Herbie, who was bigger than I was. My hands were reaching for his face and he was tearing at my clothes, and for what seemed an eternity we struggled in the snow, which no longer seemed cold. He called me a nigger again and again. I stopped fighting for a moment and took off my coat, to free my arms. Herbie looked at me as if he didn't know what I was doing. He just stood there and let me take off my coat.

Then I attacked him again. I got close to his face this time, and swung with all my strength at his nose and eyes. My fist somehow snagged on his face, like a hook in the mouth of a fish. I could feel the impact with his nose in my stomach and bowels. Something had happened. Anyone who has ever caught an opponent in the middle of the face with a fist will know how it felt: it was like digging into something soft and puttylike. Incidents like this can throw a shape onto words, and now I knew what it meant to knock the stuffing out of someone. Before I fully realized what was happening, I looked up and saw Herbie running around the yard cupping his nose between his hands. When he took his hands away, they came away red. It looked as if someone had sprayed red paint on the spot where his nose was. The blood trickled down onto the snow, and he seemed panicked by it. He ran around and around, saying I'd broken his nose. I felt very panicky myself. Someone would surely come and hurt me. Herbie ran into the house, and his larger brother came out. He took a look at me and at the ground where we'd been fighting. I was sure he was going to attack me, but he didn't. He looked scared, too. He went back inside and left me alone in the large yard. It was suddenly cold. I put my coat back on and walked home. It was the last time Herbie, or anyone else in his family called me that name.

I never told my mother about the fight with Herbie. My behavior was already far outside the reach of her approval or disapproval. I felt that the incident shouldn't have happened, but it had, and I was glad that I'd handled it as I did. In some part of myself I wanted to hurt him even more, and it was this I was ashamed of. I knew I couldn't tell my mother I'd hurt a white boy. The words formed in my mind: "I hurt a white boy." Something changed in me. But I couldn't tell my mother about it, because I felt she could never understand what hitting a white boy meant to me. I also couldn't tell her that I'd hit him for calling me a nigger, because when she called my father a nigger she got hit, too. And while I hated my father for beating her, I knew his beating her wasn't quite the same as my beating this boy. But the boy had used the same word that she used, and, no matter how tenuously, a link had been forged between them.

Being called that name had made me flinch somewhere deep inside. It had made me thirst to feel that I was equal to or better than any white boy who lived nearby. But I now knew that this was not the way I would be regarded, and that I would have to fight to be regarded in the way I wanted to be. I recognized that I'd been cast out of my mother's world and into my father's by some judgment I couldn't change. I think that somehow I was happy about it, because it clarified who I was and who I belonged to.

Around this time I remember Mark asking me whether I was going to tell people I was a Negro or a white boy. I'm not sure exactly why I was so fast to answer that I knew I was a Negro, but it seemed to me that Mark was not pleased with my answer. Mark was being called names, too—"liver lips," the white boys at school called him. I don't know if Mark ever fought back or had the desire to beat up anyone who called him that name. I do remember that he and I began having fistfights for the first time. Whatever pain he took in, he tried to push over to me. But even then I suspected that because of his inner refinement, the instinct to hurt other people was just not in him. It wasn't in his makeup to lash out with his fists as I did. Even when he would try to lash out against me or wrestle me down, I could tell there was no passion in his attacks. Mark swallowed his anger. He kept it inside. I could not. These differences marked a turning point between us.

Many unalterable things happened within me because of that fight with Herbie, as well as my fights with Mark: a greater distance was established not only between me and the white world in this little town but between me and my mother, and me and my older brother. I knew that I was defending not just myself but also the part of myself that identified with my father. If there was a conflict within me about choosing sides in a larger racial quarrel, I tried to resolve it by telling my father about the fight, even though I felt I was betraying my mother by telling only him. I needed to be able to tell another male that I'd hurt this boy with my fists, and that it was all right, wasn't it?

Dad smiled. "You've got a lot of heart," he said approvingly. He said nothing more. I was ten years old. A week later, he bought me a typewriter and told me he wanted to see anything I wrote on it. I was mystified. I put the typewriter away on a shelf in the closet. Thinking back on it now, I feel that this was what eventually set me on the path of writing: I would learn to use words to save myself from other words that hurt me, to defend myself from the complex consequences of being hurt. I would also use words to conceal, to wound, to move myself to action.

Of course, none of this was apparent then. I was far more interested in exploring my new surroundings, and the next-door neighbors were only the beginning. The house at 7 Bettswood Road seemed at first to be full of mystery. It was a very large white place set back twenty yards or so from the street. It looked like a cozy barn. There was plenty of land in the back—nearly an acre, enough for about three quarters of a football field. There was a garden under the snow, with bushes and plants poking out, and a large freestanding two-car garage about thirty feet behind the house, with old-fashioned barn doors that swung open on big rusty hinges. There was a back porch, too, and a finished basement. There was a small crawl space in the attic, a place to hide and play games in. Beyond the knotty-pine paneling in the basement was another room large enough to hold a Ping-Pong table. There, my father would regale us with stories about his experiences on troop ships during the war.

In the attic was a small crawl space where we would hide and play games. There was also a huge cedar closet for storing winter or summer clothing. Almost immediately it overflowed with my parents' things. Mom put boxes and boxes of cashmere sweaters in a corner, for later unpacking, and hung one of her leather coats—a gray one lined with fur, from the years in Chicago—on one of several long poles that stretched across the closet. All her summer clothing was hung there as well—silk blouses, taffeta dresses, belts, skirts of glen plaid she'd designed herself—and boxes of shoes she believed would come back into fashion someday were piled to the ceiling.

Dad's things were less abundant. He frequently and recklessly weeded out his clothing. Sometimes when I was taking out the kitchen trash, I'd find half a dozen starched white shirts with his initials—ABM—monogrammed on the pocket stuffed carelessly into the garbage can. Dad always wore suits to work, and he had many of them. Most were in somber colors of exquisitely tailored silk, wool worsted, or blends. He always left the house looking like the son of a well-heeled haberdasher, impeccable and flawless. There were dark blue suits by Petrocelli and Yves St. Laurent, and the occasional gray suit purchased, along with shirts and shoes, at Brooks Brothers on Madison Avenue in Manhattan. There were dozens of pairs of shoes, all on trees: brown suede lace-ups; slip-ons and lace-ups punched and overlaid in classic wing-tip designs; cordovan leather wings with laces and slip-ons with tassels; pebble-grained Beltrami and Bally shoes in brown and black. Many of these he stored in the attic closet simply because it was better not to wear them in winter. I never saw my father in galoshes, though. To him, wearing galoshes would have been in poor taste.

Bow ties were also not worn. Most of his straight ties were kept on a hanger in his closet. There were military stripes, finely knit silks, and simple wool patterns. He also stored his various weapons there: a .22, a shotgun, and a handsome Winchester 30.06 deer rifle. Later, there would be many others. These, as much as the clothing, were items he kept immaculately clean and oiled, as though they were equally important to his manly self-image and confident self-protection.

About two weeks after we moved, we were able to start our classes at Tracey Elementary School. It took about forty-five minutes to walk there. Every morning Mark, Mike, and I would leave together, while Mom and Dad were driving in to New York, about an hour and a half away. In a very real sense, my parents had accomplished their dream of trading into respectability: out of the old brownstones and into the leafy suburbs. But the dream of a better education for their children was still some time away, at least for me.

I was in trouble almost from the moment I entered Miss Martha Poor's* fourth-grade class, and I knew it. All those years in the city, when I had shut my teachers out and shut myself down to any guidance from white authority, meant that I was probably reading on a second-grade level, if that. Mrs. Sitwell, it seemed, had found out my lie as soon as she received my transcripts from P.S. 166. She placed me in a mixed class of black and white students who were very nice but were intensely afraid of the teacher. Miss Poor reminded me of the Roman Catholic nuns I'd encountered during my last year in the city, when I'd pretended to be a Puerto Rican Catholic so I could get out of school on Thursdays, the day Catholics were let out to attend catechism.

That first day, when Mrs. Sitwell marched me toward the back of the building and downstairs to a room in the basement, I looked into Miss Poor's face and saw my own terror. She was tall, thin, and severe. Her eyes bulged terribly, the result, I would later learn, of a thyroid condition. Some of the kids had a cruel nickname for her, "Marble Eyes," others called her "Miss P." I looked at those pale, watery eyes, and they reminded me of a frog or an unpleasant insect, like a fly. I disliked her intensely, so much so that I recoiled when I had to shake her hand. She stiffly waved me to a desk.

The class was in the middle of working on some simple arithmetic problems. I copied the problems from the blackboard and got nearly all of them wrong, not so much because I didn't know how to add but because I was more interested in studying the other students, the tiny classroom, the books crowded on the shelves, the overhead lights, the windows showing the sun shining outside—and wondering whether or not I'd make any friends.

Miss Poor turned out to be as unsparingly harsh in her manner as I had imagined she would be. I knew the basement classroom signified that these were not the brightest students, and some part of my dislike came from an instant revolt at being put down here to learn. I felt I was being watched in a cage—an impression that was confirmed for me as I saw how my fellow students cringed whenever Miss Poor asked a question. To me, her questions were like barked commands, and her unsmiling manner chilled me to the bone. She spoke with a thick South Boston accent, in a voice like an air-raid siren. She carried a long wooden pointer with a hard black rubber tip, but she never used it as a pointer. Instead, she used it on the students like a cattle prod.

When Miss Poor wanted someone to prove an arithmetic problem at the blackboard, she would call out a name from her list, as though she could never remember our names. The students were afraid to raise their hands, and when their names were called they would quickly go to the blackboard, do the problem, and sit down. If they didn't know the answer, as several students seemed not to, they froze in front of the class. They feared being revealed as idiots who couldn't get anything right. Her habit of calling out another student's name while the first was still floundering gave her command over a demoralized class. And the process was repeated again and again, until someone got the problem right. I hated her more and more, because she seemed to enjoy humiliating us; this seemed to be her objective, rather than teaching us anything.

One afternoon I raised my hand in the middle of some drill and asked Miss Poor why she was a miss and not a missus. She calmly answered that it was because she wasn't married.

"Will you ever *get* married?" I then asked.

The nastiness of my tone must have struck her like a slap in the face. She winced visibly. She asked me if I'd finished the drill. I told her that my eyes were bothering me, which was true. I was supposed to be wearing my glasses, but by the time we moved to Connecticut I'd "lost" nearly a dozen pairs. Miss Poor looked at me for a moment, a look that was the hardest, most baleful and withering stare I'd ever seen. It frightened me.

"Come with me," she said.

I followed. For the rest of the afternoon I was made to stand outside the classroom door.

The next day, to show the other students I was not afraid of anyone, especially not of this teacher, I asked Miss Poor why she was called "Marble Eyes." I felt triumphant. But I looked around and saw that everyone I'd thought would be amused was looking at her with stony cold fear. Nobody was laughing. Our private joke was now mine to bear alone.

"Come with me, Mr. Minerbrook," she said quietly. Again I was forced to stand outside the classroom.

Later that afternoon I was taken to see Mrs. Sitwell, who asked why I had wanted to hurt Miss Poor's feelings.

"Do you know what a thyroid is?" Mrs. Sitwell asked gravely.

"No."

"It's an important gland in the body, and if it doesn't work it causes the eyes to bulge and the hair to fall out," Mrs. Sitwell explained.

Then she bore in deeper. Did I know that people got very sick when they had a thyroid that didn't work? No. Did I know that Miss Poor had been on sick leave for most of the school year because of her condition? No.

Mrs. Sitwell finally stood up and said I should feel ashamed of myself.

"Why?" I said. I wouldn't let her have control, and I wasn't going to back down. She told me to go back to class. I felt I'd triumphed over both of them.

The next day, any trace of softness that might have appeared in Miss Poor's face when she looked at me was utterly gone. For the rest of the term I was cut adrift. Nobody would speak to me. The friends I had hoped to cultivate fell away like meat off a boiling bone. The five months I spent in Miss Poor's class were a kind of hell. Every bit of my bravado was stripped away. I cared deeply that I was flunking most of my tests. I hated feeling stupid, but I was too embarrassed to ask for help. I was too afraid, and too ashamed of being considered without talent, and that feeling turned to something like dread as I failed one examination after another.

I failed every subject that term except art and physical education, and even in those Miss Poor gave me only average grades. I would have to repeat the fourth grade. I'd never tasted such bitterness or defeat before. I felt that nothing I could do was any good. As any child who's been through it knows, few experiences are worse than being left back in school. It is worse than getting slapped by a teacher, or forgetting your lines in a school play, and is more shameful even than throwing up or peeing in your pants in the middle of a class.

All the kids I knew, even the ones who were just as rebellious and afraid or who had done as badly as I had, shunned me, a confirmation of my new status as a failure. If my parents knew about any of this, or were ever contacted by the school authorities, I never heard about it. When report-card time came around I either lost mine or tried to alter the grades. When they finally did learn I would have to repeat a grade, we never spoke of it. It was like a secret that was too shameful to admit. I never received any criticism from Mark, either—an act of kindness on his part that I have never forgotten. Years later, he would tell me how disappointed he was, but at the time he said nothing. I felt as if there had been a death in the family: mine. Everyone pretended that it hadn't happened, and that was the worst kind of punishment. It was like calling for help from a deep cave, only to hear your weakening echo endlessly bounce back to you. It was worse than trying and failing at something. I recognized that I hadn't really tried at all, and I felt that nobody would ever ask me to try again. I felt as though it had been inevitable that I would fail, that my simply being put in a class with others who were labeled slow learners had been an invitation to give up, to surrender to fate. I was sure there was some really frightening defect in me—a feeling that has never entirely left me. It's the fear that nothing I do will ever be good enough.

But worse was still to come. When my classmates learned that I'd been left back, it seemed as if every student with a need to dominate others was picking a fight with me. That was my introduction to the idea of the pecking order. I was now lumped together with students to whom I felt superior: darker-skinned Negroes who spoke more slowly than I did; whites who were poor. I was cast among them, and it was humiliating to be judged a failure among failures: I tried to assure myself that I wasn't like them, but this snobbery and prejudice did not rescue me. The next year I was seated in the back of the class, and when I raised my hand to be called on, the teacher routinely ignored me. I was now part of some faceless, nameless mass of rejection and worthlessness. I wasn't worthy of attention. Such children always know who they are. They also know who the other children are who are cast in the same light. I learned to shun these others who had failed or been left back. Once I tried making friends with another kid who had been left back, but I found the experience so uncomfortable, his reflection of my private shame so clear and intense, that I soon withdrew from the alliance.

What I didn't know then was that being left back was probably one of the best things that could have happened to me. It made me realize that if I were ever to succeed, or to feel proud of myself, I'd have to do it on my own. Anyone who says American education doesn't encourage the most rigid style of conformity is lying. I began to watch the most successful students in my class for clues as to what they were doing. I noticed that the teachers didn't pay much attention to the black or Hispanic students. Somehow, success consisted of not being identified with these students, of being identified instead with white students and their behavior. Whites, as I understood it then, were natural achievers because they were white. Browns and blacks were not, because they were not white. For the first time in my young life, I wanted to be among the achievers, even though not one of the achievers was the same color I was. How far I felt from them! But my brother Mark was among them, and I came to resent the fact that he was achieving success and I was not.

When I entered the fifth grade the following fall, I was terrified as I'd never been before. But the fates were finally on my side. I got a teacher named Mrs. O'Malley,* a gentle woman with a ready, encouraging smile. She somehow calmed me. I didn't feel judged by her. I didn't seem to have to strain so hard to please her, or maybe it was just that she didn't act displeased all the time, as Miss Poor had. I responded by working much harder. Mrs. O'Malley seemed to see that I was making an effort, and she must have known why. That was all I needed. I discovered that I was better at my schoolwork than I had ever thought I could be. Slowly I began to come out of my old self, and for the first time I could take pleasure in the work. I began to read poetry, remembering all the poems my parents knew and the stories Mom had told me about the way they'd used poetry to help one another through their early troubles. I loved funny poems, particularly those by Ogden Nash. I liked Langston Hughes, too. I made up this poem, which I called "Other Children," after reading a poem by him:

> *Some children live in palaces*
> *Behind an iron gate*
> *And go to sleep in beds of gold*
> *Whenever it gets late.*

And way up north the children live
In houses built of ice
And think that beds made of fur
Are really very nice.

In countries where nights are hot
Without a single breeze
The children sleep in bamboo beds
All fastened to the trees.

Some day I'll travel round
And visit every land,
And learn to speak the language that
Each child can understand.

They'll want to ask me questions then
I'll want to ask them others
Until at last we understand
Like sisters and like brothers.

Through black friends I made at school, I began to explore Norwalk's black community on the strength of a racial passport that allowed me to go anywhere I pleased. They lived in several areas of Norwalk, always in their own enclaves, away from whites. One was a neighborhood near downtown where a few dozen black families lived, including the family of Calvin Murphy, one of the town's finest athletes. I was attracted by the wonderful way Calvin's family and friends played basketball and other sports. They were always the fastest, the bravest, the ones who played with the greatest authority and confidence. Their friends John Ivy and Jimmy Wrenz were especially good. They'd all been raised since early childhood playing sports together, and watching them play basketball during our lunch recess was truly inspiring.

I started to play basketball, too, and as my proficiency grew I spent more time around these athletes, near their homes. They would always ask me what race I was, bluntly and plainly. I would tell them that I was a Negro but my mother was white, and that seemed enough to make them open up to me. I'd never met any Negroes like them before. They were loud and affectionate with one another. They were watchful, too, and learned each other's language tics very fast. They communicated not only with words but with their whole bodies— through gestures of the hands, face, neck, back, and elbows. Their conversations were like whirlwind dances of voice and physical motion, all done so fast it made your head spin. How unlike my father's staid and conservative habits of speech and gesture. If I was a Negro, they would ask, why didn't I talk with a deep southern accent, as so many of them did? I talked like a white person, they said. I explained that I was born in Chicago and had grown up in New York City, and this was how New Yorkers spoke.

As an interracial child, I felt that I was in some ways equally invisible to both the black and the white communities of Norwalk in a way I had never been in New York. Here, it was more comfortable for the black children I knew to relate to other black children than to relate to me. The same held for the white children. And there were few Hispanics in Norwalk at the time, so there was no middle cultural ground for me. You had to choose which social swim you wanted to be part of: either you were black or you were white. There could be no Mr. In Between.

Skin color made a huge difference to the black and the white students alike. It was a lesson driven home for me by an experience with a girl named Rita Gonzalez.*

Rita was a pretty girl with nut-brown skin whose body was already blossoming into womanhood. But her manner did not in any way match her soft, interesting curves. Rita liked me, I knew, because she would make jokes about me at school. I'd get notes from her, folded into dozens of triangles and passed under the desk, asking me if I liked her. Sometimes the notes would be from Amalia Pope,* her cousin. Yeah, I liked her. But did I "like" her? Amalia wanted to know. Yeah, I'd write back, I really did "like" her, not knowing exactly what she was talking about.

One day Rita called me on the phone and asked me straight out, "Are you black or are you white?"

I had no question about my identity. I had learned in New York that having a black father meant that I was black. The experience with Herbie Ornachev had confirmed it. And I had relatives in Chicago who stayed in touch with me. I felt I belonged to them, somehow, since my mother's people had never claimed me at all.

I told her that I was black.

"You know," she said, "you could pass for white if you wanted to." *Pass?* No one had ever said anything like that to me before.

Then Rita told me I had "good hair." I'd never thought of hair as good or bad, but she said that Negro hair was bad because it had to be burned and combed with hot irons to make it "lay down." Otherwise, she said, it would "go back." Go back to what? I wondered. I was mystified. She spoke of "grades" of hair, "shades" of skin color, of "talking white." She seemed to be speaking a foreign language.

There were other lessons of race to learn, including a few vivid incidents that occurred when I was in sixth grade. One day I was playing tag ball with some students during recess, including a boy named Matthew Jones* whose father was a successful politician. Matthew was a favorite of the teachers at Tracey, one of those students I ought to have wanted to be like, and in some respects did. Matthew threw the ball too hard, and it hit me in the middle of my back and stung. It seemed to me that he had intended to hurt me. I made angry faces at him, and he shouted at me from across the circle we were playing in, "What are you going to do about it?"

I didn't mind what he said so much as the provocative way he was gesturing at me and waving his arms in a come-on-let's-fight stance. He kept pointing his fingers at his chest and then at the ground. His gestures somehow told me that I was supposed to tuck my tail between my legs and apologize. But as he repeated them I felt something boil up inside me. If I'd learned anything in the city, it was the language of violence. One declared one's intentions simply through movements and gestures such as his.

It was the first time I ever "saw red." I ran straight at this untouchable politician's boy and belted him as hard as I could in the middle of his soft stomach. He made a sound—*oooff*—and I heard the air rushing out of his nose and a little grunt at the back of his throat. I was pleased. It was over now.

How wrong I was! He clutched his stomach and then grabbed me around the neck. I tried to twist free, which hurt my neck—though that didn't matter, because I had taken the pride out of this white boy. What pleased me most was the cruel joy of knowing that I'd torn him down in public and in his own eyes. No one had ever challenged him like that before. I even liked it when a frowning teacher rushed over. Matthew was crying now, and that surprised me. I was twelve years old, old enough to know instinctively that I would be punished for having stepped over the invisible line that separated me from people like Matthew Jones. I felt ashamed only for having gotten caught punching the boy so openly, instead of challenging him to a fight far away from any teacher's prying gaze. I noted that in the future I would have to be more careful.

The consequences were immediate. The teacher who was supervising the recess pried us apart, blowing her whistle like a traffic cop.

"Who started this?" she demanded. She seemed to be addressing the other black students who had gathered around.

Suddenly Rita and Amalia, who had been acting as though they were my new best friends, began shouting and pointing at me, with their hands over their mouths.

"Scott started it," Rita said.

I felt instantly betrayed. None of the white students agreed I was to blame, only the black ones. But it seemed to be what the teacher wanted to hear. I was sent home, where there were no repercussions.

To my surprise, the white students acted more friendly toward me after that. It was as though they'd wanted to knock this pesky son of privilege off his stilts for a long time, but couldn't for fear of reprisal. The black students who'd acted so tough and talked so loud had seen what I'd done, but were suddenly silent and distant. There was no praise from them. It was all part of this strange new racially divided culture I was learning about. It was okay for blacks to beat each other up, to talk mean and loud to each other—I'd seen that at almost every recess period—but the white kids were never to be touched. The white kids were safe behind an invisible barrier guarded even by blacks, and I had crossed that line without severe consequences.

Other strange things happened that year. I worked harder on my studies, haunted by the terror of failing again, only to find the blacks now accusing me of "acting white." They said I wasn't a Negro after all, but a white person calling himself a Negro's son. That hurt. I could say nothing in response. It felt to me like another kind of betrayal, though it occurred to me that maybe *they* were the ones who felt betrayed. Maybe they felt that my small efforts at self-assertion embarrassed them. It was certainly clear from then on that I could never completely belong to their society. I didn't know the rules.

I also found it curious that many of the same students who hectored me for trying to act white would put on their own special "colored" acts to please the teachers. It happened most often during lunch period, when one of the teachers who was very strict with the black students during recess would allow them to gather in the lunchroom and play their radios loud. The radios were never confiscated. The teachers would even urge them to dance, and they did. They threw their very souls into it. But the white students were never encouraged to dance, even though some of them were eager to show how good they were. Whenever the white kids tried to join the dancing, the teachers ordered the radios to be turned off.

It also struck me as odd that the black students were not encouraged to excel in academic subjects. Virtually the only activity they were encouraged to do well in was organized sports. The teachers didn't appear interested in the dark boys except when they picked up a basketball or a baseball glove or fought one another. On the athletic field, they were always the heroes, and students who were cowed into silence in the classroom often assumed an alertness and mastery that hadn't been there before. I wanted approval at all costs, so I began to play sports with the black kids as often as I could. If I exerted myself as strongly as they did, perhaps I, too, would be rewarded with the teachers' smiling attention.

Dad had played basketball in college, and that gave me yet another incentive. I went all over Norwalk trying to learn the fine points of the game. South Norwalk's black ghetto was one place where basketball was played every day, and I started going there regularly. In Washington Village and the other housing developments there, the competition was fierce and exciting to watch. There was Rudner

Court, where I would go on weekends, and frequently on weeknights, to play with young men like Vandy Moore or "Hot Rod" Lopez, who had "the juice." Vandy was balletic in his moves under the basket. Hot Rod never missed from the corner—the ball just magically whispered through the net.

During those first years in Norwalk, when I was concentrating on where and how I fit in, my parents became absorbed in their abiding dream of being home owners. My father's skills as a carpenter, electrician, and jack-of-all-trades blossomed, as though this was exactly where he belonged, tending his home. It seemed to me then that it didn't much matter to him whether any of us got in trouble at school. What was most important was that he'd done his part by removing us from the pitfalls that could have swallowed us in New York. Now it was up to each of us to seize the opportunities he'd made available. He would acknowledge our scrapes, but he wouldn't get involved. The move also helped him define himself as a fully formed man of his generation—home owner, father, husband—a generation that saw itself through its achievements and its unprecedented material success.

But Dad was also a Negro, and this set him apart. In these years before the civil rights movement burst with full force and gravity onto the conscience of all Americans, his achievements had the extra sweetness denied to the previous generations of his family. While they, too, had pooled their resources and winnowed their talents, they ultimately sacrificed more than any other group—with the possible exception of Native Americans—to lay claim to their rights as Americans. That was part of Dad's identity as a black man, and his moving to leafy Connecticut meant that he had achieved something not only for himself but for the generations before and after him. There was money to be made, and making it would erase the stereotype many people held that blacks didn't know how to make money or how to handle it. Dad was making it for his mother and for other members of his family—proving to them that he could be successful, just as they had always wanted him to be.

But they and others like them knew that success bore the cost of a fearful social isolation. This was something I was only beginning to understand. Few other black men were accomplishing what he was, in these days before passage of the landmark legislation that all too briefly began to level the playing field between blacks and whites. Dad was already doing it on his own, and as a forerunner, he paid the price of being among the first of his generation to penetrate the white suburbs. He could find few friends here, and with no other Negros he could relate his experiences to judging either his performance or the great distance he had traveled from Chicago. Sometimes he seemed to be traveling so fast and so far that he didn't leave time for friends. Perhaps he didn't really feel the need for them, being a loner by nature.

I remember my father at this time as a man consumed by ambition. He seemed obsessed with moving ahead quickly to satisfy his personal hunger for affirmation. He thirsted for the symbols of success, even more than the rewards of a happy life. He was doing something that raised his opinion of himself, not only in his own eyes but according to the lights of American society. In a certain sense, the fulfillment of his dreams was no more than the long-overdue realization of a promise to all black men. But that didn't diminish either the sweetness of his victory or the price he had to pay for it.

The more important thing to me, though, was that the emotional distance I'd always felt between us was growing. I believed my father was ashamed of my whiteness, and showed it by keeping his distance. I felt that he was afraid I would betray him because I could not understand what it meant to be black, and that he was proud of only the part of me that reflected his drive to achieve success. I know now that such distance is common between many fathers and sons, but with my father and me, race seemed to add a special depth.

Having a home of his own was at least some compensation to him for all the succor he could not get from us. His home was the one thing he had to show for his own labors as a black man—as opposed to his children, who didn't completely belong to him. He now had a place to focus his dreams and the hard work he put into them. And so did my mother, who was also the first in her family to achieve so much. This was an important bond between them.

Under the focus of their work, many of the old frictions between

Mom and Dad seemed to disappear for a while as they labored to build a future for themselves and for us. Mom had come from a family that was wanting in physical comfort and Dad from one lacking in spiritual and emotional comfort, and they were now self-confidently creating the comforts they'd never had.

Early every spring, with a winter chill still in the air, Dad would be the first in the neighborhood to throw himself into a home-improvement project. One of the small miracles of these years was the way the house was so completely transformed. The previous owners appeared to have left hastily. They had ripped out wall-to-wall glass mirrors in the dining room but hadn't got around to replacing them. My father quickly covered the ugly scars with pecan-wood paneling. He and Mom went to a nearby Ethan Allen furniture store and came back with a large, heavy cherry-wood dining table that filled most of the room. Dad hung a wooden chandelier from the ceiling, and put up all kinds of pictures on the walls. On weekends, Dad laid down brick paths in a herringbone pattern that led to the front steps. He threw himself into cultivating the back garden, which had been planted in rhubarb and other vegetables. He set me and my brothers to work, pulling weeds for hours on end. There was a lawn to be mowed, and the clippings had to be hand-raked, bagged, and taken to the dump. The bushes in front of the house had to be kept trimmed so that not a single loose strand stuck out. One afternoon a truckload of fence posts and rails was delivered, and Dad spent the next weekend putting up a rail fence. A higher post with a lamp on top, and a timer, was installed, with the light set to go on just as the last rays of sun flickered out.

My father worked like a man possessed, as though he was afraid he might die the next day and leave some task unfinished. He broke through an interior wall on the first floor to remove a closet and create an open hallway that ran from the front door all the way to the back of the kitchen. He opened up new space everywhere. One afternoon I came home from school to find the entire kitchen had been remodeled by a hired carpenter with Dad's help. It all happened so fast I almost didn't recognize my own house. I would return home from playing with friends on Saturday afternoons and find new tiled floors, new cabinets and countertops, new overhead lights, a new bathroom, a new stove, a new door here or there. He even installed a telephone that rang like a front-door chime. He was truly happy while he worked.

The house took on a sense of order that helped me feel we were finally setting down roots and striving, each of us, to improve ourselves. But it was a lonely kind of life, too. In a way, my parents were so united, so lashed to the mast of their work, that an even greater space grew between them and us. I saw my father mostly on weekends, when he would weigh himself and the rest of us down with an increasingly challenging regimen of tasks to perform.

Through our first three years in Norwalk, Dad continued to set a punishing pace for himself. He was a lion at his insurance work and was being groomed for promotion. Shortly after we moved he had changed jobs, and the new firm, Allstate, had sent him to Boston and to Hartford for special training sessions that lasted several weeks. Every time, he came home saying proudly he had graduated first in his class. He shone like a bright silver dollar. Success and a growing stream of money were just the kind of therapy he and Mom sorely needed.

Mom in those years helped to create the national reputations of several clothing design firms. Before the move, John's blindness had thrown her into bitter and deep depressions. Now, after she got home from work, she would collect him, somewhat jealously, from Thelma, our black housekeeper, and help him explore the house. John was a late walker because he lacked the visual cues crucial to learning balance and coordination, so as Mom walked him from room to room, John would clap his hands to experience the auditory sensation of space. He would roam the house with her, tinkering with locks and slamming doors to see what they sounded like. Mom would give him things to touch, play music for him, and try to describe such concepts as color until she dropped asleep from exhaustion, with John in her arms.

I loved to watch John as he explored. He would run the bathwater, hot and cold, and explore those sensations. He was a rather silent child, slow to learn language, but he seemed to be taking in every sound, every touch, every taste, even the breeze coming through open or closed doors. One day when he was five, after he'd carefully felt his way around on his hands and knees many times and knew every corner of the house by touch and sound, he simply determined that it was time to walk.

Around 1965, Mom and Dad decided to place John in the Boston Institute for the Blind, where he could learn Braille and could acquire the skills he needed to live independently. It was a difficult parting, but Mom knew she couldn't harbor him at home much longer. She didn't know how to teach him what he needed beyond the rudiments, and she knew she had clung to him too hard.

John's absence only seemed to make my parents throw themselves more intensely into their home improvements and their careers. And as if these weren't enough, they now adopted the exhausting routine of driving several hundred miles to Boston every Friday evening to pick up John and bring him home for the weekend. Then, on Sunday afternoon, they would make the trip in reverse. In addition, Mom traveled to Boston regularly on her own to visit John.

During the winters, when there wasn't much outside work to do, my father would allow the interior work to fall into a hiatus, partly because he preferred the outside work but partly because the strain of the long trips to Boston was taking such a toll on him. Then, each spring, the cycle of work and travel would begin again, and neither of my parents let up the pace. Dad approached the house as he did everything else in his life: with total concentration and abandon. Maybe he needed to forget the special pressures of having a blind son and an interracial family. In any event, the work was a way to direct his focus away from himself.

Incredibly, he even took on more jobs. He began to work in a bakery on weekend nights. I loved it when he'd bring home wonderful hot rolls with white icing on top, Danish pastries, cookies, and— my favorite—fresh rye bread with a thick crust. But something was turning bitter in me, too. I appreciated all he was trying to do, but I felt that he was well aware that he was using his work to run away from me and my brothers. He would come home from the bakery early in the morning and prepare hot oatmeal, rye toast with butter, and milk for us, while telling us that no one had done that for him when he was a child. This unhappy memory ruined the gesture for me, and I would leave the food uneaten. It seemed that the only way he could attend to us was in a hurry or through what he produced. He could never give us affection directly. Affection was an emotion reserved for women. And who could reproach him for overworking to provide for his family?

When he got bored with the job at the bakery, he found other jobs. He worked for a time as a drill-press operator in Milford, and on stamping equipment at a plant in Stratford that made operational systems for guided missiles. He worked like that on and off for years, relentless and driven, like a protean madman whose efforts never drained him but only made him work harder. He never seemed able to simply be at rest.

At length, I began to notice that he was getting less and less joy from any of this. The more he did, the more intensely he threw himself into each new, almost insanely ambitious project: a new driveway, a basketball rim and backboard for me, new windows to be painted and installed, a garden and trees to plant, and such hobbies as hunting and fly-fishing to fill any spare time. One summer he and Mom bought thousands of dollars' worth of camping equipment, loaded it in our new station wagon—a Buick Skylark—and drove us all up to Canada for a week of camping. We never used the equipment again.

Dad simply had less and less energy for the strenuous emotional work of fathering a household. After years of constant fix-up projects on the house, he had to spend longer hours to accomplish the same amount of work. He was running out of steam, and he began to drink to keep himself going. He drank more and more heavily. His insurance career didn't require him to be in an office regularly, and by balancing the paperwork for his job with his other tasks, and catching short naps in between, he managed to sustain himself for a time.

Increasingly, though, as he spread his energies over more and more projects, he began to lurch backward into the emotional chaos of those earlier years in New York and Chicago. Ever more violent fits of temper seized him, and he became dangerous to anyone who ventured too close. He would bring home a huge clump of rhododendron flowers to display in the living room, and then he would break the vase in a fit of anger because it wouldn't hold them all. Or we would be eating a steak dinner Mom had prepared, and if he didn't like the taste of the food he would threw all of it—plate included—into the garbage. His weekend work schedules became more and more rigid. He would go to his weekend job half drunk and half asleep. At his drill-press job one night, he pressed down too hard on a drill bit he hadn't tightened properly, and the bit dug deep into his finger. He had to use a pliers, he said, to pull it out.

The year I entered junior high school, the physical beatings began again in earnest. They always started off with Mom and Dad having a few drinks to unwind after their long week and to get ready for the busy weekend ahead. Often Dad would lash out at Mom without warning, beating her with his fists. She would fight back, crying and calling out for Mark or me to help. We would beg him to stop, and he did at first. But before long he stopped listening to our pleas, and the beatings became worse. I couldn't understand how this could be happening. Dad had seemed to be doing so well at his jobs and his work around the house.

Suddenly he would spend a huge amount of money on expensive furniture, wallpaper for the bathrooms, bedding for the bedrooms, and on liquor to wrap himself in a sense of security that he was in fact losing. And just when the renovations on the house reached their peak, gifts from Katherine began arriving again—Pfizer beefsteaks from Kansas City and Chicago; melton duffel coats with horn fasteners from Brooks Brothers. She sent Dad a credit card for G. Fox, an expensive Hartford department store, and he would run up a charge of thousands of dollars in clothes—mostly for himself. He always seemed to be trying to consume more and more things, to fill up some ravenous hunger in himself.

Dad was always especially hard on Mark. One weekend, as Mark and Mike and I were busy in the garden with our endless weeding, Dad lit into Mark, asking him why he'd developed such a mean attitude. Mark was just beginning to date, and was struggling with his racial identity. He was finding it hard to finesse the issue of racial loyalty, and once asked Dad how he could declare himself a Negro if his mother was white or declare himself white if his white relatives hated him. At school, he was taking his share of abuse from both the blacks, who didn't include him in their circle, and the whites, who nicknamed him "Bird" because he whistled to himself a lot. Mark consciously walked his own path, and was trying to keep his balance between these two worlds. He was often sullen and withdrawn.

That weekend, as we weeded, Dad attacked.

"What are you?" he challenged Mark. "Some kind of hinckty nig-gah?" "Hinckty" meant you were acting evil. Mark was moody some-times, but never evil.

Dad proceeded to cut Mark down. "I didn't raise you to be a hin-ckty niggah, boy. I didn't raise you to be a niggah at all. You come from people who aren't niggahs, boy, and don't forget it." Mark tried to stand up to this, but Dad beat him down with his insults.

We grew even more terrified of Dad than we'd been in the city. Sometimes, on weekend afternoons, he would say he wanted to take us on a long ride in the country. We'd end up going to New Haven, where he would buy us all new hats we didn't want. He drove so fast that we thought we'd surely be killed. When we got home he would play rock-and-roll or jazz records, Miles Davis or Cannonball Adderley. At night he would take us to the drive-in movie theater— everyone but John, who'd be left with a baby-sitter. Mark and Mike and I always sat outside in lawn chairs and listened to the movie over the small speakers. Before long Dad would be pounding on Mom. We would hear the slaps, and her pleas for him to stop. Then he would really let her have it. We became experts at recognizing the punch that would end the movie and start us on the silent drive home, Mom weeping and bleeding and Dad strangely calm.

Somehow, as the renovation work on the house tapered off, Dad's energy exploded. He began creating new tasks for himself and for us. His rules regarding the weekend work became increasingly strict. The garden always needed weeding in the summer months, and the new cars—his Volkswagen Beetle and a Lincoln Mercury—had to be washed, hand-dried, and waxed. He put up an American flag at the front door. He dug up the lawn and replanted it, and the new grass had to be kept clipped as neatly as a manicure. We weren't allowed to use anything but bamboo hand rakes to pick up the clippings, along with hand spades to keep the edges of the lawn trim, and hand shears to keep the bushes neat. We developed blisters on top of our blisters. Dad said it was good for us. "Make a man out of you," he would say with a laugh, *heh heh heh*. If we balked because we were tired, or didn't complete a task to Dad's liking, or tried to get out of something altogether, as I often did by simply disappearing on my bike, he became irritable and then violent.

There was always cleanup detail afterward, when we would have to sweep the driveway with a large push broom with six-inch bristles. But we were allowed to use this broom only after we'd swept off the largest pebbles with a smaller broom. We had to sweep in smaller and smaller strokes—just so—to get rid of every speck of dust.

Then Dad decided that he wanted us to paint the house red, white, and blue. So we painted two sides of the upper story barn red, the lower story white all around, and the front and back of the upper story a light blue. It was an odd and funny-looking combination, but of course it was done according to his orders. From morning until evening, we were kept busy. Dad showed us how to use the various brushes—one for the window trim, one for the wooden slats of the doors, another for the soffits and the wooden trim around the doors, and so on. Yet he pushed himself just as hard, Mark and I agreed, while he put us through our paces. I think Mark would have given Dad his right arm if Dad had asked for it. I was less willing, but would never have said so—I was too afraid. Mark never left Dad's side. He rose with him and laughed with him. But there was always something in Dad that Mark simply could not touch.

One afternoon, after our work was done, Mark and I started playing around with Dad's freshly washed red Volkswagen, rolling it up the driveway and down again, taking turns steering. Suddenly a window slammed open in a bedroom on the second floor, and Dad was cursing at us. He looked so tired, so at his wit's end, that his eyes and even his teeth were flashing with rage. He called out to us to get our asses in the house—in a hurry.

When Mark and I came in, he sat us down and calmly told Mark he didn't appreciate what Mark had been saying under his breath—answering back, talking so smart. In fact, Mark had done nothing of the kind and was thunderstruck at the accusation.

Dad took off his belt. Holding it in one hand, he began slapping Mark with the other. Mark didn't cry out, and Dad just kept slapping, not saying a word. It was like one of those World War II movies in which a prisoner is strapped to a chair and slapped, his face jerking from side to side. Finally Mark tried to cover his face, but Dad pulled his hands down and slapped him still harder.

"You think you can protect yourself?"

Bang! He hit Mark hard on the face.

"From me?"

Smack!

"No, Dad," Mark said. That got him an even harder slap. It broke my heart to see Mark taking so much punishment and trying not to cry.

Dad called Mark a liar then, and Mark burst into tears. Dad smacked him some more, putting so much force into each blow that his feet rocked forward and he nearly lost his balance. Mom was nowhere around. I was glad. She would surely have intervened and taken the blows herself.

When you get beat as a kid, there is a rough etiquette involved. For the beating to make sense to you, the punishment must fit the crime; otherwise, it is unjust and unforgivable. The worst thing a beating from your father can do is make you come to see him as a smaller human being. You begin to pity him. Then there is a massive loss of respect, not only for him but for yourself, and you begin to hate him. Each blow cuts you down further, as well as cutting him down further in your eyes. Your feelings for that person die a little more each time you are abused. You stop feeling anything after a while. You begin to understand that the adult who has beat you is just a coward taking advantage of you because you're smaller. No fall is worse for a child than this: to understand that the beating isn't meant to correct your behavior. It isn't out of love. It's simply to give the abuser a sense of release.

After about five minutes or so, I urged Dad to stop. Mark hadn't said a word to deserve a beating like this, I told him. He turned on me with a very hard, stinging blow that made my ears ring inside.

"Did I ask your opinion, you little motherfucker?" He cursed so hard, he spit. I could smell the nicotine on his breath.

I told him again that Mark hadn't said anything, and I didn't see what he was so upset about. Mark begged me to shut up, but it was way too late.

Dad began slapping me in earnest. Soon the slaps themselves stopped hurting. I simply turned myself off, and went into a kind of trance where the slaps didn't hurt. I stopped hearing them. My father's curses seemed distant. The only thing that hurt me was the injustice of it and the pain of seeing my father lose control.

When Dad saw that I wouldn't cry, he took it as evidence of deeper defiance—and it was. He struck over and over, until I couldn't tell anymore if he was slapping me or someone else who shared my name. He stopped when that person's nose began to bleed. I looked down and saw blood dripping on my shirt. It was my blood. Dad stopped. It was over.

Dad said he was finished with us. I certainly was finished with him. Mark was sobbing, less because of the punishment, I knew, than because of his utter despair that Dad could be so unfair and so lost. I knew this because Mark had always tried to justify what Dad did, tried to ignore his faults. But not this time. This beating broke his heart. We never talked about it. I simply got up and went upstairs, washed my face, and put on a clean shirt. The day's work was done.

Shortly after this, Mark moved out of the bedroom he and I had shared. He moved into the attic alone, and kept his door locked at all times. That beating was another kind of turning point for us as brothers. Unlike me, Mark could not fight back. He loved his father too much for that. He was no better at fighting my father than he was at fighting the kids who challenged him at school. He bore it. He always did. I could not. I raged against my father. Mark and I never quite forgave each other for the different directions our lives were taking. I could not reconcile myself to his love for our father, nor he to my growing hatred of him. We were jealous of one another beyond words. But what finally broke us was that we had been so utterly unable to protect each other. We could never speak of our shame, or name it in our father. So we drifted further apart. Mark continued to stay at home on weekends to help Dad, but I did not. I began wandering all around southern Connecticut on my bike. I would go off into other counties or towns, or into the white neighborhoods of west Norwalk. But mostly I spent my time in the black neighborhoods of South Norwalk, where I felt as safe as I should have felt at home.

LaVerne and Alan, 1969.

Me, during my high school football years.

SEVEN / The Colors Between Us

I love and I hate; you may ask why this is so
I do not know, but I feel it and I am tortured.

—CATULLUS

On the board behind her desk, Mrs. Kathleen George* wrote in bold Latinate script, "*Lingua Latina mortua non est.* The Latin language is not dead." No, she said, in reminders that came to us as ritually as a prayer, "*Lingua Latina resurgit.* Latin is coming back."

That wasn't true, of course. Yet there was something about her optimistic love of lost causes that made me like Mrs. George. I admired her strenuous efforts to make her first-year Latin students believe that, despite the inroads of popular culture, which was steering students toward French and Spanish and Italian, we were the ones going in the right direction. But the enrollment figures did not support her faith. There were only eleven of us in our tiny first-year class, not the usual twenty or thirty of previous years. The school board was thinking about eliminating the Latin program altogether, Mrs. George said, and what a pity that would be.

I came to Latin for my own special reasons. Beyond the question of whether learning the language was a lost cause or not—for me the element of lost causes added a certain piquant romanticism to the discipline—Latin was the language of military conquest and domination. It was the language the Romans had spoken, and they had ruled the world. It was a language of power, self-confidence, and nobility. For me, it was the language that embodied all my fantasies about snobbery and moral superiority. I believed that only superior people could speak the language, or at least read it, or so the history books seemed to say. I liked the idea of being able to speak Latin like a Roman Catholic bishop, of being able to converse with, say, some papal dignitary and see his startled face as we discussed matters of religious or historical import. Latin was the open door through which one entered the kingdom of the successful, the smart, the witty, the wise, I thought. It was a symbol of respectability, and it divided the world into two parts: those who spoke Latin and those who did not. After my elementary-school years, when I felt I'd failed myself, I desperately needed something I could put on like a new skin. Latin would be part of that new skin, and when the elementary-school teachers asked us what foreign language we planned to take in junior high, I did not hesitate for an instant. Other languages could come later; since Latin was the basis of all the Romance languages, they would be easier to master if I knew Latin. I'd worked this out pretty much for myself.

There was also this: as the violence in my family escalated, along with my growing recognition that I had no power to change my parents' actions, I desperately needed ways to distance myself from their drama. I was looking for something to engage my imagination and to help me build some degree of liberating self-esteem. I wanted to break with my own tendency to show hostility toward my teachers, too, for I knew that this only led to failure.

One avenue I'd found was to spend a lot of time in Norwalk's movie houses. I quickly became immersed in the large and varied array of escapist fare—everything from the *Three Stooges* movies, which I loved, to the James Bond films, whose tantalizing sexual innuendo I half guessed at and half understood. I liked the ever-smooth Sean Connery, who sipped his martinis "stirrednotshaken," pronounced words like "pussy" as *poussie*, and drove around in a car that squirted oil at the various enemies he was always trying to evade.

In my hungry fantasy life, the films that made the deepest impression were always those about what might be called "the glory that was ancient Rome." I was completely taken by them. They inspired in me the most profound fantasies of authority and personal power, far more than films about Britain and its wars on the open seas, and certainly more than the insipid Disney films I'd seen in the city, which attempted to coerce children into being good by showing them what happened to kids who rebelled or refused to fit in.

The movie I loved best was *Spartacus*, the story of a rebellious Roman slave. I especially liked the long segments where the character played by Kirk Douglas is trained to be a gladiator because of his unbending spirit. I identified deeply with his character and with the intense athleticism of the gladiatorial training. My favorite part was when he has been trained to such a peak of perfection that no punishment can harm him.

In one crucial scene, Spartacus must fight an African warrior, played brilliantly by the late Woody Strode. To my eyes, the African warrior was far superior to Spartacus. He possessed much greater dignity and finesse. It was the only movie I'd ever seen in which a Negro was allowed such dignity and permitted to die a warrior's death. The film's combination of cruel death by the sword, of white slave revolts, and of African warriors depicted as noble and brave brought home to me the awareness that long before my time there had been another kind of life lived by people with whom I could identify in my imagination.

But it was an image of endurance from *The Fall of the Roman Empire* that made the greatest impression of all on me. The film was about Roman legions pillaging and burning cities—pretty standard fare. In the crucial scene, James Mason, who is playing the part of a general, thrusts his open hand into the flames of a fire to prove some point. He keeps his hand there as the flames lick at it, and his face betrays not a flicker of emotion to dim his heroic act. He simply looks straight ahead, and when one of his fellows cries out, "Are you mad?"

he says something like, "Only for the sake of Rome." He wins his point. In that instant, I was a convert. I believed I could have will-power like that. And such willpower would demonstrate how worthy I could be—worthy of attention from my parents, and praise from my teachers. No other movie scene held my young attention more strongly than this one of a man betraying no emotion while holding his hand in a fire. Here was proof of the possibility that a man could control any human weakness and steel himself to any pain. He could free himself by willing himself not to feel. Here lay the bedrock of my innermost fantasy. I wanted to train myself to be exactly like that— unfeeling to pain.

After seeing that film I tried to copy what I'd seen: I cut my leg with a knife, I attempted to burn my hand over the stove, I hit myself with a stick, all the while doing my best to ignore the pain. I eventually gave it up. But on my first day in Latin class I felt I was about to learn something else that would give me the magic of self-control and the power to dominate my environment. I felt, quite consciously, that something weak in me would be strengthened, and that this would help rescue me from the encroaching fear any young African-American has: that the world stands against you unless you find your way out, there will be no way out, and you will die. As a result, I invested far more in learning the language than most of the other students in my class.

I know now that if I was clinging to a kind of fanatical faith in learning a disciplined language as a means of escaping physical real-ity, the way had been well prepared for me. My father's family had always embraced an obsessive self-discipline to prove themselves while numbing themselves to the pain of their experience of race on the South Side of Chicago. And my father reinforced these traits in me.

Around this time, I hurt my ankle playing a pickup game of foot-ball and was walking with a decided limp. As hard as I tried to conceal my discomfort, my father zeroed in on it. "Why are you limping?" he demanded. I told him. He said that black people were never sup-posed to show what they felt. He said that the art of concealment—

of physical pain as well as emotion—was important for a Negro to know. "Master it," he said, "or it will master you." He told me that he never wanted to see me limping again. Once again, I made the connection in my own mind that if I could discipline myself to learn the language of these people who had conquered the world, I could master myself and my weaknesses, which seemed so painfully obvious.

Some months later, I chipped my kneecap. I never told anyone about it. That fragment floats free beneath my kneecap still, but I've gotten used to the pain. It is part of me.

And there was one other thing, too: quite apart from the mental conditioning, the language had a kind of snob appeal for me, an exclusivity, an air of superiority that I took inside myself as I mastered the work. To be able to prove that I was superior was new and intoxicating to me. The fact that most of the white students weren't taking Latin and were amazed that I was—and was doing well at it, to boot—was a lesson for me in intellectual intimidation. How easily the whites were intimidated, and how deep their respect when they found out how well I was doing! And how differently the black students viewed this. If there was any question in their minds about my acting white before, I found that there was none now.

"If there is one thing you will learn in my class," Mrs. George intoned that first day, "it will be concentration." It was like a door opening for me.

She then changed the subject to the work at hand.

"Can anyone tell me what English word might come from a Latin word such as *resurgo?*" Resurgent? That was a new word, too.

"Yes," said Mrs. George, with a smile that filled her face with radiant light. "So you see, class, Latin has enriched the English language in a way that few other languages have." For the first time in my academic life, something terribly exciting seemed to be taking place. Mrs. George went through a long list of English words and phrases based on Latin. Some of them, like *manus manum lavat* ("one hand washes the other"), showed she meant business. "There is a literal meaning to this simple sentence and a figurative one," she said. "One hand washing the other can signify the relationship of student to teacher, soldier to general, a wife to a husband, a child to its friend." Her meaning was clear: do your work and you will be fine.

Mrs. George was a small-boned woman with a large bust and small, almost boyish hips. Her legs reminded me of a bird's legs— maybe those of a stork or some other wading bird. She carried around a big black leather bag that was half as large as her torso and as black as her hair. In the middle of a class she would grab her bag and mince away for ten minutes, returning with a friendly flush on her cheeks, which she attempted to cover with makeup. But it never worked. We all knew she was a heavy drinker.

On one level, Mrs. George was quite rigid. Anything less than excellence was failure to her. She was the first teacher I'd ever had whose standards were so absolute, and nothing could tarnish the esteem in which I held her for that. So if she kicked her bag in the middle of parsing a verb such as *bibo* ("to drink") and we heard the sound of glass hitting the desk, I didn't care.

One of the phrases Mrs. George made us memorize was *mens sana in corpore sano* ("a sound mind in a sound body."). About the time I learned this phrase I decided to begin lifting weights. Norwalk was a sports town more than it was a scholar's city. And since the best athletes there were black, I reasoned that I would gain further entry into that community by training myself to become an athlete. At first I had no interest in Norwalk's Negro community other than the connection to sports. On weekends I continued my long trips into South Norwalk, where the most skilled athletes lived and played. As I learned more about basketball, I discovered that excelling in sports was not just a matter of physical agility, as the whites I knew seemed to believe. It was far more about living in that intellectual and physical moment when a player must decide how to exploit an advantage, where to place his body, how to intimidate an opponent, and how to accomplish these moves with speed and efficiency. There was a lot more behind it than simple physical power. Sports was about mental control. It was a form of artful self-expression that had nothing to do with verbal dexterity but everything to do with what you willed your body to say. It was about steeling the body against physical cowardice, as Roman soldiers did. It was important to be able to show that you were the kind of person who stood up to pressure and exhaustion by seizing control. It was all about the dance of imposing your will on your opponent.

For me, there were other vital issues at work. I had to show that my newfound intellectual interests had not made me weak. My black friends were growing physically stronger, and I had to keep up with them. It troubled me that the double standard I'd noticed in elementary school had now become an ironclad social rule: black students were expected to excel at sports but not at academics, and as a result, most were lions on the playing field but easily intimidated in the classroom. I felt that these students were going to become intellectual half-men, and I was determined not to become one of them. They knew this, and so did I, and I sensed a lot of resentment from them about it. If I insisted on the freedom to hone my mind, many black students seemed to feel that I was setting myself above them. They made it ever-clearer that I might be among them but would never be one of them. If the white world insisted that I had to be doubly fit in mind to compete with whites, the black world seemed to insist that I be doubly fit in body to compete with my black friends. When I visited their community in search of physical challenges, none of my white friends followed. I was grateful. Their presence would have drawn even more attention to my "whiteness," of which I was already quite ashamed. To cope with these worlds so far apart, I found that I had to learn to speak two languages—that of the body and that of the mind.

If Latin was the path to help me build intellectual self-esteem, my English classes sapped my self-confidence. I might know the Latin roots of words and how to conjugate Latin verbs, but writing and reading in English were clumsy exercises for me. I could have had no better teachers in speaking English than my mother and father, both of them highly literate and possessing great verbal dexterity. But I was a very slow reader, and even slower in writing. I read my first book from cover to cover only toward the very end of elementary school. It was *The Boy's King Arthur*, a kind of abridged version of the Arthurian romances. My cousin Barbara had given it to me. I loved the language of it, and in private I memorized long passages.

But my English teachers seemed to be making a concerted attempt to kill the wonders of the language. Instead of Mark Twain or Ambrose Bierce, for instance, we were introduced to one stultifying text after another. *Johnny Tremain*, a kind of romance about a New England boyhood, threatened to put me in a coma. And in our social-studies classes, there were still no books about the achievements of African Americans. In fact, the social-studies textbooks seemed to use words in a way that excluded Negroes entirely from the tide of history, except as African Bantus or pygmies, or in their ever-present guise as slaves. I could not identify with that at all. My home life had taught me otherwise. I wanted to read more about Negro history. On the advice of my father and mother, I began traveling into Manhattan to visit the library at the Schomburg Center for Research in Black Culture in Harlem. I always came home angry. I would ask my teachers why the things I was reading about in Harlem weren't in our schoolbooks in Norwalk. They always seemed amazed and rather taken aback by these questions. Fortunately, my grades did not suffer because of this.

The attitude of many of my teachers seemed to be that I was not worth their efforts. I was "ineducable," as one of them told me. Her name was Mrs. Nottingham,* and she was my English teacher in the eighth grade.

Mrs. Nottingham was a tall, broadly built woman. She looked like an overstuffed steamer trunk, and her voice sounded as though she'd just swallowed a goat. She taught an upper-level class, and I was the only Negro in it. Whenever I asked a question, she would avoid looking at me directly, as though she couldn't bear the sight of me. I tried to avoid her eyes, also. What they said to me was too discouraging. I came to think of her as one of the gorgons from Greek mythology— those female characters whose gaze would turn a man to stone.

But I could never avoid Mrs. Nottingham's judgments. In the middle of the school year, I decided to run for class president. Everyone seemed greatly surprised by this—my black friends, my white friends, my teachers. A Negro didn't do such a thing, I was told. But I felt that Negroes *did* do such things: I was a Negro, and I was doing them.

Each candidate for president had to write a speech to be delivered at a huge student gathering in the auditorium, and English class was where the speeches were rehearsed beforehand. I was afraid my effort would be a failure, but I wrote out a longish speech nonetheless. When other students read their campaign speeches to the class, Mrs. Nottingham greeted them all warmly. When my turn came, she took off her glasses, let them drop to her desk, and clapped her hands over her head as though she was getting a terrible headache.

"Go on," she said, as I walked to the front and began reading.

I think I stumbled a bit over some words—my handwriting wasn't very good—but before long I was finished. Mrs. Nottingham cleared her throat loudly. She put her glasses back on, put her hands under her chin, and looked out at the class.

"Did you hear that, class?" she said, as I stood waiting for her praise. "That was the most crude and vulgar speech I have ever heard. It was utterly unworthy of a student running for student government." She waved me back to my seat.

Nobody in the class breathed. They were all stunned into silence. She plowed on. "The vulgarity of that speech disgusts me." She said a few other things, but by then I had tuned her out. No one in the class dared speak, and soon another student was droning away. A few days later I won the election, and I knew the incident in English class had helped me win. And the next year, I was elected president again.

My involvement in sports made it easier for me to connect with other students. I saw myself as a scholar-athlete, like Bill Bradley, the U.S. senator, who was then a student and basketball star at Princeton. Norwalk, along with much of southern Connecticut, was home then to some of the finest athletes in the nation. It was becoming a big basketball town, almost to the exclusion of other sports, and was the hometown of the phenomenal Calvin Murphy, who in less than five years would lead Norwalk High School to state championships and himself to a professional basketball career. To us, he was "Murph." He twirled a baton. He was a power. His girlfriend was called "B. J."—which stood for "big juicy," Murph said.

To a novice like me, who was just beginning to see the possibilities in knowing how to play this game, Murphy was almost a god. The high school, a great dinosaur of a building that smelled of age and dust, opened its doors early on Saturday mornings, and my friends and I would hurry over there just to watch Murphy practice. At this time he was teaching himself how to dunk. He wore a pair of fifteen-pound weights on his ankles everywhere he went. He even played in them sometimes. In these practice sessions, he would have a friend hold a basketball just above the edge of the rim, and, taking off his ankle weights, Murphy would practice dunking for hours from differ-ent angles. He still didn't have enough strength in his hands to palm the ball—that would come later. We would watch intently as this superbly coiled dark black form took five steps from above the key and then leaped almost from a standing start until his elbows were above the rim. *Thunk! Thunk!* It was like watching a dance in space. I felt connected to this extreme discipline. This was the physical equiva-lent of the kind of excellence I, in my own way, wanted to achieve.

If I was trying to steel my body, it was partly so that I could face the mounting violence at home. For all its hard-won elegance and charm, the house at 7 Bettswood Road had become a prison for me. Summer and winter now, the whole family machinery was frozen in a single, hypnotic ritual. My brothers and I would go to school, come home, and wait for Mom to get back after her long commute from New York City and for Dad to arrive from his work. None of us could call the day over until Dad got home and showed us whether he was in a good mood or a bad one. I could take one look at the lines in his face, around the jaw, the mouth, the eyes, and know just how the evening would go. I learned to taste blood in the air the way a fish tastes everything it touches in the water. Often, now, the days ended badly. There were constant fistfights between him and Mom. There was almost a rhythm to the violence; when they approached the vio-lent climax of a quarrel, it was like the climax of sex. The next morning I would often find drops of blood on the kitchen floor—always my mother's.

During these years—1964, 1965, and 1966—the entire atmosphere of the house became polluted with the feral tension of their ongoing war. I was learning from them that sometimes love and hate are so finely intermingled that it is impossible to distinguish which is the driving emotion, and that sometimes these emotions arise out of sheer mental and physical exhaustion. There seemed to be a point at which the bitterness turned to a kind of addictive sweetness: they would rather fight than not fight because that was the only thing left between them.

More often now, Mom was suffering professionally because of the emotional seesaw at home. She lost several jobs because her employers couldn't afford to keep a fashion designer around who frequently showed up in dark glasses that poorly hid her bruised face. I'm sure my father humiliated her in this way because he was jealous (though he would never admit it) that she was making more money than he was. He needed to control her. And the violence always succeeded, though she fought against it constantly.

At that time, there were few shelters or other places where women could go to escape domestic violence. A woman's home was supposed to be her shelter. Mom, living at the edge of isolation because she had married out of her race, was shunned, and in return she shunned those who shunned her. She didn't know where to turn. She was drinking heavily to dull her pain, but her pride wouldn't allow her to leave my father. That would have been conceding defeat.

Slowly something in her personality changed. A tense gloss settled over her spirit, and she went into a kind of shock in which she seemed unable to process what was happening to her. So many things were beginning to go wrong. My younger brother Mike was especially upset by all the violence—I think more so than either me or Mark or John—and began to have disciplinary problems at school. For instance, he had one teacher named Mrs. Banlaster,* and he called her "Miss Dambastard" to her face. His teachers pegged him as a troubled youngster, and Mom would sit through conference after conference with them. Mike was overweight and was embarrassed about his body. Dad, who was slim, would shame him by grabbing his gut and laughing. Mom would try to stop him, and it would provoke another fight; she shouldn't tell him how to be a father, he said.

Mom would drink during her train ride home, just like the corporate executives and other commuters who used the bar car as a place to anesthetize themselves against the day's hardships and the demands awaiting them at home. She bore it all to preserve her ideal of a family, which was becoming less of a family month by month. Some part of her, I think, could not face the fact that she was profoundly depressed by what was happening to her dream. This part of her knew that the marriage was failing and the family she'd struggled so hard to keep together was failing, yet she kept trying to hold it all together. I admired her will and her tenacity, but those qualities came at a terrible price. She was sacrificing too much of herself, it seemed, for there to be anything left over. The drinking was her way of keeping her personality from flying apart under all the pressure.

My relationship with my brothers was changing. I felt that their pain compounded my own, so I began to distance myself from them. Virtually the only form of communication between Mark, Mike, and me now was a game called tap-and-smash, in which we'd physically punish each other for fun. We would begin the game by tapping each other lightly on the upper arm, in the place where the muscles of the shoulder and the arm twine together. We would slowly increase the severity of the punishment. The taps became hits, and the hits became harder and harder, until we were pounding each other. The key to winning the game was never to show any feeling. Sometimes we would miss the arm and hit each other in the chest, on the back, wherever. A player wasn't supposed to say anything, but had to take it, we would joke, "like a man." It was a grim method of training to keep our emotions deeply submerged.

We were mirroring our parents, but something else was involved, too. We were becoming like boxers who are getting the pulp knocked out of themselves but can't understand why anyone would want to stop the fight.

Just as they did when we lived in the city, the conflicts between my parents were taking on more overtly racial overtones. But it was clear that this was only because the two of them were falling deeper into their private pits of despair. Mom would have enough of getting hit and would call Dad a nigger. We'd tell her to stop calling him that. She was actually inviting punishment, but in reality it didn't matter anymore what she said. Almost anything—from a subtle demand to a word of praise—seemed to make my father mad. It was all part of the daily drama.

Soon Dad was beating her not only with his fists but with pots and other household objects. She would be carted off to the hospital and sewn up, but no one asked her how she came by her wounds. Most terrifying was that none of us found it out of the ordinary, after even the most severe beatings, for the matter never to be discussed again. This was the pattern that developed: After a beating, the house would settle down for a few days or weeks. Things would become less strained between the two of them, and between Dad, me, and my brothers. Then the cycle would repeat itself again.

A terror one week, Dad would be voluble and expansive the next. He would bring home T-bone or sirloin steaks from Manhattan. In the summer, he'd come home loaded with corn and potatoes and peppers, red and green, to cook on the outdoor grill. As we settled down to eat the bounty, he would make a point of telling us how much money he'd saved by cooking everything at home. "Four times the price," he'd say, with great enjoyment. Quite apart from saving money, we rarely went to restaurants because people stared at us, and that made the tension even more overwhelming. It was just as well that we stayed home.

The renovations on the house were nearly complete now, and Mom and Dad busied themselves hunting for furniture and antiques—one thing that gave them great pleasure in doing together. They frequented art exhibits at the Silvermine Guild Arts Center, which was nestled away in a corner of Norwalk where few blacks ever went. One of their finds was a bronze statue of three women whose bodies were merged together as though in a muslin winding-cloth. It was titled *Daughters of the American Revolution*. Dad said he bought it because there was a small fleck of bronze on one of the ladies' backside. "See," he said. "The ladies don't know how to wipe the shit from their own asses. It must be hard for all three of them to squat at once." They also bought an original canvas entitled *All the Brave Explorers*, a painting of a sailing ship with a tall, battered mast. It made me think of their marriage.

One weekend Dad loaded Mom, Mike, and me into the car, and we drove up into Litchfield County, where Dad said he wanted to search for a large wooden American eagle for the front of the house. He wanted a very particular kind, a Lacy eagle crafted by a certain wood-carver he'd read about in *Smithsonian* magazine. We drove for hours until we came to a large barn along a country road. The Dutch door on the barn was open, and inside, from one wall to the other, hanging from the rafters and in every corner, we saw beautiful wood carvings of birds. Most of them were eagles, but some were shorebirds with stilts for legs painted in cool hues of gray and blue. Mom said she liked these the best. Others were birds of prey, and Dad seemed very taken with one of them, which he believed was an osprey. An old white man sitting behind a worktable had been watching us closely, and Dad walked over to him and asked the price.

"Not for sale," the man said, looking significantly at Mom. "For any price."

Dad gave his familiar chuckle, but Mom was stunned. Her face became set and very pale. They left the barn together. "Let's go!" Mom shouted from the car before the rest of us could even get in.

Some weekends, we would drive into Manhattan and go to a live show at the Apollo Theater, Harlem's heart and soul. I loved to go into the city for these jaunts, partly because of the music by artists like Otis Redding, James Brown, the Temptations, the Supremes, the Four Tops, and others, but also for the sheer vitality I felt in the culture of Negro people like my father.

But Dad seemed to enjoy disrupting these outings by creating needless dramas. There was always a line of people in front of the theater, dressed to the hilt in their finest threads—silk on silk, rabbit-skin hats, men's shoes polished to such a fine sheen that you could see the passing traffic in them. Dad would ignore all these people who had waited for hours to buy tickets. We would park the car a few blocks away and walk along the line slowly, on display for Dad's satisfaction. When we got to the ticket booth Dad would say to the cashier, "Are those tickets I ordered ready?"

It always caught the cashier the wrong way. She would stare at him. Then she would stare—hard—at Mom, Mark, me, and Mike. Then she would stare back at Dad in an accusatory fashion. He would watch her with increasing hostility and would say, "I said, are those tickets ready?"

By now, all the people toward the front of the line would be watching this little scene unfold. The cashier would tell my father there were no such tickets. He would instruct her to call the theater owner, who, he said, was a friend of his. Years later, Dad told me that back in those days he had been meeting at the Apollo on weeknights with a political club formed by a small group of influential black men— among them David Dinkins, Percy Sutton, and Charles Rangel— who were laying plans for the future of the city's black districts. But there, in front of the theater, I felt embarrassed for the cashier, for Mom and my brothers, and for myself. I'd have preferred to wait on line, but Dad liked to shove us in the faces of the crowd. He liked to make a game of staring down the poor cashier so that when the doors opened we would be the first to walk in. I could always feel the hundreds of angry eyes on our backs.

In the theater, I would see my father lose himself in the performance. He would take off his jacket, loosen his tie, and clap his hands to the music. At moments like these, I felt I was watching a person who was truly alive. He was so rarely able to let himself go in a way that wasn't harmful to himself or to us, and watching him loosen up like this made me realize how hard the life he'd chosen had become for him. If only I could give him some of what he got at those wonderful shows! But I never could. No matter how much anyone gave him, it was never enough to fill that ravenous hunger eating at him. But the shows at the Apollo could, even if only briefly, and I was always glad when he took us there.

Dad was often so full of rage now that it was hard to recognize him as the same man who seemed so happy in Harlem. He'd take us on roundabout trips sometimes to see his various insurance clients. Beforehand, he would pop into various drugstores and emerge with bottles of prescription medication. He would nip from a bottle as he made his rounds. He left a bottle behind once, and I saw that it was codeine. He was taking it to free himself of his craving for heroin, which he'd "kicked." During their fights Mom would use his former addiction as something else to taunt him with.

Nonetheless, Dad continued to do well at his work. It was as though he truly believed that he was doing no harm to anyone, and that the horrible torment going on inside him was not dangerous at all, but was a perfectly acceptable way to live. And he was right about that. It seemed perfectly normal to him. He had achieved a kind of dream—a successful black man living among middle-class whites on his own terms. He had no one to warn him that he was entering a downward spiral of addictive overwork and overindulgence. As long as he could continue to perform his job and other duties while leaving the impression that nothing was wrong, nobody would intrude. Any signs that his world was afire were lost on him. He was too giddy with his success—and his exhaustion—to notice.

One day he came home and told us he was going to be on television. He'd been selected to be on a game show called "Love or Money." I remember how excited I was by this. When I got home from school on the day of the show, I rushed into the library, where my father's desk was, and turned on the TV. There he was, a handsome, well-dressed, elegant-looking Negro, a charming smile playing over his face as he was introduced to the audience and the nation. Not a care in the world, that expression said. Like a boat on a serene lake in the summertime.

In the end, Dad did so well at the game that he was given the choice of bringing home either cash or a star-sapphire ring. "Will you take love or money, Mr. Minerbrook?" the host asked him.

"I guess I'll take love," he said.

After I turned off the television, I took a few steps over to Dad's desk, opened a drawer, and found a handgun in it. I was shocked and fascinated. I told no one about it. That evening he gave Mom the beautiful star-sapphire ring he had won. She lost it a week later.

By the end of my third year in junior high school I was living a split life whose separate lines did not intersect. I was excelling at school now. I was involved in sports. I'd been urged by the minister of our church, who knew of the turmoil at home, to apply to the Mount Hermon prep school in Massachusetts. I wanted desperately to go there, to get away from Norwalk and my parents' troubles. But I felt stuck. I was afraid to leave home for fear of what might happen to my mother if I wasn't there to deflect some of the punishment my father dished out. I was so ambivalent, I deliberately flunked my entrance exams. My teachers knew none of this. I was too loyal to my parents to let anyone but a few select friends know what was going on. Fortunately, my teachers noticed my interest in math and science. They invited me to join the math club, which made the work more interesting. I also began drawing sketches of the human anatomy, using *Gray's Anatomy* at the public library. This, I came to feel, was a side of my personality that needed to be excellent, in emulation of my father's pursuit of excellence.

I was now spending even more time with my black friends from South Norwalk, sometimes spending whole weekends there. Being with them was in many ways as close as I could come to a feeling of acceptance, a feeling of what it would be like to be part of a normal family. I had come to feel less and less comfortable around the white students who wanted to be my friends, because they considered me an "exceptional Negro," not like the other black kids they knew. I'd also begun to feel that nothing I'd achieved was as important as the deep friendships I'd made in the black parts of the city, where I didn't have to be a scholar or a star, where I could lose myself in being just who I was—someone who could not be claimed by anyone but myself. In South Norwalk I was allowed free passage. It was where I experienced most of the rites of adolescence. My friends and I bought liquor from the resident bootleggers. We got drunk together and played sports together. We had crushes on the same sweet young women. Somehow, being able to disappear into this ghetto soothed something deep inside me. In South Norwalk, I didn't have to think about my parents' problems. I didn't have to prove that I was carrying the legacy of their ideals, ideals that they no longer seemed to understand or consider worthwhile. I felt that my parents did not understand what I was going through because they hadn't grown up interracial. I didn't want to be told by the whites I knew, as I regularly was, that I was "getting the best of both worlds." I was very glad to leave Norwalk's white world behind. I was glad to have a place to go where I could simply feel the great joy of being alive.

Around this time, my mother began phoning her family in Caruthersville again, after many years of leaving them alone. I hated it when she did this, since it only seemed to make her more upset. I related her family's insensitivity to the cruelty of the Mrs. Nottinghams, Miss Poors, and some of the other teachers I'd had. I would think about the folks in Caruthersville and be glad I was attached to a community that embraced me as a human being, in spite of the whiteness in my face.

I had my own crew. Their names were J. C. Torian and Walter James* and Cyril Pikers.* We drank whiskey and smoked pot. We talked a lot about taking heroin. We got drunk, skipped school, and played basketball in our bare feet in freezing weather. We roamed the night streets of South Norwalk together, got bitten by the same bedbugs, and listened to the same music. It was at the home of another buddy, Mickey Outlaw, that I first heard a singer named Gene Chandler. He sang:

> *I just can't stop these rainbows*
> *Innn mmyyyyyy hearrrrt.*

His songs expressed the ancient need of a people to be saved and to save themselves through faith in love, through a belief that they could be loved. There was a deep, passionate ebullience in the music, and it thrilled me. I yearned to be so completely joined with the world identified by this music that I began dressing like the young black men I knew in the streets of South Norwalk: silk slacks, silk shirts and socks, silk underwear, rabbit-skin hats, all in bright colors of purple and rose and tangerine. I ordered Stacy Adams shoes from the tiny advertisements in the back pages of *Ebony* and *Jet*, which also touted skin bleaches, hair straighteners, lip-reducing surgery, long-haired wigs, and pamphlets on how to interpret dreams for profit.

I had white friends, too, but not as many. My best buddy from that world was Jerry Christopher,* a gentle guy whose kind family smiled a lot and cared deeply about him. Jerry and I played football together. He was a good defensive player, but he couldn't catch a football for beans.

Jerry had a strong independent streak, and that was why I liked him. But I felt I could be only partly myself with him. He would chase after smug little white girls, with their blonde hair and stiff smiles, and he wanted me to do the same. I gave it a halfhearted attempt, but emotionally I was far too distant from that world. I found the whole environment of baited, repressed sexuality offensive and corny. The white kids all seemed so prudish and afraid of their bodies, when what they really needed was some good exercise. And I felt that at heart they were actually perverse in their sexual attitudes and habits. The guys talked all the time about "getting to third base," and this metaphor repulsed me. There was no poetry in it. The Beach Boys were not poetry. The Five Stairsteps were. Jan and Dean were not poetry. James Brown singing "It's a Man's, Man's, Man's World" certainly was. In these years before the birth-control pill gained favor, first among white women and then among the more careful black ones, the young black women I would meet at block parties or house parties were far more sexually cautious than their white counterparts. Their courtship rituals were far more elaborate. But slow dancing with them was always more exciting than the groping the white kids did at their rec-room parties, because the black women I knew were not afraid of being touched. The black kids I hung around with would hold each other with a desperation and a passion that made me feel as if I was part of something alive and real, part of the give-and-take of mutual need. Nothing was faked, as it was with white girls, who seemed so afraid of their sexuality. We got no sex. But we never asked, "Did you score?" the way the white guys did. I hated those questions. They seemed demeaning to every feeling I had. Sex was not baseball.

Inevitably, Rudner Court in South Norwalk was where I learned about the greater implications of sexual experience. There was little raw sexual contact, though there were many rumors about pregnancies, and you knew one had really occurred when this or that young woman disappeared to "visit her aunt." Mostly, sex was a lot of hot touching, intense practice—which was fine, because we all knew that was as far as it was likely to go unless the woman "really loved you."

The girls I dated thought I was "cute," but I was always falling in love. First I was in love with a basketball player named Ruby Slade.* Ruby was short and thin, but she was known throughout the black community for her promise as an athlete, and I liked that about her. It also amused me that she had achieved a certain acclaim at a man's game while I had not, and I felt that the reversal of gender roles was a bit strange. I was embarrassed, too, that she could whip me at basketball, despite my fastest moves, simply by playing consistently—something I never did. I would watch her play, those long, thin hands of hers sure with the basketball and certain in her skill, and I would feel a great pride and admiration. Ruby had such a warm face and such eager eyes, and her body was lithe, and when we danced together I saw forever. That was the way we talked. We dated for several months. I had a great sexual hunger, but she wasn't going that way. I was rather jealous because everyone admired her. When she went away to college—she was several years ahead of me in school—I was so mad that I didn't even bother to see her off.

Next I fell in love with a young woman named Swan Lambier, mostly because I liked touching the smooth roundness of her behind—which she'd let me do for a while before pushing me away.

Then I fell in love with a brown-skinned beauty with gray green eyes named Beverly Nelson,* but she had foul monster-lion breath, and that was enough to keep me away.

I finally lost my virginity in the photography lab of Norwalk High. A good Jehovah's Witness took me, and that was that. I was fifteen, and I discovered that sex—which I'd known little about—was not like sports at all.

It was 1966, and the slow songs we danced to were beginning to tell stories of love and loss. Not the usual kind, in which one loses at love, but the terrible losses of young men who never came home from the jungles of Vietnam. I began to notice a thinning in the ranks of young men I knew, just slightly older than I was. They were going off to war, happy to be in the military because of the steady pay, and proud to serve their country. Vietnam claimed men from many of the families of the women I was dating. It was my introduction to the sorrows of the war. In some ways, the war added intensity to our fear that we would probably die young. We had to get our living done early, before we were claimed by the streets, by the military, by the hardships of Negro life.

Many of the songs played at our dance parties were full of the deep foreboding that captured what was to come. We were on the very edge of a precipice—of sexual experience, of war, of departures of one kind or another—and we somehow knew it, and that made our dancing softer and more intense. Such feelings never seemed to touch the whites I knew. I would become aroused while dancing almost as a matter of course; there was nothing to it. There was no shame in having an erection. It belonged to the moment, and when the moment was over, my partner and I thanked each other rather formally, and that was it until the next dance. The young women I danced with seemed to become aroused as well, grinding their inner thighs hard against my leg for the long minutes the slow songs lasted. And when the songs were finished, they simply walked away, fanning themselves. You talked only during the dancing, when you asked your partner nonchalantly about herself. If she liked you, you found out more about her later from her friends, or you asked her if you could call her. If she liked you, you called.

I fell in love with a young woman named Jean Randall.* She was tall and gangly, fair-skinned with freckles, and had very long legs. But she wouldn't sleep with me, so I dumped her. It didn't matter to me that I broke her heart.

For us, the dancing and the promise of sex were about trying to escape the world that was closing in around us even as it opened up for whites. Usually the male desire to escape had nothing to do with saving himself, but with throwing his life away. If the war didn't get him, drugs or an early death by accident often did. I began to see that young black men learned these things early on from older men, who embodied the culture of defeat that had existed in the years before the civil rights movement.

There were many things I wanted to escape. As I struggled through my first year of high school, my home life began to come apart in earnest. My father's attacks on my mother took on the quality of mania. They were both drinking constantly now, and Dad would beat her with the barrel of a loaded rifle.

In fact, with so many riots going on in so many cities, I felt that my parents' troubles mirrored the racial troubles of the entire nation. Mom and Dad were locked in a hypnotic death dance that began every evening after they came home from work. It ran alongside of the "Evening News with Roger Mudd." Drinking was the prelude, and, by eight or nine o'clock, the murderous waltz inevitably followed. There appeared to be no way to stop it. Mom would call the police, and they would come to the house and tell her that there was nothing they could do. "It takes two to tango," one officer said, after a blow from Dad had split her lip open. Years of overwork accompanied by too much alcohol had pushed him far over the edge. He seemed to be coming closer and closer to killing his wife. Mike was now suffering from a neglect that seemed to wound him more deeply than ever, and I was almost always away from home, trying to concentrate on my studies.

In my second year at Norwalk High, my Latin teacher was Jessie Pollard, an eccentric character who complained constantly about how the Latin curriculum was being undermined. Yet his courses covered a great span from the oratory of Cicero to the poetry of Virgil, Horace, and Catullus. I liked Catullus best, because he was so wildly passionate, so careless, and so unafraid to say what he felt.

I also began singing choral music, with a wonderful music teacher, Charles Matts, whose training helped me and many other students prepare for competitions. One afternoon he remarked that he'd taken Latin, too, and had enjoyed it. I'd become quite priggish about my Latin studies. Who did he like best? I asked. Oh, just a few important quotes are what I remember, he said. "In mudeels are. In pinetar is. In oak noneis." It took me quite a few minutes before I figured out the joke.

When I played sports now, it was to hurt and damage other players. In football, I liked to play defense, because I could punch and elbow the other players. It didn't matter whether they were teammates or opponents. I enjoyed lashing out. I felt as if something was breaking apart inside my head, but I didn't dare tell anyone about it. If I was injured during a game, so much the better; at least it would distract me from the constant mental anguish of being afraid my parents were trying to kill each other.

Increasingly I was drawn into their disputes. I'd get into fistfights with my father to make him stop beating my mother. One evening he called me down to the living room and without warning smashed his fist into my mouth. The blow neatly split my lip. "Hinckty nigger," he said. "See if you like a little taste of that."

I can't imagine that I was a very easy person to live with during this time. As stubborn as the Caruthersville folks, I would goad my brothers with insulting remarks. I called Mark "Mr. Lame-o," because he'd broken his arm at the elbow and couldn't throw a ball straight. I would make my mother so angry that she would take school-yard swings at my head, missing as I dodged and ducked. She threw a frozen ham at me once. I laughed when it cracked a kitchen-cabinet door, and I found it even funnier that it might have killed me if it had hit me in the head. I liked the feeling of being almost permanently high on adrenaline, the body's own danger drug. But emotionally I had shut down.

In the summer between my sophomore and junior years, Mark was selected to go to Kentucky to work among the impoverished. He had his bags packed so fast it made my head spin. He was out the door without saying good-bye. I received occasional letters from him, which were somewhat elusive and hard to understand, but he seemed to be happy and doing well.

When he returned six weeks later, he was a changed man. His hair was long and combed into a huge Afro. It looked great! He was wearing an oversized jacket, blue jeans, and sandals. He sounded smooth and polished, like a Park Avenue lawyer. He smoked filterless cigarettes, Lucky Strikes, and I noticed that the knuckles between his first two digits were stained a caramel color.

Dad hated such expressions of individuality, and he kept after Mark for weeks. He said that Mark was a "hinckty bastard" and that there was no room for hinckty bastards in his house. He lit into Mark

for having Jewish friends—"kike bastards," he called them. He called
Mark a sissy and slapped him around a lot. As usual, Mark took it
silently. He swallowed his emotions. It was his last year of high
school, and I saw very little of him. I was proud of him, but we no
longer spoke much, except when it came to the fighting at home.
Despite my best efforts to keep from getting sucked into my parents'
quarrels, Mark and I often found ourselves taking sides over who
had started a fight and how it had ended. Their quarrels became our
quarrels. Their violence compounded and intensified ours.

My life changed again in 1968, thanks to a friend named Elsie
Wilcox, an instructor at a day camp where I had worked during
my first two years of high school. Elsie invited me to join a group
of students who were going to Germany, Scandinavia, Poland,
Czechoslovakia, and the Soviet Union for the summer. The travel
fellowships were sponsored by the Friends World College, a Long
Island–based school supported by the Quakers. Our group landed in
Prague just as the Red Army was invading the country. I witnessed
a revolution and a counterrevolution. I saw tanks in the streets. In
observing how people lived in other places, I received a more valuable education than I could ever get from any social-studies book. I
came home full of stories. But nobody in Norwalk seemed interested
in hearing them.

The situation at home had grown worse while I was away. Dad's
drinking had finally begun to poison his brain. He would get into his
car and speed to his after-work job at a defense plant outside of New
Haven, pursued by the state police. He never got caught. After working eight hours there, he would put on a business suit and attend to
his insurance job, drinking constantly. It was a wild party for him.
One weekend, driving to his defense-plant job, he edged the car over
120 miles an hour, and the engine threw a rod. He enjoyed retelling
that "very funny story."

When he chased Mom around the house now, it was with a rifle.
He had gone hunting with his deer rifles that winter and had bagged
his first buck. But he returned home hysterical over not having killed
the deer cleanly, as they did in Hemingway stories or in the manly
literature of *Sports Afield*. He'd wounded the beast and had to chase

it, and the animal had howled its death song, and before it died, Dad said, it had looked him in the eye and begged him to finish the clumsy job. That experience sent him over the edge. He had seen himself in the animal and was afraid. For weeks, he cried like a child about his failure to make a clean kill. "Buck, buck, oh, buck," he raved as he drank himself to sleep.

He was losing control of himself in other ways as well. He wrote in black paint on the wall above the stairwell, "Billy is a liar!" Nobody knew what it meant. He began an art project that consisted of daubing concrete onto a strip of wire mesh measuring eight feet by three feet that he'd nailed to the wall. After the concrete dried, he painted the top half titanium white and the bottom half jet black, with a bloodred line less than half an inch wide in between. I was quite certain it was his way of warning us about the potentially fatal violence to come.

He cried frequently over the death of his cousin Robert Lawrence, Jr., who had been selected as the first black astronaut in the Gemini program and had been killed the previous summer in a plane crash. For long months Dad had showed little reaction to this event, but now it seemed to send him into a paralyzing grief. "The crackers got Bob. They assassinated him," he said. He would break down crying and calling out Bob Junior's name.

All the years of drinking, on top of the obsessive hard work in building his career and improving his home, made him experience a kind of continuing nervous breakdown. He began to hallucinate. He would urinate in a corner of his bedroom and then go off to work. Once he walked across the street to where a young Italian neighbor was sitting with his girlfriend. He accused the young man of calling him a nigger and punched him, dislocating the man's shoulder. He laughed as he did so: "Heh heh heh heh heh."

As if to add salt to our wounds, that was the summer Ocieola paid us her surprise visit. There'd been no preparation for her arrival, and it only brought up all my old bitterness about her rejection of us.

"Who is this white bitch?" I said to myself when I saw her. I felt, rather than remembered, the associations of my first contact with her many years before, when my childish hopes had turned to a complex hatred of all she stood for: the physical and emotional abandonment of black children by white people, and much else. No one hates more than the rejected. I blamed Ocieola for not being available as a family member when I needed her most. I'd needed her during the years in New York City, when it wouldn't have mattered to me that Ocieola was white, the way it mattered now. But she had disappeared from my life, and she'd become "that white woman." I thought she must be playing a cruel trick on my mother, coming to see her at a time of crisis not to help but to remind her of what she need not have lost had she remained "in the fold." So I watched closely and considered Ocieola's motives.

She had come to visit the daughter who had never given up hope of finally being accepted by her family. I wanted no part of this. Maybe Ocieola was ready to forgive and forget, as her daughter apparently was. But I was not. I was deeply bound by the past, which now made me feel that Ocieola was just another white person trying to claim what she no longer had a right to. I wanted to protect my mother, but there was no way I possibly could. Should I say something? It was too late.

I certainly disliked Ocieola, but that was only part of what I felt. I also felt something of the irresistible ties of blood and saw a kind of hope in Ocieola's eyes and in the gentleness of her manner. She had suddenly appeared at our house, and I couldn't find any words, in love or accusation, to use against her. I was too frozen by my deeper confusion to say anything useful. The simple fact was that it seemed too unrealistic to hope that her visit would change anything. It would only increase the tensions. I was too numbed by all the fighting even to acknowledge her courage in making the trip.

"Hello, Scotty," she said.

"Hello, Ocie," I said.

"How is school?" she said.

"Fine."

"That's good," she said.

"How long are you going to stay here?" I said.

"I don't know," she said. "As long as your mother will have me, I guess."

"Great," I said.

"Well, I'm sure you have things to do," she said. "We'll talk another time, I'm sure. We have so much to discuss."

That talk never happened. I think Dad was too bitter to play host to a woman who didn't like him or his children, and who now claimed the blood loyalty of his wife, the woman he needed to control. And he was, I felt, fully justified in this. Whatever it was, when I got home the next day, she was gone. Nobody asked why. We didn't dare.

Later that same summer Mom's younger brother, Huddie, came for a visit. It lasted for four days of cordiality and heavy drinking. He and my parents seemed to hit it off fairly well. But Dad finally got tired of being nice to Huddie and told him he had to leave. Dad drove Huddie to the train station in Norwalk, bought him a ticket to New York, gave him twenty-five dollars, and told him to be gone. That was the last time I ever saw or heard from him. I wasn't sorry. To me, Huddie and Ocieola were nothing more than white crackers who had shut me out of their lives—so I shut them out of mine.

I didn't have the time or energy to care about these kinds of family problems anymore. I had a regular job—trying to stop my father from murdering my mother. Whenever he started in on her with one of his periodic explosions, I would hold him tight and try to talk to him. She was no longer his wife; she was his battered spouse. It was as though every bad intention Katherine had ever had toward Mom was contained in Dad's fists and feet. Katherine was getting her boy back.

Their quarrels now lasted weeks, it seemed. After an argument Dad would drive away and be gone for hours. One time he was arrested for drunk driving and spent the night in jail. Mark, who had just started college, still loved and admired his father immensely. He would come home for a weekend, listen to Dad's version of the latest quarrel, and take Dad's side. I felt obliged to be Mom's ally, mostly because I couldn't stand to see her being beaten. I couldn't side with my father, even though I identified with him as a black man in a world that hated black men. But I couldn't abandon my mother to his violence. I was split in two. I loved my father, but I hated him and wanted him to die so that I wouldn't have to fight him anymore, or have to take part in a quarrel that was not mine. Where I had once believed that my parents' marriage exemplified racial unity, I now felt that their marriage was the embodiment of racial hell. When Dad beat her now, it felt like a kind of abandonment, as though he was giving up on all he'd worked so hard to create. He was giving everything away to a madness I couldn't understand. When I'd stop him, absorbing the blows myself and getting kneed in the groin, or slapped, or chased with a knife, he'd accuse me of being white, of "sucking up on that white tittie."

I began to feel only weariness for them. I thought they were both using race as a way of avoiding their deeper personal problems. They were enacting every stereotype of a tormented interracial couple, and I hated it. They were lost, and so was I. But we could never discuss any of this. With the conspiracy of silence that so often lies at the center of addictive behavior, we were simply not allowed to mention these insane episodes. Dad would wake up the next day and go to work as though nothing had happened. I tried telling him that he was killing himself and his family, but he would dismiss me as nonchalantly as he would dismiss a cop giving him a parking ticket.

I have a picture of my father from that year, when murder shadowed the lines in his face. It was taken at a beach one summer day, and he is laughing, wearing a peculiar grin. His eyes are hidden behind a pair of fancy round sunglasses. I felt then that there was no one behind those glasses anymore. My father had disappeared, and I was disappearing with him.

More and more often I went to Rudner Court and the other black communities looking for sexual and emotional solace. I was a member of several small gangs that broke into stores, usually for liquor or small change. We got drunk on wine a lot. At the same time I was having greater success than ever in my studies. I was absorbed in my plans to become a doctor; the healing arts exerted a strong emotional tug during that period in my life. I was also reading Latin prose and verse, and becoming less interested in sports. The thrill of athletic competition, which had once buoyed my spirits, now seemed like just another kind of battle, and I was too sick at heart over the collapse of my parents' marriage to participate in any kind of battle.

During my senior year I dated a very beautiful young woman named Sandra.* Her father was Dutch, and though he didn't fully accept me, he didn't stop Sandra and me from seeing one another. When I was making love to her one evening, we both lost control. Afterward she began avoiding my calls. One afternoon she finally took a call from me and said she was pregnant. Before I knew what I was saying, the words came out: "Are you sure it's mine?" I don't think I've ever been so brutal in my life. I was unashamed. I justified my cruelty by convincing myself she was pushing me, needing me when I had nothing to give. I thought she was trying to trap me, just as my parents were by trying to pull me into their insanity. She had a saline abortion, and we never talked to each other again.

For support, I invited the friends I made on my trip to Europe for a reunion one fall afternoon in 1969. It wasn't at all well timed. Dad began berating them the minute they arrived. He launched into an anti-Semitic attack on one of the young men. Then he started to drink. That evening he cut Mom so badly with a razor that she had to be hospitalized. He was so out of control that everyone had to leave. When Mom got out of the hospital, she pressed assault charges against him and had him committed to a mental institution for a few days. It was the best thing that could have happened. Personally, I was hoping the wardens would never let him out.

That was enough to get Katherine on a plane from Chicago, where she was living again. When she found out her dear son was in a mental institution, she immediately blamed Mom; LaVerne, because she was white, was overreacting. Katherine sprang Dad from the hospital, and within days he was beating Mom again. No matter what he did, Katherine justified his actions. Having a white wife and half-black children was too hard for any man to bear, she said. How could a white woman understand his problems? Personally, I began praying for his death in earnest. This wish weighed heavily on my mind throughout my senior year in high school.

A few weeks later, when Dad was chasing Mom around the house with a knife, I took an empty Chianti bottle from a shelf in my room and charged him just as he was chasing her into their bedroom. I held the bottle over his head and said that if he didn't stop, I'd kill him. I meant it. All the hatred and anger and pain I felt over his decline were focused in that instant on the bottle over his head. He brought the sharp edge of his knife flush against my stomach and assumed the stance of an infantryman about to gut an enemy with his bayonet. We stood there for several long minutes. Then, as if by mutual consent, we both backed down.

I recognize now that my father was hallucinating during that episode. For a long time I thought his aggressiveness was directed specifically at me. But I have come to understand that he was fleeting in and out of madness, just as my brother John's vision had fleeted in and out when he was an infant. There was no operation that could cure my father's blindness, though. If anything, we were all so afraid of him that we couldn't tell him the single thing he needed most to hear: he'd become a monster, plain and simple. That wouldn't have stopped him or saved him, I don't think, but it might have slowed his descent. It certainly would have been better than Katherine's explanation, which only absolved him of any responsibility for his actions. By this time I held him completely responsible. I pitied him, which, in a son, is worse than hatred.

Pitying my father caused my own world to fall inward, like a wall caving in during an earthquake. I tried getting still farther away, hitchhiking to Vermont on weekends, or going into the city, but I always had to return to the hell at home. I looked for safety among the whites I knew, simply because they lived in a safer world than mine. So many of my black friends were also in pain—the pain of learning that they were growing up unvalued. I felt unvalued, too. No matter how much I achieved, it didn't seem to be enough to make my parents stop killing one another.

I had always dated both white and black women, but now I was dating whites only, because they seemed safe. They didn't share my emotional or physical damage. I knew that the only reason some of them liked to be seen with me was because there was a certain cachet in dating a black person. But I didn't mind, as long as I could be in a place where I didn't feel I was going to die. Maybe, in this regard, I was imitating the way my father felt when he was dating my mother. But when Dad noticed my dating habits he accused me of being a traitor. Maybe that was how he had felt all along about having a white wife and half-white children. Maybe that had always been part of his burden.

I retreated even more deeply inside myself. I withdrew from friend-ships and from many of the things I loved to do. I stopped playing any organized sports, even though they'd been so effective for a while in helping me focus my attention away from the insanity at home. I simply had no will to compete anymore. In some part of myself that I had only a vague notion of, I stopped playing basketball because I had rejected my father's example. I stopped believing in him. I didn't know whether that hurt him or not, and I didn't really care. I was calling attention to myself, but nobody asked why. At some point success begins to work against you. I didn't know how to reach out to other people, and they probably assumed that I needed no help, since I asked for none. That made me feel even more lost.

I was barely able to keep up my grades, though I managed to main-tain a narrow semblance of sanity in my behavior. After spending several nights in a church to escape beatings by my father, I took my Scholastic Aptitude Test. I did well on it.

That spring, between nights of sleeping at the homes of friends and in churches whose windows I could force open, I began working on my college applications. I don't even remember filling out the application to Harvard. The only reason I applied there was because my father threatened to beat me if I didn't. One weekend afternoon, he entered the bedroom where I no longer slept, slammed his fists into the wall and ceiling, and told me what would happen to me if I didn't apply.

"Up now!" he shouted. "Up now, motherfucker!"

I completed the application. On it I said I wanted to be a doctor. I thought that if I could help someone in pain, heal someone else's wounds, it would help me nurse my own. More deeply, I wanted to be a doctor because my father had always said he wanted doctors in the family. It wasn't enough that Mark was already on that road. It was an old dream of Katherine's, and then of his and my mother's, that I carried in me. It was a long time before I rejected that dream as theirs and not my own.

By the time I received the letter notifying me of my admission to Harvard, I could feel neither exultation nor doubt. I couldn't figure out why I had been accepted at Harvard. I didn't feel like a Harvard man. It seemed like a great chance to study and to be away from my parents, but that was all. I had stopped believing in everything, even my own dreams. All that was left was my will to survive.

That summer I picked up an odd habit that was my own peculiar form of protest. I would let my hair grow into an Afro and then get it all cut off. It was my way of ridding myself of any racial identification with my father.

One thing that saved me was my friendship with a young woman named Felice Lesser, whom I'd known since my junior year, when we'd taken chemistry together. She was a ballet dancer, born to the art. She was also Jewish, and I had many fistfights with Dad over dating her. He accused me of being a Zionist and attacked me because, he said, I should have sided with the oppressed Palestinians and their goal of driving the Jews into the sea. He called me a rat and told me I should work for the Central Intelligence Agency. I was in love with Felice, as well as with her mother and sister—kind and generous people, whose presence in my life then provided the only solid ground I knew. The Lessers were the only people I told about being admitted to Harvard, apart from my parents and my younger brothers. I didn't tell Mark. He didn't ask.

It was a summer of violent ends and violent means, both in the nation and in my personal life. My good friend J. C. Torian died in a car crash, the top of his head thrown back into the rear seat of the car he was driving. I don't really remember how I got through the last two months of high school. I don't remember my high school graduation at all, or whether I even went to it. I know I never received my diploma.

I stopped seeing Felice in the fall of 1970, when I left for Harvard. I learned that one of my best friends, Cyril Pikers, was drifting into heroin use. I lost track of Walter James and all the others in South Norwalk who had meant so much to me. I didn't care about anything or anyone. I only wanted to get away from Norwalk and from my family and from anything or anyone who knew me. I cut my hair.

I left Norwalk in September of 1970, and I have returned only once, in 1990, with my wife and two children. I wanted to remember all that I had lost and all that I had gained by growing up in that city of dreams. I thought of a line from Virgil's *Aeneid: "Forsan et haec olim memenisse juvabit."* It meant "Maybe one day it will be pleasing to remember these things." Looking back, I recognized for the first time that until that moment I had not experienced the keen pleasure of survival.

Me, in Harvard's Freshman Register, Class of '74.

EIGHT / # The Black Tables of Harvard

> *Men become civilized, not in proportion to their*
> *willingness to believe, but in proportion to their*
> *readiness to doubt.*

> —H. L. MENCKEN

When I entered Harvard University in 1970, one of more than a hundred incoming African-American freshmen, there was an expression the black upperclassmen told us to remember: "Harvard has ruined more niggahs than bad whiskey."

This declaration, spoken in a solemn tone, was almost a gesture of secret confidence. It was proffered like a fraternity handshake, as though we'd automatically become members of an exclusive club whose doors had swung wide in welcome. We were supposed to feel grateful for this sage advice. I was not. I was sure it was a bad joke. But the phrase was repeated often, sometimes with a dash of humor, sometimes with a knowing air, like the deeply felt *ummmmhummm* one heard in the amen corner of a black church. The first time I heard it, I asked if it was supposed to be taken seriously. "No joke," the brother replied. I asked him if he could please tell me what it meant. "Figure it out for yourself," he said. And so I was left with this strained hint that the university most people would kill to get into wasn't such a good place for black people. No. Not at all. I repeated the phrase to myself, trying to make better sense of it. Did Harvard students drink bad whiskey? Surely that wasn't Harvard's fault.

What the phrase meant, of course, was that Harvard was a racist institution that intended black people no particular good. That idea was cynical and shocking enough. But the truly disturbing thing was that it seemed to be generally accepted that Harvard *did* ruin black people. Rumors of personal failure were constantly bruited about as a warning of Harvard's danger to *all* blacks. There was the case of the brother from Indianapolis who had come in as a math genius, and after two years of striving had a nervous breakdown. There was the case of the brilliant and ebullient sister from Philadelphia, who went into such a deep depression one winter that the last time she was seen in public, on the arm of her powerful attorney father, her blank face recognized no one. These cases were the coin of the realm. The general idea was that if you survived Harvard intact, it would only be because African Americans supposedly possessed keen instincts for survival. Harvard just did things to black people.

I don't think I was scared when I entered Harvard, but now I saw that others were, deeply so. I wondered at the deep pessimism and anxiety, and considered whether I might become one of those whose life would be washed away. I think what disturbed me most was the speed with which my fellow African-American students cast the institution in the harsh light of a racial adversary. It shocked me that many of us—who were among the first large group of black scholarship students to enter Harvard—seemed rattled by having the chance to prove our worth in this intensely competitive environment. Being black in a white institution was suddenly seen as dangerous; Harvard would get the better of us, cause us to fail.

There was a general belief among us that Harvard would be one thing to white students, the ones who came from wealth, who came from the private academies like Exeter and Andover and Choate and didn't worry much about "gentlemen's Cs," and quite another to black students, regardless of their talents or heritage. Harvard would never claim us as its own. We were its stepchildren. As I heard this characterization repeated over and over, the message I got was that the blacks had cast themselves as eternal outsiders looking in. Once we got out, after four years of very hard work—those of us who made it out—we would be marked as strangers to our own people. The communities from which we had come would no longer welcome us. How deeply discouraging it seemed. These beliefs undermined many black students, and were probably just as damaging to our spirits as the real article of race prejudice.

During my first few weeks in Cambridge, I observed that many of the African-American students came from the pampered middle and upper classes. They were the very blacks who were the most assimilated in their values and culture. I hadn't known many such blacks in Norwalk, and hadn't liked most of those I did know. They tended to be spoiled crybabies who whined and complained a lot. They lacked any scent of the street.

Eventually I came to see that many of these pampered black students were accustomed to the same privileges as the white students. It had made them soft. Having whites judge them negatively hurt them to the soul. I met blacks whose parents—doctors and lawyers—owned homes on Martha's Vineyard. I was astonished to learn that there was actually an insular little community of blacks on that island. In the summer they attended camps run by an organization called Jack and Jill, where they met other sons and daughters of well-to-do families clinging to their tiny niches of black privilege—the cream of the Negro elite.

How strange all this was! I had come to Harvard expecting a monoculture among blacks. They would all be like me: quiet, self-confident, self-motivated, reflective. Some were. Many were not. I felt the stirrings of intolerance in myself, and I was uncomfortable to find it there. The very richness of black culture I'd heard about had never come so close to me before, and I decided to keep my distance, to watch and learn.

My previous social life had taught me that I should wear my blackness proudly but quietly. Here, many black students announced themselves as different by assuming loud, boastful, gritty personae that thoroughly conflicted with their personal backgrounds. They seemed eager to portray themselves as "streety niggahs," when at best they were merely dabbling in false identities. Dressed in floppy hats and screaming bright colors, blasting music from their dormitory rooms, smoking marijuana—though not nearly as much as the white students did—they seemed to be imitating the worst kind of stereotypes of blacks, the very stereotypes they'd been raised to disprove. Yet most of them were very good students, with solid work habits. But in public they wore masks that contradicted the hard-won habits they'd come to Harvard with. They seemed not only scared but deeply intimidated by Harvard, almost to the point of believing what so many of the white students seemed to be saying—that blacks didn't belong at Harvard at all.

Their defense was the world of the "black tables," at which they segregated themselves from whites and bitterly denounced them. But what was the point of being at Harvard if it wasn't to get what my father called "the keys to the white man's city"? The black tables seemed to have been created as a place to find safety in a briskly competitive and even hostile world. But they offered only a false security. They created a separatist identity, and often seemed like little pools of bigotry every bit as pronounced as that of the exclusive white clubs, which had by then gone underground. I'd even received an invitation to join such a white club—the Fly Club, it was called—to which I never responded. I tried to avoid the black tables, and vowed to follow my own path.

This was the period of a great burst of political activity around certain worthy social causes. The Black Panther Party for Self-Defense, and their efforts toward such causes were held in the highest esteem. But I knew at least four young African Americans from the most comfortable homes who, when they tried to join the party, were reduced to running around the block, doing sit-ups and push-ups, and performing scut work around the headquarters. And yet the passion of these students for ideas like "revolutionary suicide" never failed. It came to me one afternoon that these sons and daughters of black privilege were trying to expiate themselves of some deeply felt guilt at the comforts they'd been given, in much the same way as the children from the wealthiest white families of Fairfield County,

Connecticut. They seemed like whites in blackface, or "manqué whites," as one revolutionary philosopher called them.

At the black tables, the most guilt-ridden of Harvard's African-American students cut themselves off from anyone in the freshman dining halls—black or white—who exhibited "bourgeois" values. Every dormitory had its black table, and each one seemed to hew to the separatist line. Blacks were not encouraged to make white friends, and whispering campaigns were waged against those who did—everyone knew who "they" were. Another way to prove one's blackness was by boasting of volunteer service "to the community," that nebulous mass of humanity in the greater Boston area that was neither light-skinned nor from the right side of the tracks. Most of these boasts were spurious. There was a certain attitude toward the black poor, in fact, that made Harvard's politically active black students sound a lot like the liberal Fairfield County Democrats who wanted to "do something" about poverty. These guilty black students felt they had to bring their poorer brothers and sisters "up to standard," as performer James Brown mockingly put it. If the black tables were intended to exclude whites, they also succeeded in excluding those blacks who sought a keener understanding of the way the white world worked.

At Harvard, black class exclusiveness wore a politically defensive pose. In this world, being truly black seemed to mean that you avidly consumed revolutionary Marxist tracts. Instead of Hobbes and Kant, you immersed yourself in such writers as the French psychiatrist Frantz Fanon, whose works I found impossible to get through or remember. And yet the brothers memorized whole sections of books like *Black Skin, White Masks*, a tormented and forgettable essay on the evils of colonialism. Another vogue among African-American students was the latest African writers: Chinua Achebe, Wole Soyinka, and others. There was nothing wrong with that, of course. A lot of this literature was exciting. But many students had an almost fanatical devotion to Third World authors. They embraced their works less for their intrinsic value than to prove that European authors were part of a dying culture whose literature was not worth reading. I couldn't understand that. Surely one should allow that Shakespeare was part of a vital, energetic tradition. I liked Soyinka too, but his work required a special understanding of Nigerian culture and politics. Besides, the idea of excluding all things European seemed foolish to me.

After long years of patiently planning my escape from a family environment in which every experience had been forced into a rigid and narrow sieve of racialized meaning, I was not happy to find the same kind of race baiting of white people at Harvard. After having witnessed through my parents the way human troubles could be falsely laid at the door of race, I certainly wasn't a willing acolyte of a racial revolution in which Third World people would suddenly assert their superiority over white people. It was a fantasy, and yet so many of my classmates seemed to fall for it.

For me, being at Harvard was a deliverance from the harsh life I'd been living at home. It was a liberation, not an excuse for petulance and complaint. For the first time, I felt completely free to make my own choices about how I would live. I was overjoyed to be anywhere except home. But now, to find blacks calling themselves "Harvard niggahs" was a living contradiction. I'd been raised to believe that one of the most intense desires of black people was to demonstrate that they were *not* "niggahs," but were human beings first and last. The notion that these privileged African-American students were imposing a deeply retrograde self-definition on themselves was stunning. And to call this progress was a delusion. It was as though the very group whose struggles for equality had created a new definition of freedom for humankind was looking for new ways to enslave themselves. White people might think of blacks as niggers—it was clear that many at Harvard did—but that was only out of a futile effort to avoid facing the fact that blacks could and did compete with them successfully at every step. Of course, these Harvard blacks might be calling themselves "niggahs" as a smart bit of irony. If so, it went over my head.

Other values were inverted as well. If Harvard made us work harder than we ever had before, it wasn't to make us earn our hard-won success, but supposedly was to burden us unduly with "institutionalized racism." The upperclassmen kept telling us that we were not at Harvard because of our intellectual accomplishments or ambitions. Those didn't count. We were there because "somebody had died for us." "You aren't here because of *who* you are," said one junior, "but because of *what* you are—a nigger." Opponents of affirmative action couldn't have put it better: blacks lacked qualifications other than the color of their skin. It was as though the whole concept of excellence was under attack, as though striving for success and dreaming big dreams were to be denigrated rather than celebrated.

At the heart of this thinking was the assertion that blacks who attended Harvard were not a leadership class at all. Nor were we the best and the brightest students the African-American community had ever produced. Even our ambition, according to these lights, was somehow shameful. That sense of shame showed up in many different ways. For instance, black students visiting the ghettos of Roxbury or Dorchester would introduce themselves not as Harvard students but as people who were "studying in Cambridge." The ghetto residents winked at each other on hearing this, but their knowing gestures seemed to escape the notice of these self-denigrating Harvard blacks. "Slumming today, are we?" the residents would ask, and the embarrassed students would inwardly cringe at the truth of it. To say that you attended Harvard was to open yourself to criticism for being a de facto elitist, and in those days being an elitist was the most shameful accusation of all. In contrast, white students bragged about attending Harvard, as almost anyone would. But not these African-American students, who labored under a perverse and destructive belief system that said it was wrong to celebrate their achievements or to soar above the heads of others.

So, if Harvard was a lonely place for black students, as it seemed to me, it was largely because they hobbled themselves with values that negated their true identities as achievers. And they were lonely. My black classmates were the loneliest people I knew then or have known since. In demonizing whites, they demonized themselves. It was as though achievement and success were suddenly "white things" not inherent to blacks. But I knew from my father's family, who had practiced at being successful for three generations, that this was nonsense, and that knowledge was my rudder in a choppy sea of self-doubt. I didn't mind being described by other blacks as "bourgeois." In fact, I rather liked it.

As much as I believed Harvard could become the source of my

personal salvation, however, the intense political struggles over identity among the African-American students meant that Harvard could
never be the place I had hoped it would be. I would learn that one
could never entirely avoid the racial obstacles that came out of the
separatism among black students. If there was a great deal of energy
spent on "identity" among the black students, there was little of the
same among the white students, who seemed to float free of any such
difficulties or ambiguities or doubts. They seemed to feel they were
at Harvard by right. Blacks should have felt exactly the same, but they
could not. They chained themselves with doubts about who they
were and imposed those doubts on each other. To me, it seemed a
poisoned atmosphere for achievement.

This is not to say that the doubts of the African Americans had
emerged in a vacuum. Racism was a shared belief among many
whites, who often seemed to feel that blacks were to be humored,
their common anger merely indulged. There was a nearly universal
consensus—even among the students I knew from Germany, Sweden, Italy, and other countries—that no matter how brilliant a black
student might be, the white student deserved to be here more. The
word "quota" applied, in their minds, only to blacks. That just wasn't
so. There were all kinds of quotas at work at Harvard, especially
among the foreign students. In fact, the place often seemed to me to
be one huge quota. There were quotas for rich whites and for poor
whites, like the friends I made from West Virginia and Georgia; quotas for jocks; quotas for chess masters; quotas for the sons and daughters of Zion, who hated quotas the most; quotas for African students
and Bengalis, for sons of Spanish ambassadors. It was understood
that the "Third World" students would go home and run their own
countries. All these quotas existed with one powerful intent: to create
leaders for the world that was just then coming into being. The aim
was to have as diverse and interesting a group of students as possible.
Harvard could have done a great deal to lessen the racial tension on
campus, I believe, if it had only acknowledged its sense of duty to
engineer its student body. It was perfectly obvious that Harvard was
responding to the lessons of the civil rights struggle by attempting to
create new opportunities for blacks, and this was perfectly consistent

with its sense of mission in the world. But Harvard never acknowledged this, and so missed a chance to make a profound point about the responsibilities of great institutions in American society. If anyone felt aggrieved by the quota system, it would have been quite legitimate for Harvard to argue that quotas worked in many different ways and for many different groups, not just for African Americans four or five generations out of slavery.

These issues aside, one thing I shared with the other African-American students was the sense of being singled out by teachers for special criticism because I was black. So when the black students' humor turned bitterly against the whites, I could not help but join in. I would hear blacks laughing at the pretenses of whites, and I would laugh, too. When whites were mocked in private, and criticized merely for being white, I listened and kept my own silent counsel. "I always thought white people were supposed to be smart," was one remark. "Look," went another, "that boy over there with the funky drawers on is your master. Hello, boss!"

At the root of such resentment, I believe, was the insult most black students felt at being inexorably tied to other blacks merely because of the color of their skin. In most cases, the differences among blacks were at least as glaring as the difference between blacks and whites. But while blacks were equally diverse in their opinions and beliefs, that diversity was rarely acknowledged. It was considered a bad idea for blacks to disagree with one another in front of whites, since the whites might conclude that "all those people do is fight among each other"—a phrase I heard from white mouths more than once. This made many black students so defensive that they weren't able to appreciate each other's varied experiences.

For me, one of the wonderful aspects of being at Harvard was this very diversity in the backgrounds of the black students. Some of them were the sons and daughters of families who had only recently emerged from a sharecropper's life in the Mississippi delta. There was one, named Thedford, from a dirt-poor Alabama family, who had had a short story published in the *Atlantic Monthly* while he was still in prep school. There was Fred, who came from Oakland, California, dressed like the rock drummer Buddy Miles, and later became a brain surgeon. There was Philip, whose family was so wealthy he spent his summer vacations at private estates in Cannes and his winter breaks in Zurich.

I also met African students who exposed me to the realities of African culture, as opposed to the culture so romanticized by African Americans of the political persuasion. One brother from Nigeria, a wonderful soccer player, would boast of exercising by chasing birds until the birds became exhausted. Another Nigerian was a beautiful and prideful fellow who would have been considered a good catch for any woman on campus. But he preferred to share his bed with slightly built young Jewish men. "I like the body hair," he told me once. "I don't have much of it myself."

I was greatly relieved, after a few months, to find that many of the students I would never have introduced myself to initially were becoming worthy friends. I made a habit of putting myself in odd places—at a banquet held by members of the English peerage, at an Israeli folk-dance festival, at poetry-reading contests and playwriting workshops—hoping to jar myself out of being predictable in my views of the world.

I began spending time around the Loeb Theater, the university's foremost theatrical venue. I met young men and women from Scotland and Poland and Sweden, some of whom invited me home with them on summer vacations. I never accepted, because I had grown too sensitive to being anyone's "black friend." Still, I enjoyed their company when I could.

I also met several students from the South, including one named Leslie* from West Virginia, who was attending the same seminar I was in the philosophy of Søren Kierkegaard. He liked to tell stories about growing up "poorer than a country mouse" and about a village philosopher named Booger Ray from his hometown. I began to appreciate what a rich place Harvard could be if only I could slip outside the bonds of racial conflict and see the place in a more creative way.

I often went walking through Harvard Square to witness the continuing drama of the community's street life, which was only partly connected to the goings-on at the school. Early on, I learned that Harvard Square had a life of its own. There were odd, faded, wasted-looking people everywhere: panhandlers, drunks, homeless children, musicians who played for small change until two in the morning. There were hippies selling hashish pipes or muttering that they could get hash oil at a good price, and macrobiotic, tie-dyed acid freaks on their way to crash-pad shelters. There was one group peddling a pornographic magazine published by a Berkeley cult known as the Fellowship of Ohm. There were members of the Black Panther Party for Self-Defense, those self-absorbed revolutionary military cadres, who boldly sold the party's newspaper under the roof of the Harvard Co-op, the university-run department store. There was the tall, red-headed woman in a long black hooded cape who sold a satanist magazine. She winked at me once. I imagined Satanic orgies, and regretfully walked away.

And there were others who just wandered, lost. One young woman had painted her face to look like a strawberry. Next to her was a man whose smudged green face paint suggested a cucumber. Some people were listening to a young black man dressed like a knockoff of Jimi Hendrix who was pounding a conga drum. "Are you alone in your freakiness?" said one girl to another, who was clearly high. The scene always gave me a special thrill, because it was such a counterpoint to the challenging life that surrounded me at Harvard.

Then there was the physical appearance of the rest of the square. The whole area outside Holyoke Center, which housed the university's administration offices, was littered with glass shards left over from nights of rioting and demonstrations by people from "the community," which one understood to be angry black working-class men and women from Somerville and environs who accused the university of being a slumlord.

I was simultaneously repelled and attracted to the place. The loud music all around grated on my nerves. Yet, even though I had come to associate loud music with my father when he was drunk and threatening to beat me, I always went back to my dormitory room whistling the songs I heard and feeling happy.

From the moment I met my two roommates, I knew the living situation wasn't going to work out. On top of all the conflicts and confusion I was experiencing, the polarizations of identity politics and race politics, I wasn't exactly the most tolerant person around. Basically, I didn't like the idea that because I was black it was logical for me to be assigned black roommates. I resented that assumption. I didn't want my roommates to feel responsible in any way for me, and I didn't want to feel responsible for them. I didn't want to feel guilty if I preferred not to share my life with them. I wanted to have the freedom to associate with anyone I chose. I didn't want to be tied down to two guys I didn't know and wasn't really interested in knowing. I was a loner. I didn't want to carry anyone's burdens but my own.

All through these first few months, I would open the door to my barracks like dormitory room and be greeted by a cloud of marijuana smoke lingering above the desks and beds. I should have tried harder to adjust to this, but my roomies seemed to assume that I would accept it automatically. I didn't appreciate what appeared to be their assumption that because I was black I had to put up with the drug habits of people I didn't know. I felt I had little in common with either of them beyond the color of our skin.

One of the roommates, a guy from Arizona, took an instant dislike to me, and vice versa. I considered him a slob. He considered me a "high yella" arrogant Connecticut snob, which in some ways I was. He would keep the record player going at all hours of the day or night. In the middle of the afternoon he would announce that he was hungry and wanted to "get high and fuck." My other roommate was a gentlemanly guy from Alabama named Micah.* We would walk around Harvard Square together searching for common ground, he from the soft-spoken South and I from clipped and fussy Connecticut. Micah had gone to public schools, as I had. And, like me, he had been an athlete and a scholar. He confessed that he was afraid he wouldn't make the grade at Harvard, and that greatly relieved me, because I was quite sure I wouldn't. I told him I felt so overwhelmed by the richness and complexity of what the university had to offer that I was afraid I would never be able to absorb the half of it.

The Arizona roomie got under my skin in various ways. He didn't seem to feel it was necessary for him to study very much. I would go off to the library and return to find that he had never left the room.

He would still be listening to the songs he'd been listening to when I left, and the reek of marijuana would seem stronger. I was afraid that his drug habits would rub off on me. On other occasions, I would return to find him entertaining one or another of the young women he knew. I was constantly interrupting these little feasts. Micah confessed to not knowing how to cope with the situation any better than I did. This Arizona roommate was the product of a prestigious prep school, the first black preppie I'd ever met but not the last. Many of the blacks who'd gone to private schools seemed to have the same bad habits—intensive drug taking, selfishness, disregard for others—and I learned to avoid them. All in all, the rooming arrangement made me claustrophobic. Fortunately, toward the middle of my freshman year I was able to arrange a transfer to a small private room across campus, at a place called Hurlbut Hall.

Early on in my freshman year I reacted to the cultural whipsaw by again cutting my hair, the main feature that had helped identify me as an African-American student. I wanted to create a breathing space for myself. I was more than what I looked like, more than the color of my skin or the shape of my nose and lips. Altering my appearance was one means of challenging the way people saw me. If I didn't wear my hair in an Afro, did that mean I wasn't black enough? In fact it did, but I didn't care. I would claim my right to make my own friends as I saw fit, choosing those I felt kindred to, black or white. If people could see that I was a fair-skinned African American, so much the better. I wouldn't try to explain myself.

That led to a number of ironic situations. Once, a black student mistook me for a white boy as I crossed the campus. She was one of the radical political types who worked out their emotional ambivalence by spouting slogans. She asked me if I knew that most of the young men dying in Vietnam were poor blacks. I asked her if she had gotten her information from *Jet*, the small tabloid magazine that passionately catalogued the rise and fall of members of black Chicago society and little else. I was rather surprised that few of the black students recognized me as their fellow. I apparently looked so different from the picture in the freshman register that when the black students saw me in person they mistook me for white. When one black freshman finally put my face together with the picture, she said, in a startled tone, "Is this *you?*" She pointed to the yearbook picture. I told her it was, and asked if there was something she wanted. "No," she said. "Just checking." These were exactly the kinds of experiences I had cut my hair to avoid.

In a way, the changes I made in my physical appearance were more fundamentally due to intellectual doubts that had little to do with race. If other students wanted to argue race for four years, let them. I wanted to know who I was, to challenge myself and find out what interested me beyond questions of race. I knew I was an American—my trip to Russia and my witnessing of the invasion of Prague had convinced me that I could never be anything but an American—but I also knew that I wanted to explore my inward territory far more than I'd ever been able to do before.

I had entered Harvard intending to study medicine, but as my sophomore year loomed in the distance I knew that I could never become a doctor. I lacked the passion for medicine that I'd once had. I'd wanted to become a doctor, I think, partly because I was attracted to the idea of being able to heal others of their sicknesses. Now I knew I really just wanted to heal myself. I attended biology lectures with a growing boredom. I felt that I was in the wrong place. As I memorized amino-acid configurations, glucose conversion chains, and other premed staples, I seemed to have become someone else. I didn't need the status that becoming a doctor would confer.

I'd lost my faith in becoming a doctor for another reason, too. It was the last vestige of a connection with my father, who'd always wanted me to be a doctor. When I told my advisers that I would be pursuing another academic direction, I knew I was leaving behind some part of myself that I didn't need anymore. I wanted to be my own person, not the person my father wanted me to become.

I returned in my mind to first causes. Long before entering Harvard, I had come upon the writings of the historian and Harvard graduate W. E. B. Du Bois, one of my few heroes. I considered what it would be like to become a historian or, at the very least, a writer. I took classes in fiction writing, and in philosophy and history as well, and found a level of comfort in myself that the study of science had never given me. At the end of my freshman year I began to think about declaring a major in English, but I decided that field was far too bound by tradition. In the English department black authors were rarely studied, nor were any other writers outside the European context. I'd read Richard Wright and Ralph Ellison and felt they were just as important as Ezra Pound or Robert Frost or Spenser or Marvel.

I began taking history courses in the African-American studies department, as well as in the history department, and finally found what I wanted to study. African history, particularly the slave trade, had fascinated me for years, and I decided to make it my field of concentration. I wanted to make sense of my own life, and the study of African and African-American history, so little understood and so little taught at Harvard then, seemed a natural choice. I think that underneath this choice was the awareness that race meant something very different to me than to most people I knew, black or white. I wanted to trace back to its beginnings the roots of the racial experience in America, to see if I could come to grips with this difficult subject in a way that would help me understand my own experience. What was the nature of racialized experience? And how had it affected me? I knew that changing my course of study so drastically might put my entire career at Harvard at risk. But it turned out that part of my great luck in attending this institution was that such a fundamental shift of interests was tolerated, even encouraged. I wondered at first why not one of the college advisers I talked to tried to change my mind. Maybe they weren't paying attention. But at Harvard students were on their own. It was assumed that we were thinking, considering creatures and that we knew we would be held accountable for our life decisions, even if they were hard or dangerous or fraught with challenges.

After reaching my decision, I found myself becoming more deeply involved in the campus debates over the nature of African-American culture and history, almost in spite of myself. Whenever I could insert myself into a reasoned historical or philosophical debate, I did so. I came to disagree more and more bitterly with those cultural nationalists who sought to elevate a racialized sense of blackness itself as an ultimate good. Where they searched in Africa and elsewhere for models of human behavior, my reading was helping me understand the true accomplishments of African-American history. I saw examples of the ways black people had survived oppressions of class and race. It became difficult to listen to the nationalists, who seemed to value all things African merely because they were African, as though no wisdom could be found in the history of blacks in America. Race was everywhere, and looking to the culture of a vaguely understood Africa for solace didn't strike me as a very promising avenue.

I discovered that, on one level, all the talk about Africa was an attempt to bully the diverse black student body into a false consensus about personal identity. One afternoon, in a political discussion about whether or not one owed unwavering racial loyalty to the African continent and the revolutions that were occurring there, a black "leader" named Jackson Leery,* a dropout from MIT and a member of the inner circle of the black nationalist poet Amiri Baraka (LeRoi Jones), alleged that every black was African. "We are an African people." Heads nodded in agreement.

I stopped him. I asked him what he meant.

"That should be self-evident, brother," he said with a special glare.

"But it isn't at all," I said. "Who in this room was born in Africa?"

The other students looked at me as though I'd just dropped a load of bricks in the middle of the circle. No one responded.

"I think that should tell you that maybe *you* aren't African," he said.

"That's silly," I said. "What tribe do you belong to?"

Leery always carried a carved ebony truncheon similar to the one carried by the dictator Mobutu Sese Seko of Zaire, one of the most corrupt leaders in recent African history. As if to emphasize his belief that all things African were excellent, Leery imitated the dictator's style, while disregarding his record as a thug and a grafter on a massively corrupt scale. He pounded his truncheon into the middle of his palm. The gesture was so silly and gangsterish, such a patent imitation of Edward G. Robinson, that I laughed out loud. I was the only one who did. That was the last such indoctrination session I ever attended.

More often now, I retreated to my private room in Hurlbut Hall.

It was small, but big enough to contain all I needed: a dresser, a bed, a chair, a desk, and a sink. There was a bathroom in the hallway, which I shared with three other students. That was not too convenient, but it was no cause to complain.

The one thing I found most helpful in calming the fierce troubles in my heart was the music of Beethoven. I felt a tremendous love in his work, and was inspired by his life story. I found a wonderful collection of classical recordings at the university's school of music and spent much of my free time there, listening to the compositions I liked best: Beethoven's "Rasoumovsky" string quartets, the late string quartets, and the Great Fugue, as well as the works of Igor Stravinsky, particularly the ballets *Petrouchka* and *The Rite of Spring*. I also listened endlessly to Mozart's symphonies and piano concerti, and I discovered his Requiem. I discovered the Brahms Requiem as well. It leveled me. While everyone else was listening to rock music and going to beer parties, I would go into Boston to take in the operas that were performed at the universities there. I loved choral music, too, especially that of Brahms, and surrounded myself with it, often going to the music library after my classes to bathe myself in light.

Having found a satisfactory academic curriculum outside of medicine, I plunged eagerly into my studies. I read biographical profiles of poets like T. S. Eliot, and I soon discovered the life and writing of Ezra Pound, whose works, from the early simpler poems to the massively complex *Cantos*, made me feel that I'd discovered another, richer world. I studied as much as I could of his work, and found myself also digging deeper into the vast body of world literature that Pound used as his sources.

I began to take a special interest in acting, particularly in the Elizabethan theater. Student-directed productions were mounted at the university's Loeb Theater, and I became involved with one group of students who put on productions there, including many Shakespeare plays. The Harvard theater community was also active in several on-campus houses, and we performed some of the lesser-known works in these smaller settings. I played Pericles in the play of that title, and Troilus in *Troilus and Cressida*. It was a joy to be cultivating talents I'd never tested before.

All during this first year, as fall turned to winter and then to spring,

I wondered if maybe I'd been allowing racial turmoil to occupy too much room in my life. I was finding that there were so many other areas to explore rather than trying to puzzle out the enormous complexities of that subject. I was taking more history courses, to learn as much as I could about the particular issues of economics and ethics that had formed racial attitudes in the first place, and that helped me put my personal experiences in perspective. I was also learning that the world of social and political turmoil was just one of many areas in which students were testing themselves and defining their personal identities. There were many different Harvards, I discovered.

After relocating to Hurlbut Hall I met a young Japanese-American student named Takuya who was pursuing his dream of becoming a mathematician. His world was quite different from mine, and I was thoroughly intrigued by it. Tak's world was a place where the most brilliant of the brilliant seemed to create new fields of reality out of the energy of their minds. In that world, new branches of mathematics were formed and developed. New branches of physics and chemistry came into being. It was a truly creative world, where invention was as natural as breathing, and it was a revelation to me.

I discovered that Tak, too, had been less than content with the roommates he'd been assigned, and we found that many of our grievances were similar. Tak was tall for an Asian, gangly, witty, and alert, and full of trenchant comments about the white people he'd met. It turned out that we were both from Chicago. Tak's father, a university professor, came from the peasant classes in Japan, and his mother, a housewife, was from the merchant-samurai classes. Before Harvard, Tak had graduated from the University of Chicago's lab school, and his ambition, he said, was to study something called "pure mathematics." It was a world peopled by such divines as Evariste Galois, a French mathematician who had devised solutions to certain algebraic equations of the fifth degree and higher. Galois is reported to have exited the world in a blaze of glory after challenging another man to a duel just as he was about to join Napoleon's army. In a letter written right before the duel in which he was killed, he outlined a new form of mathematics he had discovered, leaving it to others to carry on his work.

I soon discovered that if my world was a contentious, bruising place, the world of pure mathematics could be a place of far greater cruelty. On our long walks together, Tak would describe the struggles he was waging for his own identity. Often, he said, solving a single problem took reams of computer paper, days and weeks of time. As I struggled with questions of my own spiritual and intellectual identity, I witnessed Tak wrestling with his work, taking in barely enough sustenance to keep himself healthy, in torment over whether he had the "sacred fire" of genius. I admired this spirit, and began to wonder whether I was challenging myself as fully as he was, or was relaxing on the ropes.

One day Tak explained more fully the nature of his struggle. He'd recently taken a course in advanced mathematics taught by a certain genius who was only twenty-two years old, he said. This young man had discovered a theoretical postulate in pure math that was the cornerstone of his present career as a teacher and consultant in the math departments at Harvard and at Stanford. As Tak observed, he taught his principles with the hauteur of a Prussian general.

As he was writing proofs on a blackboard, Tak went on, this teacher noticed a very young student, no older than fourteen, sitting at his desk and waving his arm in the air. The teacher tried to ignore him. This went on for long minutes, Tak said, until it was clear that something unusual was in the air. The teacher was obviously avoiding the boy, and everyone was curious to know why.

After a few more minutes the teacher interrupted his scribbling. He asked, in the way that only a snotty twenty-two-year-old genius can, "Is there a problem?"

"I see an easier way to do that equation," the boy said.

It was, Tak said, as though the teacher had suddenly been unmasked as a fake. He had been writing out the very section of a problem he had discovered and upon which his reputation rested. For this young student to say that there was a simpler way of doing the problem meant that the so-called genius had not seen his own work clearly enough, had overlooked a vital part of his own concept. No one had noticed the imperfection until now, the holes in his invention. In that instant, his entire career lay in ashes at his feet. His future was past. "It was like watching a murder," Tak said. "There was no hiding place."

Tak struggled and struggled with his love for math that year. As I watched him, it made me realize that I was not giving myself completely to my own efforts. I had been coasting, faking it. Maybe I'd needed time to coast, but that time had to end soon. I hated the idea that I might have been just going through the motions, not doing the hard work of discovery. It wasn't that I felt I owed a better performance to those who were paying my bills. I felt that I owed myself a better performance.

By slow degrees, my studies led me to an enthusiastic reading of the history of the slave trade. Scholars were then beginning to train their sights on the experiences of the slaves themselves. I soon found myself deeply immersed in the studies of slavery in America written by Eugene Genovese, Kenneth Stampp, Stanley Elkins, John Blassingame, Philip Curtin, and others. From there, I turned to various African writers who had produced fascinating accounts of what the institution of slavery was like in Africa. It was a rewarding, if circuitous, route.

I decided I would set my own course of study. Around the middle of my sophomore year, I discovered a collection of George Orwell's essays called *Such, Such Were the Joys*, which encouraged me to be honest with myself and do what I wanted to, regardless of the consequences. The idea that I might one day want to write history became stronger, and I enrolled in the African-American studies department, where courses in economics, history, and literature might help me arrive at an understanding of the slave trade from an African point of view.

Among the scholars who were contributing a new sense of what the African slave trade was like was a professor named Kenneth O. Dike (pronounced "D. K."). He taught in the history department at Harvard, and I eagerly enrolled in his courses. His study of the African slave trade in the riverine regions of West Africa was considered a classic work of historical research. My study of it led me more deeply into the works of other African scholars who were writing about the conditions within Africa that had allowed the European slave trade to become an international enterprise in which morality was of scant concern. This, essentially, was the focus of Dike's and other African scholars' work.

It was a peculiar period in African-American studies. Partly because it was still a very new field of research, and partly because it had grown out of a political movement that demanded a scholarly reconsideration of Africa's crucial role in world history, African-American studies had yet to produce anything resembling a body of first-rate scholarship. Unfortunately, the African-American studies department did not always attract the best minds. There were a few historians, like Dike, who were happy to play consulting roles in the new department, but most of them preferred to remain in the more established history or English departments, which weren't suffering from so much controversy. The department was blanketed by charges—many of them true—that it was more concerned with race politics and questions of racial identity than with scholarship. Was the department to become a sinecure for politically strident ideologues who would loudmouth Harvard for its perceived racialist practices? Or would it attract first-rate scholars who were interested in shaping a solid curriculum grounded in mature scholarship?

In fact, African-American studies was one of the few areas that allowed students to take courses in many different departments. Dike believed that this was a great advantage, even if the department's too-young and too-noisy leaders often seemed to make scholarship a secondary concern. After I had taken several courses with him, and had grown increasingly obsessed with questions of freedom and unfreedom, of morality versus cold economic calculation, Dike agreed to be the adviser for my undergraduate thesis. But he warned me, "Be careful about how you propose your topic. There are certain sensitivities there." I didn't think to ask him what he meant, and finding out on my own proved to be a valuable lesson for me.

Dike's thesis of the slave trade ran roughly as follows: If one studied the slave traders in Nigeria who became prominent in the international commerce of slavery in the nineteenth century, it was clear that they came from a vital and robust tradition of trading within Nigeria itself. There had always been a market for slaves within

Nigeria, although slavery here was profoundly different from the chattel slavery practiced in Europe. When the European demand for slaves reached its height, during the late eighteenth and nineteenth centuries, it was Africa's internal markets in trade goods—from palm oil to iron and copper, from cowry shells to English cloth from Manchester—that were instrumental in establishing the trade networks from the coast to the interior. The control of these internal markets at first remained in undisputed African control. As the demand for slaves began to surge, forcing other trade goods into a secondary status, the Africans were able to adapt and enlarge these trading networks for the new trade in human life. But as the European demand for slaves became so overwhelming as to promise great wealth to the slave dealers themselves, European power over the internal trade networks increased. By setting one African kingdom in competition with another, the Europeans forced the Africans to pour more of their resources into stemming these internal conflicts. Massive depopulation weakened the African political structures, and ultimately the Africans lost control of the trade. To say, therefore, that Africans were not themselves partly responsible for conducting the slave trade, and thus for the enslaved condition of Africa itself, that evil European immorality was wholly responsible, was a fiction and a patent misunderstanding of history. For better or for worse, Africans and Europeans had worked closely together to form the trade links, and both had benefited at the expense of the mass of Africans.

Of course, this historical reality conflicted explicitly with the tenets of black nationalism, which essentially blamed all black people's problems, both here and in Africa, on the greed and corruption of whites. That being so, black nationalists believed that it was foolish and self-destructive for any black person to turn to Europe for self-definition. Black people should instead turn solely to Africa for their identities. But what if a study of history showed that Africans were just as responsible as Europeans for promoting and carrying on an immoral slave trade? What if Africans weren't thinking about morality at all when they sold other Africans to the slave ships? Blaming white people for all the problems of black people only made the whites loom more powerful than they actually were. Why not accept the role blacks had played in the demise of African culture that resulted from the slave trade? Wasn't that a more "empowering" strategy than placing blame?

Apparently not. I developed a thesis topic drawing on Dike's work among others, but when I discussed it with the head of the African-American studies department, Euart Guinier, he only nodded vacantly and smiled. He had no questions. I was rather disappointed that he didn't express any excitement over the way I was approaching a controversial subject that directly or indirectly had shaped the lives of black people around the world. Nevertheless, I took his silence as assent. Over the next two years, I read the diaries of escaped slaves who had been traded by Africans to the Europeans. They described their experiences in great detail and in powerful narratives. I studied the diaries of slave traders like Tippo Tibb, a link between the African traders and the European buyers on the coast. I explored the ideas various historians had developed about the strength of African internal markets, and Dike directed me to research papers detailing the intricate economic markets in ivory, gold, and, finally, slaves that had contributed so much toward making the slave trade a prosperous business.

When I told my parents about changing my major from pre-med to African-American history, Mom was upset. She asked why I had abandoned a medical career. I reminded her it had always been more her dream and Dad's than mine. Dad wouldn't talk to me, but Mom claimed that he took the news casually and with great indifference. Either way, their reaction didn't much matter to me. They were living their lives as they saw fit, and I was doing likewise.

It was about this time that my father moved back to Chicago, leaving Mom, Mike, and John in Connecticut. Mark was attending Clark University in Worcester, Massachusetts, where he was still pursuing a medical career. In 1972, at the end of my sophomore year, Mom decided to sell the house in Connecticut and move to Chicago with John and Mike to rejoin Dad. Once again, she found herself in the middle of the same old emotional triangle. Katherine was openly hostile, and Dad was putting more and more financial demands on her. Katherine was having trouble making ends meet on Harold's salary, and Alan's appearance in Chicago complicated her life immeasurably. Dad took a job selling life insurance on the South Side of Chicago. He was a fine salesman—he had always been good at every job he held—and in short order he was one of Prudential's top salesmen. But his drinking never stopped, and the old pattern of abuse against Mom resumed. I would receive occasional reports from Mike about her difficulties, but I had problems of my own and couldn't do much for her anymore. It tore me up inside that I couldn't, but her troubles with Dad now seemed like distant considerations to me. I was creating a life of my own, and I knew I had to break with that part of my past in order to survive.

Meanwhile, I had become politically involved in the issue of Harvard's investments in South Africa. The college owned stock in Gulf Oil Company, among others, and I was among the many black students who felt that this was wrong. How could Harvard claim to be a liberal institution when its investments were buoying up companies doing business in nations whose reign of racial oppression should have marked those nations as international outlaws? Harvard, we felt, should divest itself of such stocks, or at least should use the power it had to campaign actively for political change in that part of the world.

I wasn't part of the team of students who planned the occupation of the university's administrative offices in Massachusetts Hall to protest the investment policy, but I quickly decided to participate. My own experience of racial oppression compelled me to take a stand. I felt strongly that I couldn't morally justify attending an institution that contributed to the oppression of African people, and I agreed that the most dramatic way to highlight the contradiction between what Harvard professed and how it acted was to occupy the building. I knew, of course, that I was putting my own academic career at risk. I weighed the consequences carefully, but I could see no other choice: if my presence at Harvard was supposed to help prove the institution's commitment to racial justice, I felt I should be one of those to test that commitment by opposing the objectionable business practices that I was indirectly benefitting from.

On the designated morning in early spring, the handful of African-American students who were going to occupy Massachusetts Hall entered the building without any trouble. I was among them. Surprisingly, the most vocal critics of Harvard's investment policy were not. I found it strange that we didn't have to break any windows to get in. No one had called the police, either—another surprise. Instead, there were two men quietly clicking away with their cameras as we climbed through a first-floor window. We sat in for nearly a week. We were proud to be claiming part of the legacy of the civil rights pioneers through this act of moral conscience.

But apparently none of us had given enough thought to the consequences of our actions. Only during the tribunal that followed did we learn what the college board of overseers proposed: it recommended expelling us permanently from Harvard. What was equally surprising to us, however, was that many voices of reason in the university—including law school professor Derrick Bell—stepped forward in our defense. They were able to convince this all-white group of men that our actions were for a just cause. Luckily, conscience and reason prevailed on the part of the overseers. As a result, Harvard did something that is difficult for any large institution to do: it admitted that its policies needed to be examined and promised to look more closely at its investments in South Africa, something it had not done before.

My junior year passed quickly. I was more focused than ever on my study of the slave trade. It seemed an ironic topic, because in an important way it challenged the logic of the African-American studies department itself. The department was a boosterish kind of place: interested only in Great African Civilizations, Great Black Americans, and Black Achievements—and certainly not interested in black people as being subject to the same errors and misjudgments as any other group of human beings. To my mind, there was something fraudulent about the claims to moral superiority of the Negro Race Men and Women in the department; equality seemed challenge enough. There was, in my estimation, no future in this way of looking at the world. I wondered when black people were going to allow themselves to come down from their glass towers of moral superiority and join the great, flawed, joyous muscular effort known as humanity. When would black people stop sitting in judgment on white people when they were just as guilty of sin as anyone?

I saw the history of the slave trade less in political or moral or even economic terms; I saw it as a human tragedy for which all races bore a measure of blame. The Africans had cared little more about the fate of their cargo than the Europeans had. Where in that was the substance of any claim to moral authority? The African nobility had profited, but at the same time had undermined its ability to withstand European domination. It was greed that brought about the ruin of African economies, African political units, and African cultures. America imported slaves to build economic empires with cheap labor, but at the price of introducing a moral dilemma that undermined its most fundamental claims as a nation of free men. At the center of it all was simple human weakness, which had spawned the notion of racial supremacy that had touched the very center of my life. None of it would have been possible without the cooperation of those Africans who were quite willing to exploit other human beings every bit as mercilessly as the Europeans were. Who, then, was guilty and who was innocent?

In a deeper sense, I knew I had learned something that gave me great personal satisfaction. When I was a boy, my father told me that he had once wanted to study African and American history and maybe to teach it. I had quite overlooked this shared interest as a link between us. My mind now sought it out, and I began to feel that if only my father had had some support in overcoming the profound sadness and loneliness that had always haunted him, he might have achieved that goal. Maybe if he had learned to value himself he would have valued his accomplishments more, and would not have felt compelled to undo all he had achieved as a black man and as a human being. He had been rejected, just as I had, by his father and by other relatives, though in a different way. I understood that my pain was not so different from his. But partly because of him, I had had the chance to go to Harvard. It wasn't a question for me of seeing myself climbing on the shoulders of some anonymous ancestor to get into college, but of climbing on his shaky shoulders.

I wanted to understand the issue of responsibility for oppression, and I discovered that this was a very delicate question indeed. History is a subtle place. We all look there to find justification for our present courses of action. But the past is a world unto itself. It has its own echoes, which are often different than the ones we hear. I felt I'd learned that by listening closely and honestly to the past I could understand the complexities of racial existence that had tainted my life. And by learning this, maybe I could find a way to face the realities that gave me pain—facing them not by the cant of false accusation that surrounded so much of black anger toward white people but by finding the things blacks and whites have in common. In pursuing the subject I loved, I had found a deeper connection with my father. It gave me a great sense of relief. The terrible rejection I'd felt from him had wounded me just as deeply as my rejection by my mother's family. By exploring the things we shared—a love of Africa and its history—maybe we could be reconciled. Maybe we could put our old ghosts to rest.

A strange drama unfolded before my eyes during the summer leading up to my senior year. I was living in Roxbury then, one of the Boston area's black ghettos. It wasn't really a ghetto, but rather a well-tended area of middle-class homes, not unlike our neighborhood in Connecticut. I liked hanging out there, and this proved to be a particularly interesting time to do so. About a dozen male and female black students from Harvard had taken up residence that summer in one of the housing projects not far from where I lived. I didn't know how they'd gotten into the project, but I wanted to see how they would survive there on their own.

With all the talk of "the community," many of my Harvard classmates were finding out through painful experience that the proletariat regarded them with profound suspicion. The "Harvard brothers," as the men were sarcastically called in Roxbury, seemed surprised by the reticence of the "community brothers." I later learned that the men of the neighborhood believed the Harvard guys were only out for easy sexual adventures—which was probably true—and the locals didn't want to be shown up by these college men with their greater access to money, cars, entertainment, and other pleasures. Likewise, the women in the projects felt that the Harvard women were slumming it to get ghetto guys who would be more "lumpen" than their classmates. It seemed to me that the suspicions of the Roxbury people were more than justified. For many of these Harvard blacks, revolution was all talk. To them, talk was almost the same as action. And beneath this was their complete obsession with "true blackness," as though, because of where they'd come from, they could never be black enough.

In their search for the authentic, the Harvard brothers and sisters seemed oblivious to what was going on around them. It was an open secret among the people in the projects that Harvard "niggahs" were good to have around, if only for one thing: they could always afford the best marijuana. If the people of "the community" wondered aloud what wind had blown these students into the ghetto, the latter seemed to think the discussion was about someone else. One student's apartment was robbed by some community brothers. The Harvard brothers did not retrieve the stolen articles and were denounced as "pussies." Another student was raped. The male students tried to lecture the Roxbury brothers about sexism and were laughed out of the projects. The Harvard brothers argued that blacks were all Africans and that Africans had no history of stealing from one another. The locals asserted that there wasn't an African within twenty miles of Roxbury, and if the Harvard brothers didn't pack their bags soon, someone might get hurt. They said that if Harvard was teaching its students that black people were Africans, they'd better enroll in the community college, where the teachers at least knew who they were.

"And what are you learning at Harvard?" I heard one woman ask a Harvard sister one evening. "You're being taught nothing but social theory. You make me into an abstraction. Promise me something. When you graduate from medical school, do something practical. Come here and start a medical clinic." But the people of the community knew full well that they were not part of any of the students' long-range plans. To be black and middle class was about leaving "the community" behind. Yet the Harvard brothers and sisters seemed to believe that they could just come in and quickly absorb all the soul they'd lacked, supposedly because they'd never been poor. I found it interesting that this line of reasoning also seemed to infect many of the young Harvard scholars who visited Africa. They would leave with high hopes of becoming more African, and would return knowing just how American they truly were. They learned that the Africans only expected them to do what Americans do best—spend a lot of money, just like the white tourists. This was all part of my Harvard education.

I started my senior year determined to do my best with the thesis I'd been working on for about two years now. It was an examination of the slave trade in Dahomey, Ghana, and Nigeria. I put every ounce of my energy into the work and finished it by the end of the second semester of my senior year. It ran more than 150 pages. My adviser, Kenneth Dike, was pleased. I'd reconstructed the way in which the existing economic markets, in place for hundreds of years before the slave trade, were merely expanded to maximize the profit from trading slaves during the eighteenth and nineteenth centuries. I showed that business, not morality, was paramount, on both the African and the European side. If anyone lost, it was the Africans, who helped shift the balance of power by depleting their human resources. The slave trade, I argued, was as much an exercise in African self-destruction as it was in European dominance of the markets.

Dike warned me again that when I was called upon to defend the thesis, I should be careful to avoid a moral debate with the professors who'd read it. How was that possible? I wondered. He stopped just short of warning me about something I already knew: that the African-American studies department was run by ideologues who were not likely to agree that Africans, whom they tended to romanticize in every way, were partly responsible for the terrible trade in human flesh. Still, I was prepared for a bracing debate over history and economics, which seemed to me more interesting concerns than moral debate. I became deeply immersed in further studies to prove my point—perhaps too deeply for my own good.

Then, out of the blue, I received a notice from the U.S. Army that I was to report to Grand Central Station in New York City for my physical examination. I had been drafted. It was 1974, and the Vietnam War was grinding to its horrible end. My selective service lottery number was 54, and somehow my student deferment hadn't gone through. This crisis couldn't have come at a worse time. I spent a week calling the various draft boards in Norwalk and was told the matter was out of their hands. I decided to rent a car and drive out to a draft board in Brighton, a suburb near Boston, where being a student at Harvard might carry some weight. I handed my notice to a man sitting at a long desk and told him that surely there had been some mistake. I explained that I was registered as a student at Harvard, and had been for the last three and a half years. He looked at me with astonishment and said, "Well, someone messed up something, because it says here you've been drafted." I asked him if it would be possible for him to notify someone that I was a student and should have received a deferment.

"I don't know, but we can try."

Those were the kindest words I had heard in a long time. A week later I received an emergency telegram saying that I had been granted a student deferment because I was enrolled at Harvard. I knew then that the struggles I had encountered at Harvard had been more than worth it. If I had been attending any other school, I might well have gone to Vietnam. Harvard had saved my life, and, even if I could not yet admit it, I was grateful. I returned to the draft office to thank the man who had helped me, only to learn that he had retired.

I continued to work on my thesis, feeling like someone whose life had been snatched from destruction. I finally submitted it, and on an early June morning in 1974 I sat down at a large round table to defend it.

True to Dike's warning, the attack began almost instantly. Still, I was astonished at how vehemently the professors of African-American studies reacted to my work. The head of the department, Euart Guinier, was not a participant in this event. My thesis had been read by three people: an English teacher, an assistant professor of African politics, and an African historian, who seemed deeply offended that I had taken only one of his courses and that the thesis did not include much of his work on the role of guns introduced into the slave trade by the European powers.

The professor of African politics insisted that I had taken a wrong direction. Slavery, she claimed, was a moral issue, not an economic one. White people, and white people alone, were guilty. They had built nations on the backs of black people, spilling black blood for the sake of their own greed. The slave trade had been run exclusively by whites, for the sole benefit of whites and the universal exploitation of blacks, and it had resulted in the loss of millions of black lives. When I asked about her sources for this assertion, which contradicted my two years of research, she glared at me as though I had slapped her.

I replied that morality had had nothing to do with the slave trade until the trade was ruled illegal by England. The laws of economics had always governed the trade, and as long as it was profitable morality was easily overlooked.

But how could I say that Africans had profited from the trade? she asked. I replied that whole kingdoms in Dahomey were founded on the slave trade, as they were in Ghana and Nigeria. If Europeans had grown fat on the sale of human beings, so had Africans. Weren't Africans as liable to avarice and inhumanity as anyone else?

The thesis readers wouldn't have it. They wanted someone to blame for the condition of black people, and white capitalists had always been a convenient target.

The irony, I felt, was that the very department that had challenged Harvard to broaden its concepts of intellectual achievement and had accused the faculty of narrow-mindedness toward blacks was itself subject to these faults. The department was tied more to ideology than to the evidence of history. I was sad but not surprised by this. Ideology had segregated the field called African-American studies and had made it narrow and mediocre, and as closed as any of the "black tables."

I realized, too late of course, that I had committed a terrible error. I had dedicated my resources to an effort that was never going to be approved and to a department that in its way was as unyielding as many of the departments it criticized. Luckily, I had enough credits to graduate anyway, although without praise for my scholarship.

Then other difficulties intervened. My parents had separated again, and while I was busy finishing my thesis I more or less stopped checking to see if they were keeping up with my bills. My father had completely stopped sending any payments. When I asked him what was happening, he wrote in a note, "When you ain't got nothing, you ain't got nothing to give." My mother had to take out loans to pay the portion of my final term bill not covered by my scholarship, in order for me to graduate. And she did so only on the promise that I would pay off the debt after I graduated.

My father, meanwhile, was in deeper trouble than I knew. Since his return to Chicago his life had spun completely out of control. Now he'd been sentenced to prison for writing bad checks and for weapons possession. I felt that he had finally landed in a place where he would be taken care of, something he'd always wanted and needed.

But he left behind quite a trail of suffering. His drug habits had finally got the better of him, and Mom had decided that their relationship could not be patched up after all. The arrangement was not good for John, either, as Chicago had few good schools for the blind. And Mike was desperately unhappy as well. Soon after Dad entered prison, Katherine and Harold moved out of the country, largely to avoid the catastrophe that had befallen her son. Everyone in my family was heading in a different direction. In a way that closely resembled the beginning of my time at Harvard, things were falling apart. Still, I'd made it through, and had discovered the things that moved me.

On graduation morning I woke up feeling elated and free. My cousin Tracy Lawrence came in for the ceremony, as did my step-grandfather, Harold. Mom, Mike, Mark, and John also came. They hardly recognized me. I'd shaved off all my hair again, this time because the Cambridge summer was unbearably hot. Before they arrived I dropped a tab of mescaline, so I hardly recognized them either.

After four years of trial and change, in which I had achieved an imperfect record at Harvard, I'd survived. I could hardly believe my luck. I had the feeling a soldier must have after a war is over and he finds that all his limbs are intact and he has survived without major surgery. I was a bit shell-shocked, I suppose, but other than that I knew I would be all right. Harvard had been dreadful and sublime, often at the same time. I had hated it and loved it; I was never bored by it, and was almost constantly surprised. Still, I was glad to be out.

I did not attend any graduation parties. I did not say good-bye to anyone but my best friend, Tak. We vowed to see each other again in five years, but never did. I would love to see him now.

I had gone through so many important changes in the last four years that, Afro or buzz, I hardly recognized myself. Some expectations were fulfilled and others unfulfilled; I had new dreams in place of old ones; I had a feeling that I was more open in my mind than I'd ever been. Harvard had left its mark on me. I had survived, and a world of experience awaited me. It was a hot summer day and I didn't want to sweat. My hair would grow back. I was in no hurry. I had the great pleasure of knowing that I had more than survived, really. In the end, I wasn't one of those black students who were ruined worse by Harvard than by bad whiskey. I had never swallowed that poisonous fruit, and I'd never felt the need to try.

LaVerne (left) and family.

NINE / Tolerance

*I am a stranger with thee, and a sojourner, as all my
fathers were.*

—PSALMS

In the fifteen years between my graduation and my second trip to Caruthersville, I started a family, built a career, and watched my parents and brothers drift further and further apart. I had grown weary of my hates—large and small—and of the stupefying power that race had exerted over my life. At best, race now seemed nothing more than an elaborate pose, a lame excuse. It seemed more important to me than ever to assert a full human identity instead of a shallow racial one. I decided it was time to try seeing Ocieola again.

So much had happened that I needed to understand. My father and I hadn't spoken in nearly twenty years. His life was never the same after he got out of prison. He was just another ex-offender now, and try as he might, he couldn't get back on his feet again. My mother was now living alone in New York City, still working as a fashion designer. My brother Mark was a practicing physician. My younger brother Mike was working his way through college. My youngest brother, John, was finishing up college. I had worked for a time as a newspaper reporter at a publication so riven by racial division that I finally had to leave to keep my own sanity. I had two children, Aaron and Terence, and a wife, Frances, whom I loved and who had given me the strength to push my own boundaries. I was trying to anchor myself as a father. To be a father is to learn to hope for forgiveness. It is to confront your own limitations. It is to accept blame and not expect praise. It is to learn to surrender by yielding to other people's needs. On that first trip to Caruthersville, I had come less as a father than as a son, a grandson, a nephew—a ghost who refused to die. Now I wanted to return with the full heart a father gives to his family. I wanted to forgive Ocieola and Clarence for being absent from my life. I truly hoped it wasn't too late.

But first I went to Chicago to see my father. He confided to me that many of the mistakes he'd made in raising a family came from a desperate feeling that he would die prematurely of a heart attack, as his own father had. "I felt so desperately alone," he said. "I could find no peace in myself. I was afraid to die, and so I nearly drank myself to death. I did terrible things to everyone." I told him I knew the feeling of being alone, and I could understand why it had frightened him so much. I asked him why he'd run away so far and so long. He said he was just scared because he didn't know how to make contact with his own children. I let it rest. That was as far as the discussion went, and for the time being it was enough. It was the beginning of trying to re-establish contact with him.

Katherine had died two years earlier in Chicago. Somehow, her death left me with a palpable urge to see Ocieola and Clarence, to connect with these people whose lives had distantly touched mine. The experience of loss that lies at the center of racial grievance seemed far less important to me than the loss of an opportunity to see my white grandparents before they died. The shadow of Katherine's death made me feel the injustice of my long, partly self-willed separation from my mother's people. The time had come when I simply had to choose not to be ruled by my ghosts if I was ever to find the means to be free.

Clarence, I learned, was living somewhere in Arkansas, hundreds of miles from Caruthersville. But where? After weeks of questioning, my mother finally admitted that the last time she checked he was living in a town called Mayflower. But she'd lost touch with him so many years ago that she had no idea whether he might have moved. She had no address or telephone number, but I might get them from her sister Raebeth, she offered. I braced myself, and, ignoring precedent, I called Raebeth. She was as evasive and discouraging as she'd been in that first contact we'd had more than a year before. On this part of the journey to the roots of my mother's family and into my own history, I would clearly be left to my own devices.

I dug out some road maps of Arkansas, but none of them showed any such place as Mayflower. I called information. The operator said there was no Clarence Smith listed in Mayflower, but there was one in a place called Lake Conway, the next town over from Mayflower. I grasped at this tiny scrap of hope and began calling the telephone number I was given.

I tried the number repeatedly, often three times a day. Either the line was busy or it rang without being answered. Finally, after about three weeks of this, a female voice answered.

I introduced myself quickly and said that I was trying to locate a relative that I hadn't heard from in many years. The woman was friendly, but unfortunately she couldn't help me, she said. I then called a C. B. Smith, a C. I. Smith, and many other Smiths. None of them could help. During a reporting trip in that region for my magazine, I called them all again, thinking that maybe the first calls had jogged memories, as they sometimes do, and would yield clues.

More weeks passed. After another talk with my mother, she finally volunteered that her father had married a woman named Ethie.* That gave me another avenue to pursue. There was an E. P. Smith, the operator said. I called the number often, without result. Finally a woman answered, but she couldn't help me, she said. She didn't know any Clarence Smith. I called her several more times, and she grew increasingly impatient. She knew no Clarence Smith, had never known a Clarence Smith, and would I please stop calling her? Finally I wrote letters to about forty Smiths in the area. I received no replies. That exhausted all the standard reporting techniques I could think of.

There was nothing for it but to go to Mayflower. After flying to

Memphis again, I rented a car and started driving, this time across Arkansas. Interstate 55 was a pretty stretch of road through lush fields and endless sky. It was very hot, and the car's air-conditioning failed with an alarming clatter that drowned out the cowboy music blaring from the radio. I rolled down all four windows, and hot dry air gushed in. When I turned onto Route 40, the landscape changed to a deeper green. The swampy Arkansas rice fields were sown in narrow, swirling, low-lying rows, like tattoos on the open land. There were no trees to block the horizon, and in the distance, maybe a hundred miles away, dark rain clouds were breaking in tattered sheets over places with names like Cotton Plant, Des Arc, Bald Knob, Beebe, and Searcy—which is pronounced like Circe, the beckoning siren who drove sea voyagers onto the rocks.

Four hours later I was in Little Rock, trying not to allow myself to fear being in a new place or to despair of ever finding Clarence. I drove into a gas station–convenience store in search of a good map and a telephone, so I could try again to locate either a Clarence or an Ethie Smith who would tell me, to my great relief, that, yes, they were the very people I was searching for.

Without the air from the highway rushing by, I was immediately engulfed in a wall of suffocating wet heat. There was no telephone. The cashier in the convenience store was a short, bearded man whose gaze rested on me for a meaningful thirty seconds, inviting the other patrons in the store to do likewise. But soon he turned his attention back to his customers, who resumed digging into their pockets to pay for their purchases—devil dogs, sodas, potato chips, ice-cream bars.

It wasn't much cooler in the store than in the car. I began leafing through the road maps, looking for Mayflower or Lake Conway. A stringy blond-haired man, stripped to his waist and with sweat staining the back of his blue jeans, brushed past me. Small, thin, and worn, he grabbed a six-pack of soda and took it to the register. The cashier was busy trading insults with a frail-looking black woman whose purchase he was ringing up.

"How much you askin'?" the cashier said, laughing.

"I ain't askin'," she said. "The customers asks *me*."

"I heard tell you was sellin' so cheap your customers thought they was somethin' wrong with the goods." The cashier chuckled and looked around for approval from the other customers waiting at the register. Some chuckled and waited for the woman's reply.

"Nothin' wrong with what I sell, dahlin'," she said. She looked at me and winked.

"Well, in that case," said the cashier, "you should try to bring the price up. Those sweet-potato pies you make are just about the best in these parts. You deserve to make a dollar on 'em."

He looked at me with a nod of approval. I saw my chance and asked him if he had a road map that would give me a good description of Mayflower and how to get there.

"If you think this heeyuh is the po-et of authority, you can't read too good." His voice was without humor. After a long pause, he continued. "This heeyuh is a gas station. Them maps is for sale."

I took one of the maps, marked "Little Rock and Vicinity." He smiled. I opened the plastic and unfolded the map. He smiled again.

"You won't find Mayflower in there. You city boys ain't as smart as they say," he said, for the benefit of his other customers. "I'll tell you how to get to Mayflower. You get back on the interstate and follow the sign going north. Mayflower is about twenty minutes' drive. If you'da been a little more polite, I woulda tolt you before. By the way, you don't have to buy the map."

I insisted. Then he insisted. Then I insisted. Then he insisted. Then I insisted. He took my money, and I left.

His directions were better than the map, which would have gotten me lost for sure. I followed his instructions exactly, and half an hour later I was in the middle of Mayflower. Which is to say I was exactly in the middle of nowhere. The closest place with overnight accommodations was Lake Conway, about ten miles north.

The Continental Motel, one of many small motels that dotted the roadside, was a clean enough looking place of one-story bungalows. The office was empty, but as I went in my nostrils were assailed by the powerful scent of curry. From the back came a tall, thin man whom I immediately took to be Pakistani. I was relieved to see him and took a deep breath.

" 'ello, mate," he said in a lively Cockney accent. I was sure it was a put-on. It wasn't. "A bit of a long way from 'ome, ahn't yeay?"

The motel owner introduced himself as Pranay Vijayargavan.* Born in Britain, he and his entire family—more than six members, including his grandparents—had immigrated to Arkansas in search of "business opportunities." His sister had been the first to come, he said, and, having scouted out the South, she had settled on Arkansas as a place to make money about eight years earlier. Pranay now ran the motel with his wife. There were, he said, quite a few Asians like himself who'd gone into "the hotel trade in these paahts."

"Here to teach at university, are you?" No, I told him, I was in Arkansas to see if I could locate my grandfather, whom I hadn't seen in more than thirty-six years.

"I understand," he said, with a warm smile. "A kind of journey to close all the loops, eh? Like taking a breath of fresh air, isn't it? Tying up loose ends and all . . ."

It was very much like that, like taking a breath of fresh air. If only I could make it happen, I knew that somehow I would feel freer than I ever had. Pranay's remark echoed in my head as I filled out the forms for my room. He briskly grabbed the room key and escorted me across the wide parking lot that fronted all the motel rooms.

Before I went in, I noticed an older white man sitting on a kitchen chair outside his room. He was looking at me. I looked back. He was wearing light yellow shorts, black knee socks, and brown shoes. His shirt was open down the front, with his ample paunch protruding from it. He was preening his stained white beard with one hand and holding a cup of coffee in his lap with the other. He watched as Pranay showed me in, and when he saw me watching him he tipped his hat and smiled. It was a strange, crazed sort of smile. Directly in front of him was a huge yellow Lincoln Continental parked about three feet from his door.

My room was dark and wood paneled, with brown shag carpeting, a brown-shaded lamp, a brown bedspread, and a very white bathroom with a cracked sink. There was a desk, too, and a hanging lamp that sent out what Victorian novelists called "a crepuscular light."

There was also a television set. Pranay turned it on.

"This is home," he said. "Feel free to call if you have any questions or troubles." And with the same crisp, friendly manner, he shut the door.

I felt an urgent need to get back to my task of locating Clarence, and I sat down at the desk with the Southwestern Bell telephone book covering Conway, Mayflower, Greenbrier, and Vilonia. It had this message painted on the cover: "The road to a brighter future begins by learning how to read. . . ."

I paged through it, and among odd names like Harvenious Smith, Slinkard, Sliger, Slover, and Lavon Smashey I saw "Clarence Smith." No address. Just the words "Lake Conway" and a phone number, the same one I'd originally been given by several phone operators. I decided to dial it one last time, on the odd chance that I might get lucky.

"Hello," came a woman's voice.

"Hello. Is this the Clarence Smith residence?"

"No, it isn't. Say, aren't you the same man who has called here so many times before?"

"I'm afraid so," I said.

"Well, it's the same as before," she said. I heard steel in that deep Ozark twang. "There's nobody here by that name, and you really should stop calling here."

I told her that I hoped she didn't think I was a crank caller. I said that I was in the area trying to locate my grandfather. "Well, he's not here," she said abruptly, and hung up.

As I walked out of my room for a breath of air, the man with the beard waved me over.

"You from Tennessee?"

No, I told him. I was from New York.

"I thought from your license plates that maybe you was. What you in these parts for?" he asked. His eyes were bloodshot. It was a drinker's gaze—I'd seen it often enough at home. "I'm just an old alcoholic," he said, smiling. "But I can tell you're looking for something." There was a great gentleness in his voice.

I told him my reasons for being here, surprising even myself by all I was saying to this stranger.

"I can tell you how to find your grandfather," he said. "I used to be a repo man for a car dealer, and once I traced my wife and two daughters clear across the United States after she quit me.

First, you're not going to get very much information with that northerner's accent of your'n." He smiled a no-insult-intended grin. "No offense, mind, but you've got to fry it up a little. Ya got to blend.

"And that head of yours. That hair. I think you'd better go and see if you can buy yourself a baseball cap or a tractor driver's cap, or get someone to sell you theirs."

He looked down at my feet. "And those shoes . . ."

I looked down. I still had on my fancy laced-up New York City work shoes.

"You have any gum-soled work boots?" I said I didn't. "Well, that would help, too. But the main thing is that accent."

"You know," he went on, "you can locate anyone you want if you really want to. In my line, it's easier sometimes than coming up cold like this. Say you're tracking people with bad credit who you've sold a car to. First, you make them give you the address of where they work. You give them one set of keys and then you keep t'other. If they're one day late at the end of the week in making their payments, you repo the car. That's what I do for a bit. You start hunting. A lot of times, if they really cut free and scoot, a bank connection will help. You get the local bank to give you any information that might give you an idea of where they might be headed, any relatives they might have listed on a credit application. If you track them, you see the car, you snatch it. If you're a professional repo man like I was, you get a flat fee. But you got to remember that you have to blend in a little. That's the way you do it . . ."

He smiled. I thanked him for the advice. After changing clothes, I got in my car and headed back to the area where I started my search, doubting if any of his tips about "blending" would help me track Clarence. I considered the matter of the accent more seriously, however. Maybe a slight change in accent would lower a few walls. I tried to make some adjustments, but I felt so foolish that I stopped.

The town of Lake Conway was little more than an exit sign off Route 65. But the lake itself is not small. It dominates the landscape, and it gave the air a sweet smell as I drove off the exit ramp and into the tiny village of Mayflower, with its one gas station and one restaurant. If this was where Clarence had settled, I could understand why: it looked much like a Caruthersville inundated by water. The lake appeared to have overflowed often. I wondered what Clarence would look like now, and in my mind's eye I tried to picture a rail-thin, stooped white man whose face I would recognize.

Not far along the road I was on now, Highway 365, laid down quite literally in the middle of a field, was another gas station and convenience store. Behind the counter was the owner, chatting with a local mailman. I asked them if they knew anyone by the name of Clarence Smith. They didn't. The mailman asked if I knew the first three digits of his telephone number.

"Four seven zero, I think." I'd written down the number of the listed Clarence Smith, on the off chance that he was my Clarence Smith.

"Well, you've got the right area, but Lake Conway is a huge place. There are more than a hundred homes in this area, and there are many, many Smiths up here. Maybe you should go to the police station."

That thought hadn't occurred to me before, perhaps because southern policemen evoked a kind of terror in me. In my mind, I saw them constantly cruising the highways at high speeds looking for trouble, their rebel cries echoing through the silent fields. Granted, that was my stereotyped fantasy, but my real-life experience with police officers hadn't been the best, either. I had been arrested once, as a boy in Norwalk, for trespassing on the grounds of a YMCA summer camp that was closed for the season. When I tried to run from the police, one of them threatened to shoot me. And my experiences with the police as a child in New York hadn't been much more encouraging. The thought of approaching the local police here gave me familiar twinges of compunction and doubt. But I was desperate. Nothing else I'd tried had yielded the slightest clue to Clarence's whereabouts.

As I drove along Route 365 looking for the local police station, the country road narrowed and wound past open fields with rolled haystacks as big as barns. Signs announced that I was in Faulkner County. Just over the county line, large signs advertised beer for sale. I went into one of the stores. A Mexican smiled and said, "Howdih, amigo. What can I get you?" When I told him that I was looking for the Mayflower police station, his face darkened. "Head back that-away. It's on the left side of the highway."

After a third pass, and a third stop for directions, I spotted the nondescript brown building. It looked as if it had been converted from a garage.

I told an officer in a black uniform sitting behind a desk that I was trying to find a Clarence Smith. Did he know of anyone by that name? He said he didn't know of any Clarence Smith, but he would make a few telephone calls to see if anyone in the area could help. I wondered if he was telling the truth. He placed a call and had begun talking when I thought to tell him that, by the way, if it would help, I believed Clarence's wife was named Ethie.

The officer looked up from the phone in surprise and straightaway told the person on the other end that he would call back.

"Well, why the hell didn't you say so, for God's sake?" I'd never heard an officer sound so cheerful. "I know Ethie Smith's house well. We're always sending police cars over there to help her out with him. He's that sickly old man."

The officer pulled out a map of Mayflower. He pointed out a bridge over the highway and said I should cross it and look for a street called Mimosa and then Lake Forest Drive. The street snaked through some woods, he said, and the last street on the right was Pine Tree. "By the way," said the officer, "I just sent a police car over there a few minutes ago." I didn't bother to ask why.

As I drove out of the parking lot and returned to the highway, I noticed a police car turn around and follow me, very closely. It was growing dark now, and the sun was casting deep shadows on the hot pavement when I turned onto Lake Forest Drive.

About a hundred yards from Pine Tree, the officer behind me flashed his lights and, through the car's loudspeaker, ordered me to pull over and get out of the car. I felt a sudden tightening in my stomach. I got out and stood near the door of my car, in case I had to make a sudden getaway.

He demanded to see my license, registration, and insurance card. As I walked over and handed them in through his open car window, I switched on the tape recorder I was carrying, as a protective measure in case something bad happened. If I was going to die or get arrested, there would at least be a recording to tell someone else what had happened.

"Whatall are you doin' around these parts?" The policeman, whose identification tag proclaimed him to be Officer Chip Gaines,* got out of his car.

I identified myself and told him I was in the area to visit family.

"What family would that be?" he asked firmly.

"A man named Clarence Smith," I said.

"I don't think you want to see Clarence Smith," said Officer Gaines.

"Why not?"

"He's had a stroke and he's resting," the officer said. Gaines was a young, sweaty, ham-fisted man with a red face and large ears.

He leaned against my car and waited to see what I would say. "You know Miss Ethie is worried about his health. She says you've come to hurt him."

"I don't want to disturb him, officer."

"I still don't think you want to see him," Gaines said firmly. "Why did you come here, anyway?"

"I need to see my grandfather before he dies."

Something softened in the officer's face. It was like a door opening. His whole body seemed to shift into a less oppositional stance.

"Well," he said, uncoiling his arms and moving back toward his own vehicle. "Let me see what I can do. Follow me."

With a sudden lurch, Gaines's car raised a cloud of dust so thick it engulfed us both. I hastened to follow him. He was moving so fast that I almost missed the final turn. Before I knew it, he had pulled into another dirt street and then into a small driveway. Just as suddenly, he got out of his car and told me to wait, then rushed inside a single-story trailer home with red flowers planted in front.

I noticed there were several neighbors in front of the house looking at me, their arms crossed, as I got out of my car. It seemed as if half the neighborhood was standing on Ethie's front lawn waiting for me.

Before I could close the car door, Gaines came out of the house, followed by a short, gray-looking woman wearing a faded purple shirt with stains down the front.

She strode rapidly over to my car with an angry look in her eyes. She was wearing glasses.

"Scotty," she said, "why did you wait so long?"

I did not know this woman. She did not know me. I was stunned that she knew my name, and her question stunned me even more. Her tone demanded an immediate answer, and it seemed pitched to the neighbors' ears. But I had no answer, and bristled at its presumption. I noticed that the officer and the neighbors were watching me still more closely, waiting for my reply.

"That's a tough question, and I can't answer it in ten seconds," I said. "What's happened in the past is past. I want to be free of that and move on. Can you understand? That's why I'm here. I'd like to see Clarence before he dies."

"Well, you cain't see him, and that's final," the woman said. "He's very sick. A visit from you could kill him. Scotty, I don't want you to upset Clarence."

I fought down the urge to curse at this small white thing who stood between me and the man who had helped to create the world I had spent my whole life fighting.

"You must be Ethie," I said. "Nice to meet you. Finally."

I extended my hand and smiled. Ethie seemed nonplussed. She looked at me and down at my hand for a very long second, and then grudgingly, almost involuntarily, she put her small, cold, bony hand in mine. The people in front of the house looked at one another. Officer Gaines folded his arms back across his chest.

Ethie squeezed my hand weakly and let hers fall quickly, decisively, almost in a reflex of revulsion, as though she hadn't planned to touch me at all. I watched her face, which showed a mask of disbelief, for she *had* touched me. I told her I didn't know Clarence had been ill. He was still just a white man to me. I had come to see him now for reasons that were larger than myself—for my children and their sense of family, which his absence had damaged. But I wasn't about to beg Ethie to allow me to see my own kin.

The neighbors seemed to be waiting for some sign of violence or temper on my part, but they weren't getting any.

Ethie appeared suddenly embarrassed. She paused again for several seconds, and then, for the first time, she seemed to open her eyes and look at me.

"You shouldn't have waited so long," she said. Silently, I agreed that she was right.

She visibly wavered, looking over her shoulder toward the neighbors and the police officer. "I'll let you see him, but only for a minute, and only if you promise me not to introduce yourself as his grandson. Now promise me that, Scotty. Promise me." She sounded frantic. "I'll let you see him," she said, "but only if you agree not to talk to him."

I smiled and agreed. It had almost become a game for me. Somehow, if I could only be patient and cool, watchful and wary enough, maybe I could use their own embarrassment, their own silent rules of social engagement, against Ethie and Officer Gaines. The trick was to say nothing in anger, to slick my way past the gatekeeper cop and the gatekeeper spouse long enough to do something I should have done long ago.

Ethie walked quickly toward the house. She led me, followed by Officer Gaines and a dark, high-cheeked, Native American–looking woman, through a screened-in porch and into a dark room so thickly carpeted that we could not hear our own footfalls. There was a ceiling fan, turned off, that hung low enough to touch without stretching. Ethie led us into a narrow kitchen, where we were greeted by a loudly yapping dachshund she called Peppy. I confess to wanting to strangle the poor animal. It was six o'clock, and still was unbearably hot.

Ethie climbed down two steps and pushed back a heavy white woolen curtain that divided the rooms and had the effect of sealing the heat in. Beyond the dimly lit kitchen was a sitting area with a television set. Seated in an overstuffed plush lounge chair against one wall was Clarence. He was asleep. The police officer and the next-door neighbor stood in the kitchen, shoulder to shoulder, watching me as I looked at him. Who was the intruder now? But I knew that I couldn't give in to the surge of anger I felt at their trespassing on this moment in my life. The officer would have just the excuse he wanted to cut the visit short and hustle me out of the house.

The nearly empty shell who was my mother's father, Clarence, sat propped up by the chair cushions, which made his frail body look tiny, almost like a child's toy. It seemed a brittle carcass, languid and spent, without suppleness or strength.

This man whom I had only once been permitted to meet, who had never stepped outside the narrow confines of his life as a white man to cast his spirit into mine, was fast asleep. His head was bent slightly to one side, his lips were slightly parted, and the skin of his face was drawn as tight as a drum against the bones of his face. The mouth was an empty socket. The eyes were shrunken and receding. A set of dentures lay on a small table. His glasses were resting on his lap. The television set next to him was turned off. How soundly he was sleeping! I knelt three feet away to look at his face and at this body, clothed in a white striped polyester shirt open at the neck and a tent-like pair of pin-striped slacks that were unhitched at the stomach. He looked well cared for.

Clarence was breathing regularly. I looked at his hands, which rested on the arms of the chair. They were perfect, a gambler's hands, long and elegant, with manicured nails, a fine, proud pair of hands. Perfect for cardplaying. They reminded me of the hands of my older son, Aaron, and of my older brother, Mark. My own hands have always seemed wide and clumsy, a workingman's hands. Clarence's fingernails, thick but carefully tended, were like the hedges in Ethie's garden. I imagined him dealing cards with these hands, and then the stories my mother had told me about him began turning in my head. Not knowing why, I felt glad that I had made this trip, as if the sight of these hands was the reason I'd come. This was my flesh and blood. I wanted to touch him, and I may have lurched forward to do so, without being aware of it.

"You don't want to wake him up," Ethie said, startling me. She was watching me impassively, and so were the police officer and her other guest.

"And remember, when he does wake up, I don't want you to say anything about your mother or the fact that you're his grandson. Promise me that. It might make him go into one of his fits."

"He's had some very bad fits lately," said Officer Gaines, almost apologetically. He was now leaning against the door frame. He looked embarrassed to be in the room.

"I call Officer Gaines here pretty often, don't I, Margery?" Ethie said to the brown-skinned neighbor.

"Yes, you do," said Margery. Margery's voice had a backcountry twang. She stared at me, her face a glacial mask.

I looked back at Clarence. "What kind of fits does he have?"

"Oh, Scotty," Ethie said, "you wouldn't believe his temper." It was half boast, half complaint. "Sometimes I have to sit on him just to keep him under control. I call the officers here to help me all the time. Scotty," she said, "why did you wait so long to come see him? It's too late now."

"Well, that's going to be a little hard to say. Maybe we can sit down and talk about it now," I said. "I came because I've gotten over the idea that it's too late. It's never too late, really, is it?"

Officer Gaines seemed to be getting more uncomfortable. He looked at Ethie. "Well," he said, "I'll be going now. If you need anything else, Ethie, anything at all, you know where to reach me."

"Thank you, Chip," Ethie said. "Must you go right away?"

"I reckon I do," said Chip, looking at me.

"I guess I'll be getting along, too," said Margery. "I'll be checking with you." Margery didn't look at me as she said this, but it was clear that she meant she'd be checking on me. "Good-bye, Scotty," she said. "It was nice meeting you."

"Your grandfather, that is, Clarence, had a heart attack four months ago, and he hasn't been right since," said Ethie, after Margery and Officer Gaines left. "We all thought he was going to die."

She walked back into the kitchen. "Can I make you some coffee?" It seemed strange, but somehow my being alone with Ethie seemed to help her relax.

After the heart attack, she told me, "the Alzheimer's" had begun to chip away at his mind, often making him difficult to control. His fits were like a child's temper tantrums, Ethie said. He would try to hit her. "I have to be hard on him sometimes, you know," she said fiercely. "I *have to*, Scotty. You don't know what kind of temper he has. Sometimes he raises his hand to me, and I have to tell him, 'You just try it, mister.' "

Pouring the coffee and sitting down at the small kitchen table, Ethie went on.

"There's one thing I want you to know right here and now. I never stole your grandfather from your grandmother. They were just about finished when I entered the picture."

I nodded my head.

"Your grandfather was the handsomest man, Scotty."

She left the room for a minute and came back with a portrait of them together. They were a handsome couple. Judging from the cut of their clothes and the seamless contours of their faces, the picture had probably been taken in the late forties.

"I was the one who made him quit gambling," Ethie said. "Did you know that? I told him it was gambling or me. He chose me. That's when we moved here. We worked, both of us, at a furniture store. I developed cancer, and they cured it. Clarence loved the work, and we needed the money."

I interrupted her. "Ethie, why didn't you or Clarence ever try to contact my brothers or me or anyone else in my family?"

Ethie sat up. "I blame your mother for that," she said. "She didn't call her father for twenty-seven years, and when she did it broke his heart, she was so hard on him. You have to understand their pride. They were hurt when your mother left them. You see, she was the one who left, not them. She kept her distance for years. And your mother and her sisters were always quarreling with each other."

I asked her how she had known it was me when I drove up to the house.

"You called here about two hours ago," Ethie said.

"You mean to say that I was calling the right number?"

"Yes, Scotty, it was me you were calling all those times. I wasn't surprised when you called and said you were here. Smiths never give up, so your persistence didn't surprise me at all."

"You mean you were the lady on the other end of the line? That was you all the time?"

"You can't imagine what telling you that did to me, Scotty, to have to tell you all them times that it wasn't the right number. It just tore me up."

"Did you tell Clarence that I called?" I heard an exasperated, angry tone rising in my voice.

"No," Ethie said, "I didn't. Why stir up unnecessary pain?"

"But don't you understand what you did? I was trying to contact my grandfather. You say his health started going into decline four months ago. I called you months ago, before that. You could have helped him and me, but you didn't."

Clarence moaned in the parlor. Ethie sprang from her chair, as though relieved to hear his voice.

"Hello, honey," she crooned. "Did you sleep well?"

Clarence mumbled something as she helped him from his chair.

"I think it's all right for you to introduce yourself, Scotty," she said.

I did so. But there was no glimmer of understanding in his face. I felt a thousand tender and bitter feelings rush in on me then.

"He doesn't remember you," Ethie said. Speaking to Clarence, she shouted, "Do you remember LaVerne?"

"That's my daughter," Clarence said.

"Do you remember her sons, Mark and Scotty?" she shouted, directly into his ear. But Clarence was gone again, like a worn-out battery that causes a radio to flicker on for a moment and then off. The radio was off now, the battery wasted away.

Sitting there in that hot room, I suddenly felt very lucky to have had the chance to make this connection. My bitterness evaporated. I had waited too long, it was true, and he had waited too long, and we had all waited too long and wasted too much time with our anger and grievances. We had simply accepted the idea that these losses were to be expected. We'd gotten on with our lives, but not really, because we had become lost to each other, and in some measure we had become lost to ourselves. In that moment, I felt a deep sadness at the loss we had all suffered, but I thought that at least some of the suffering hadn't been in vain. This trip was about feeling whole inside myself, despite the time it had taken for me to do so.

We had all put off a reconciliation that should never have been put off. Families quarrel. Sometimes they split apart, as mine had.

There were always a thousand excuses for that, and for my family race had been one of the more powerful excuses. There were always reasons that seemed good at the time. But there was no justification for what had happened in my family, really. It was cowardice and lack of passion, fronting as bravery, and it was going along with what other people told you was right. It had made us incapable of feeling. We were like people without any sensation in their hands, or without a sense of taste. We were dead to each other and to ourselves, and race had been our excuse. What had always seemed a necessary pose suddenly seemed a tragic waste of life.

I had needed a grandfather, but that was a pleasure Clarence could not allow himself because of his ideas of race. He had blamed race to make up for my mother's absence from his life. He'd been as much a prisoner of his fear as I was. I had wondered about Clarence my entire life, wondering what he was afraid of, and my bitterness over his fear had allowed me to make him into a monster he never deserved to be, any more than I had deserved to be one of the cast-off members of half my own family. I wondered then how it was that there could be such a thing as having a grandson who was the wrong color, and how much Clarence had lost in thinking that way. I would never know now. I had waited too long. I had been the wrong color to him, but more important, I'd learned to live with it, because that was what black people did.

Clarence was an old man, close to death. Ethie had him up from the chair now, shambling toward his place at the kitchen table. He shook like a leaf. His life had meant nothing to me. His arms were outstretched to keep himself from tripping over his unsteady feet. I moved to hold him up and felt the warmth of his shaky body, my flesh and blood. It felt odd being here, odd, and like an extraordinary piece of good luck.

I held onto his arm and guided his feet up the steps into the kitchen. I felt a lightness of spirit then, forgiving him for the past. Every inch of movement seemed such a mortal struggle, but I was able to support him, and it made me feel very important. I hadn't been strong enough, either, or brave enough. I hadn't had enough love to break through that wall of silence that had seemed so profoundly oppressive. But in this moment all that was in the past, and we would have to make the most of the time we had left together. I pitied this old man, and I felt a kind of love for him—until now a grandfather in name only—and I sorrowed for his having come up in a world where his choices were so limited, so finite, so brutal. He'd had to wait so long for a grandson.

Ethie and I eased Clarence gently, gently into his chair in the dim kitchen. Ethie turned on a lamp over his head, and I noticed for the first time that his disarranged hair was silver, like the hair of the black relatives I had loved and feared and who had loved me. I looked again at those hands, grown so weak with the years. I stepped down the stairs to retrieve his glasses and slid them carefully on his face.

Clarence looked at me and then looked at Ethie. "I've been an honest man all my life," he said, in a voice so weak it took everything I had to hear him. He was addressing no one in the room as he spoke those words, and I couldn't help feeling a twinge of resentment.

"That's right," said Ethie. "He was an honest man. He never lied to anyone." But I felt that he had lied about me. In Clarence's mind, it must not have seemed a lie to deny the existence of family members if they were of another race.

"I've been a very lucky man," Clarence said to no one in particular. He was talking about his days as he had lived them, and those days had not included me. I wanted to let this go, but it was proving very hard.

"I can see you have in a way," I said. "You've been taken care of very well." I felt grateful toward Ethie for having stuck with Clarence, even against the advice she'd received to put him in a nursing home. Here he was comfortable, at least, and had someone who loved him and cared for him.

"I would drive for miles and miles with John sometimes," Clarence said. But his voice trailed off.

"What did you do for miles and miles?" I asked, hoping to make sense of his words.

Ethie looked at me and shook her head. "He's gone again," she said.

"I never had an accident," Clarence said.

"That's not true, Clarence. You and I *were* in an accident once. You see, Scotty, sometimes he makes sense, and sometimes he don't."

I put my hand on Clarence's and said, "It's good to see you, Clarence. I'm glad we got the chance to see each other." Ethie shouted for Clarence to give me his hand. "It's Scotty's hand," she said. He did as he was told. Holding Clarence's hand somehow made me feel closer to him, helped me to understand that he was beyond questions now. He was too old to be bothered answering anyone's questions.

"Hello, grandson," Clarence said. He looked at me and smiled. "Pleased to meet you."

"That's your grandson, Clarence," Ethie said, suddenly happy and amazed that Clarence recognized me. "That's LaVerne's son," she said. Clarence faded out again, and we took him back to his armchair.

Ethie said that in the forty-one years she and Clarence had been married he had enjoyed near-perfect health, had had surgery once, but other than that had never needed to see a doctor. "You thank the Lord every day for good health," she said.

"You know," she said, "I'm so sorry for the way things turned out. It wasn't right. It was hard on them all when your mother left. They all felt so abandoned. She made it so hard on everyone. She's got nobody to blame but herself."

But people leave home all the time. It doesn't mean that anyone has the right to nullify their existence, I thought. I didn't carry the thought any further, for the subject of race seemed far removed from our conversation. It was time to put all that aside.

Ethie spoke of her quilt-making skills and showed me several of her creations. They were beautifully made starburst and pineapple patterns, and she said she had made them to keep off the cold in winter. I imagined Clarence wrapped and warm in one of them, and I decided I liked Ethie, after all, for staying with Clarence, alone by this lake, in winter and hot summer. Ethie said that my mother had always been an independent spirit, just like Clarence. She went into her room and brought out four pictures of Clarence's family, which she told me I could have reproduced if I promised to return them. She spoke of her own hardscrabble childhood in Dardanelle, Arkansas.

She talked about all the things Clarence had told her—how my mother would paint pictures of the Mississippi with her brother, Huddie, how sick her sister Betty Lou had been as a child, and how hard times had been in that part of the South when they were growing up. Clarence had worked as a foreman in lumber mills and furniture factories to support them, and in her view he had done as much as any man could to raise a family. He was a gambler when she met him, in 1949, and had been a gambler for twenty years before that, she said. She had liked Clarence's father, who died in 1970. Tall and good-looking, she said, he was known to his relatives as "the old gentleman."

Clarence had tried his hand at sharecropping, but he didn't like to get his hands dirty. He went back to gambling. When he quit gambling in 1952, he went to the Texas oil fields to work. He moved to Hayti, Missouri, in 1961, where he opened a gambling club called Smith's Bar. Then he sold it and moved to Mayflower, where he worked making furniture until age seventy-six, Ethie said. Their air-conditioning and heating bills often threatened to overwhelm them these days, she added. I could see she still loved and respected this temperamental man, even after forty-one years of marriage.

I made another promise to myself: I would not lose touch with this decent woman who had taken such good care of my grandfather.

I asked her when she had learned about my parents' marriage. She said that Ocieola had kept it from Clarence for a year, until he'd learned about it that day at the baseball game as a dirty joke from Ocieola's friend. LaVerne had phoned Ethie and told her about the marriage when I was one year old.

Ethie also told me she had called the neighbors after I phoned that I was in town, and they'd been scandalized that I would even try to make this visit. They were all sure I had come to harm Clarence and Ethie both. That was why so many of them had been in the yard, she said. "Everyone knew you were coming. I didn't know what to do."

She asked about my brother. I told her I had three of them. "You have three brothers? I didn't know." I started to tell her about them, but she interrupted me and said, "Scotty, don't go where you're not wanted. Don't go anywhere people don't want you to go. You won't change anything by doing that."

Clarence awoke then, and Ethie and I helped him again to the table. As she fed him, Clarence said to me, "It's so good to meet you, Scotty." Then he drifted off into his dreams.

It was dark when I left the house. I wanted to find Officer Gaines to see if he could tell me more about Clarence and to ask him how he knew I was in town. As I crossed the bridge to get back to the police station, I realized that he had been following me all the way from Ethie's house.

He stopped, and I pulled over next to him. We both rolled down our windows.

"Have dinner yet?" he asked.

I hadn't, I said.

"Well, why don't we get something to eat? There's a few things I want to tell you."

We drove to a local eatery. The only eatery in town, in fact. We both ordered Cokes. Gaines told me he was trying to get a new job as a state trooper.

"You know, I've got the second highest number of arrests for people driving while intoxicated. I've been shot twice, in the left hip both times. I've killed a man."

I asked him why he had followed me to Ethie's house. He said that after I called her, Ethie had frantically called the police, worried that I planned to do her and Clarence harm. He said that when he went into Ethie's house they had agreed that if I made trouble he would arrest me.

"I hadn't planned on letting you go anywhere near the house. But you know what changed my mind?"

I said I didn't.

"It was when you said you wanted to see your grandfather before he died. I had a grandfather who died on me like that, before I could say good-bye. I know what that was like, and I didn't figure I could be a part of something that would have it end like that for someone else."

I thanked him. If it hadn't been for him, I realized, I would not have seen Clarence at all. We promised to stay in touch.

I drove back to the Continental Motel, marveling at the miracle of discovery I had experienced. Two days later I was back in my own home, trying to remember everything that had happened to me, grateful to the deity who had allowed these things to happen as they had.

Clarence died three months later. I sent flowers, and a card thanking Ethie for having taken care of him so well. I called her once or twice after that. But the next time I tried to reach her I was told that the number had been disconnected.

Ethie had moved away, and, try as I might, I was never able to find her again.

My family in 1988. From left: John, Alan, me, LaVerne, Mike, and Mark.

TEN / Grace

Faith may be defined briefly as an illogical belief in the occurrence of the improbable.

—H. L. MENCKEN

I don't remember much about the drive back to Little Rock the next morning. I wasn't taking in much of the exterior scenery, because of my new feelings after meeting the white man who was my grandfather. Something had changed in me. I felt I'd begun to close a wound. I felt I had fulfilled some small part of my parents' dream to mend the terrible wound of race, a journey they had started but could not complete.

I was on my way now to Caruthersville, to see if I could find a way to visit Ocieola, my white grandmother, who had chosen to keep me out of her life for nearly three decades, and whom I had kept out of mine just as long. I had made her bear the weight of all those years from my early childhood, when I thought she didn't want me because of my darker skin, on through the years when I hadn't wanted her, because to me she had become just a white-trash hick living some-where in the South. I wondered how my life would be different if I had known Ocieola, if we had been less willing to give each other up. What lay between us now was time.

Race cannot succor deeper human desires. I wanted to be recognized as human by my own flesh and blood; to recognize my own grandparents and be granted my humanity by them without shame or apology. I, who had been born with the blood of both black and white tribes, had struggled too long with the ambiguities of my heritage to feel ashamed or arrogant about the emotional territory they had conveyed to me. People may not like their own flesh and blood, but at least most of them can articulate the reasons for their distaste. Somehow we had lacked a language even to do that. Both Clarence and Ocieola would soon drop from the narrow precipice of life. I wanted to know what my feelings for them were before it was too late.

The trip to Arkansas had given me a small triumph of spirit. And with it came a small hope that I might heal my deepest and oldest wounds. Perhaps I could finally address the deep racial fears that had flooded the basement of my soul and lingered there like stagnant rainwater. My childhood had been spent puzzling out a racial rift that was never of my own making. And as I grew older I became blind to the possibility of living without an abiding anger that derived from color hate. This was the effect of race on me: I lost sight of my power to see myself as a human being. I should have made the trip earlier, perhaps, but I hadn't tried. Race had made such a journey seem impossible. It was only after that first, unsuccessful visit to my mother's hometown that I had seen how deeply fragmenting the issue of my color had been, and how much of my own dreams had been lost. I wanted to stop wasting time. I was finally able to bear the weight of my own responsibility for allowing so much hatred to come between myself and my mother's family, for allowing fear to destroy my own sense of human connection.

None of this would have been possible without that first journey to Caruthersville. I wrote a brief essay about it afterward for the magazine I work for, *U.S. News & World Report,* in which I summarized my stunned disappointment at the outcome and my hopes for an eventual reconciliation. I expressed my anger at the rejection I'd experienced and confessed to an urge to burn an old picture of my mother's family in revenge.

Quite a number of letters came from readers in response to the piece. Many expressed the opinion that I had no business digging up the past, that it was best to "let sleeping dogs lie." Others said I should be ashamed for my "genetic wishful thinking." These readers seemed to think I had always wanted to be "white." They missed the point: I'd been rejecting all forms of racialized thinking.

One letter in particular made me laugh. The writer, a retired army lieutenant colonel then living in Springville, Alabama, said:

> *The results of miscegenation are predictable and are sure and certain. . . . The Cardinal, the Dove, the Blue Bird, all live in my front yard. They do not fight — neither do they interbreed. Coyotes, domestic dogs, Red Fox, Grey Fox, are all canines — but in their natural state, they do not interbreed. I would say to Mr. Minerbrook that in the real world we do not always reap the harvest of what we have sown — the majority of our harvest may have been sown by many, many generations. That is family.*

Another letter said:

> *I feel he should not have made the trip after the many definitely unwelcome warnings. I question: had he looked like his mother's side, had he been raised among his white relatives, would he have been this persistent in seeking out his black relatives? I doubt it!*

Others said I should go cry on my mother's shoulder, since she was the one who had married out of her race.

But several were more supportive. One writer was glad that I hadn't burned the picture of my white family. Some said they had black relatives in their own families, buried many generations back. One, from a woman in Atlanta, said she'd had a slave-owning great-grandfather who'd had several children by a black woman whose name was lost. A son of this union had traveled with his father as a "boot black," for the father didn't want him sold. "It matters not how I got here," the woman wrote, "but that I have arrived. . . . I admire black men and white women a lot who have the courage to love and to be together." After reading that, I didn't feel quite so alone.

Another writer, from Illinois, said that if I promised to "try to teach your family, descendants, friends, neighbors, and colleagues not to be bigots, I promise to teach mine. Keep trying. Someday, we'll get them all. Hope."

And so it was that I found myself heading back to Caruthersville on a hot July day roughly a year after my first trip there.

Driving north from Memphis again, I was more alert to the exterior landscape. I was surprised at how dramatically the fields around Caruthersville had changed. On that first trip, the lowland delta had been planted with soybeans. Now, instead of the verdant soybean fields, this whole region of northeastern Arkansas and southeastern Missouri was planted either in cotton or in an African form of corn called milo. In preparation for the trip, I'd read several farm-journal articles about the so-called "Africanization of American agriculture," the planting of African grains used, as milo was, for animal feed stocks. In the warm summer sun, milo grows from a single stalk out of a densely green, cabbagelike bush, and it turns a sulfurous yellow as it ripens. Planted row upon row in the damp Arkansas climate, it almost glows.

Closer to Caruthersville, I passed Steele, Arkansas, where the Japanese had created thousands of jobs for local workers at a steel-making plant. I now saw vast fields planted in a low-lying, naked-looking crop. It was the new breed of genetically engineered cotton, which doesn't grow as tall as its ancestors but bears far more fruit and is easier to harvest by machine. Soon the whole field would be alive as the cotton bolls burst open. Just outside Caruthersville, I spotted an old cotton gin being refurbished after years of disuse. It was one of many signs that cotton was making a comeback in these parts. I would later learn that this was due to a growing demand for the reengineered plant, which produces a stronger fiber.

Despite the revitalization of the cotton industry, Caruthersville seemed to have slipped still deeper into decay. Driving down Ward Avenue again, I thought the streets looked even more desolate. I had made an appointment for later in the day with the editor of the local newspaper, the *Pemiscot Post*, to find out more about the town. In a way, because of my first journey, I had lost some of my fear of Caruthersville and of what it had always represented to me. I wanted to know more about these people, to make them less abstract.

I had resolved to somehow talk my way into Ocieola's nursing home this time, and I thought I might get a clue from Raebeth's husband, Will. I wanted to speak to him outside his home—and away from Raebeth's influence—so I headed to the place where he worked.

In the year or so since I'd seen him, Will, a slight man of medium height, had let his hair grow almost to his shoulders. It looked great on him. Now he more nearly resembled one of the Native American chiefs he'd said he so admired. On the walls were a dozen portraits of them, mostly war leaders and peace advocates: Chief Joseph of the Nez Percé, who surrendered after being pursued to exhaustion by the American cavalry; the Lakota heroes Kicking Bird, Black Elk, and Sitting Bull, the Apache leader Geronimo, and other war chiefs. But their presence here spoke of a resigned man who had kept his spirit alive through these black-and-white portraits of dead men—men who had warned an unhearing America of what it could become and had become, a nation at war with its own blood. Will was part of that war, and so was I.

His workplace was neat and spacious. Soon he came out from behind a counter and looked at me. There was no look of surprise, either of friendliness or of hostility or regret, on his face. He merely looked weighed down by his private burdens. He didn't extend his hand to shake mine.

"Well, hello," he said. "What can I do for you?" He laughed.

I said I wanted to talk. His burdened face became even more downcast. The expression said, "I will bear my burdens silently if not gladly." He invited me to sit down next to a desk in a small corner near the entrance.

To warm him up, I asked what significance the portraits above his desk had for him. They were the last of a proud race of people, he said; the United States shouldn't have done what it had to them.

I asked whether that wasn't just as true of the way America had treated the Africans, whose labor had been exploited without mercy or compensation while giving the nation its economic and political substance and shape. Will smiled and said he supposed that was true.

Several customers came in as we sat there, and he dealt with them in a friendly, relaxed, and competent manner, giving no indication that he felt any awkwardness about my presence.

"You know," Will said, leaning back, "when your story came out in the magazine about your being black and having a white family in Caruthersville, we didn't know anything about it until a certain woman in town saw it. People started asking questions about who the people were in the picture. One woman, who is very well connected here in town, came here and said she thought she knew who the people were, because she thought she recognized their faces. She came here and said, 'Do you know any of these people here?' "

Will took a long deep breath and stretched back in his chair. It was clearly difficult territory for him, being linked with someone who, in his mind, had married out of her race and had nonwhite sons who were now grown men. The chickens had come home to roost.

He brought his chair back to its natural position and looked at me. "Well, the best thing I could say when she asked me if I knew anyone in the picture was, 'Naw.' She said, 'Well, I'm just going to find out who it is.' She knew who it was, you see. She called everyone, got everyone in town calling around. She went to the post office and asked them whether there was a person in any nursing home in town they might know who looked like the person in the picture. The next day she came out here and started going on about it again, about how she was going to find out who it was, and then I had to sit her down and I said, 'Let me stop you right now,' I said. 'Let me tell you all about it.' I said, 'It bothers Raebeth so very much, and I didn't want to say anything to anyone about it, and that's why I lied to you.' "

There it was, then: my life as a lie these white people had to tell to protect themselves; my life as some fearful thing that could embarrass them, shame them, cause them pain. I was suddenly glad to be back in Caruthersville, simply to hear that the feelings I'd grown up with as a child and a young man were not illusions, but were quite real.

Will continued. "I told her, 'Yes, I know who it is, yes, in that nursing home.' I said I wanted Raebeth to know about her questions first, and everything, before I talked to her again. So she said, 'In that case, it won't go any further. I won't say anything more about it.' So I went on and told Raebeth, and she said someone else had already called her about it, someone who had already discovered who she was. And Raebeth got all shook up. I said, 'Don't get all bothered and all and everything.' I said to her, 'The best thing to do is to stop it right now. Say, "I'll tell you who it is right now." ' This lady knew your mother and everything, and she said, 'Well, where is she now?' and I told her and everything. And she said 'Well, it won't go any further. I won't ask and I won't try to find out any more.' Some people were trying to call her to find out. The whole town was. She's the kind of woman, you know, who when she wants to find something out she'll find out. I told her, 'I'll just tell you right now. Put an end to it now.' "

I felt an odd rush of emotion—both sympathy and rage—when he finished. To be told your life is someone's secret is a painful thing. I found it hard to sit still and hear Will talk so innocently about protecting his wife and himself from the embarrassment of my being alive. It brought back all my frightened childhood feelings of being unwanted by Mom's family because my father was not white, because I was not white—and therefore not acceptable to them—and all that anguished rage at the teachers who reminded me of these people. In that moment, I felt such hatred for Will that I wanted to kill him in his office. I wanted to kill him for all the people in my father's family who had been marginalized and locked out because they were not white. I wanted him to die for making me feel as I did in that instant. But thinking this way only made me feel things I didn't want to feel anymore.

I had considered long and hard the pain my return to Caruthersville would cause my mother's sister. Was it really necessary? I had decided it was necessary to me. I was filled with a strange, stinging mixture of pride, hot anger, and shame at the thought that this small man could affect me so strongly that I wanted to take his life. He talked on, but I couldn't hear him. I couldn't listen. It was all I could do to say a prayer: Please, Lord, I came here to overcome myself. Please don't let me hurt this man as I've been hurt.

I took a deep breath and tried to listen. After a moment, I realized

that Will had been reduced to trying to defuse the impact of my assertion of a human identity that went beyond race. He would have to
face the prospect of seeing his friends and neighbors turn against him
because a deep, deep secret had been revealed that might place him
in the same predicament my mother had been put in. His embarrassment was simply another mountain for me to cross, and my presence as a family member was another mountain for him, too. I hoped
he'd make it. I knew I would.

I thought of other things as well: of how little I knew about the
South, of how little I knew about the country that had shaped my
life. In the North, people talk to each other in stutter-step memo-
randa. We don't linger in conversation. It makes us uncomfortable.
But here, in this small town, the rhythm of conversation had its own
life. People were less careful in what they said and how they said it.
They revealed themselves, their weaknesses and strengths shielded
only by their fear of shame and humiliation.

The South was different in ways that I had not understood until
now. It was a place of open secrets. By coming into town and asserting
my identity, I threatened to reveal the secret that would redefine
Raebeth and Will in the eyes of their community, and thus redefine
their place in the narrow hierarchy of Caruthersville.

Will continued in his polite manner. "As soon as I knew about
your story, I felt funny. People stuck that picture in my face out of the
clear blue sky and said, 'Do you recognize this person?' Then they
asked me, 'Do *you* know this Scott Minerbrook?' And I said, 'Naw.'
Well, what could I say? Somebody else had seen the picture and
recognized Raebeth and called Raebeth and told her, and Raebeth
had already seen it and she hadn't said a word to me about it. She
hadn't said a word to me about it. She already knew, you see."

Even now he was trying to keep his wife out of trouble. I felt a
twinge of admiration for his chivalry. Still, I hadn't come this far only
to go away.

"What is Raebeth afraid of?" I asked.

"Of people talkin'," he said. "People can be real mean. She's afraid
of what people would say and what people would think."

I changed the subject to Kay, their daughter. I asked him to tell
me about her. He said she had three kids, aged eighteen, twenty-six,

and twenty-seven. I wondered if I would ever meet them, and I asked Will if he thought they'd be interested in meeting me. "I don't know," Will said. "They don't know anything about you."

It was time to bid Will good-bye. But before I left, I told him that he had made a mistake in his life. Maybe we both had: denying our own flesh and blood had only made us all poorer. The distance between us had made an important part of both our lives a lie. There was no difference in our blood. "I suppose you're right," he said. "But you don't have to live here."

The *Pemiscot Post*, my next stop, had run story after story about one of the region's major employers, a wheel-manufacturing plant, that was moving out of town. A few months before, the Climax, the bar where Clarence had worked before starting his own business, had burned to the ground, in a suspicious fire that had killed a fireman. Economic confidence had been further shaken by false predictions of a coming earthquake, which had sent the residents into a frenzy of hoarding and had caused the schools to be closed.

On my first trip, I hadn't had time to meet with Ralph Clayton, the editor of the *Pemiscot Post*, the larger of the two newspapers that cover the Boot Heel region of Missouri. I had heard, through my contacts in the news industry, that he was one of the most devout, even strident, defenders of the Boot Heel.

Recent stories about the area hadn't been flattering. One, in *St. Louis Magazine*, had opened with a general description of the town of Hayti, Caruthersville's next-door neighbor, and a complaint from one of its eminent citizens, C. W. Reed. Reed, who was then a sixty-seven-year-old farmer, said that he was "tired of the newspapers always painting us as this feudal land of peons." But the piece had quietly asserted that such was indeed the case. It was a town of "poverty so visible and appalling (if you know where to look) that you can't wait to get in your car and drive away and forget you ever laid eyes on the place, erase the broken shanties and scratchy roads and skinny dogs from your mind as if they were nothing more than another episode from 'The Twilight Zone.' "

I entered the small newspaper office and asked for the editor. Out came Clayton, a short, stroppy man with a gleaming pate and a pair of dark glasses that gave him a thoughtful look. When I asked him about the town's apparent problems—its hardscrabble rural poverty, its dying economy—he bristled.

He complained that every year the *Kansas City Star* would send a reporter to do a piece about what he called "the dusty roads of Pemiscot County." He said the Boot Heel was a politically and economically neglected section of the state. There were few jobs here, and those who had them kept them, so there were few prospects to attract job seekers. Caruthersville's public officials tried hard to attract new business, but it was hard, since the out-migration of talent was so brisk. I thought of my mother having left Caruthersville so many decades earlier. The result, Clayton went on, was a fierce competition among the neighboring towns for what jobs and state services were available.

"People think of us as 'old dusty roads,' " he continued, "but we've got some paved ones, too. The problem is that when they send a reporter down here from Kansas City or St. Louis, we always end up being described as a community of washing machines on the front porch. One reporter was so dumb, she wrote that as you come into Caruthersville you could see the crane of a shipyard over a rise. Well, that isn't a rise. It's a levee. She didn't even know the difference between a rise and a levee."

Clayton went into considerable detail about the wrongs of the past. He allowed as how the whole idea of putting the Boot Heel in the state of Missouri had been a mistake in the first place; the region should have been part of Arkansas, which he described as the area's true spiritual geography in any event. "We would have been happier," he said. "If you look at the map of Arkansas, you can see we were cut out of the state."

Sitting with him at his desk in the *Post*'s front office, I had difficulty concentrating because of the strong solvent fumes coming from the printing presses in the next room of the single-story structure.

Clayton complained some more about neglect by the state and about how nobody at the state level understood this county where he'd spent his entire life. "The University of Missouri says that Pemiscot County has one out of five who can't read or write. It may be true, but how would they know? We're on the top of every bad list there is, and nobody seems to want to do anything but beat up on us and not help us."

After another fifteen minutes or so of this, I parted with Clayton by asking why he had repeatedly returned to the issue of his grievances and why they seemed uppermost in his mind. "Well, when everyone dumps on you the way we are dumped on," he said, "I guess it kind of gets to be a habit."

As I walked out into the full heat of the afternoon, a black woman stopped me in the parking lot and pressed a piece of paper firmly into the palm of my hand. She was smiling at me. I thought she was probably an evangelical, or maybe a salesperson, or maybe she had followed me out of the building and was flirting with me. I was surprised by her approach.

Then she introduced herself as Justine Clark,* an employee of the newspaper. Did I have a minute to talk?

"Sure."

"Are you Scott Minerbrook?" she asked.

I nodded.

"You need to come see me as soon as possible," she said. Her voice was freighted with warning. Where? I asked. She looked at my hand without saying anything, and when I indiscreetly looked at the paper she said, "Don't look at it until you get into your car." It all seemed like part of some peculiar intrigue.

When I got into my car, I saw that the paper bore the name J. Clark, along with an address and a telephone number.

I called the telephone number a few minutes later from a pay phone.

"Are you Justine Clark?"

She said she was. "How soon can you come to see me?" she asked.

I told her I was on my way to interview some people at city hall — an excuse to evade her. I asked her what she wanted to tell me and why she sounded so urgent.

"If you meet me at the following address, you'll see." She gave me another street number and name, and said I should meet her there at five that evening. I agreed to do so.

I decided to take a drive out into the countryside, past Braggadocio and out as far as a town called Cotton Plant. I thought about all the stories my mother had told me of her life in Caruthersville, and how those stories had shaped my attitudes about race and about myself. I thought about the world she'd entered after leaving Missouri, and the way she'd strived to improve her life. She'd chosen a life far more complex and dangerous than the one in Caruthersville had ever been, full of excitement and difficulties, and she had raised a family of four boys on sheer strength and a will that could never be defeated. In some measure she had achieved her dreams, but she had never completely achieved the one that mattered most: to create a family of her own that *was* her own. In many important ways race had cheated her, too. She had half-black children who didn't understand where she'd come from. I understood the power of my need to see this place—to see for myself what she had risen from.

I drove back into town and found the house where Justine Clark had asked me to meet her.

I was greeted there by a tall black woman who was dressed as if she was on her way to a church service. She introduced herself as Denise Kent,* and welcomed me into the house, which she said she owned. I had thought I was going to Justine's house, but Justine apparently had a scheme.

Denise invited me to sit down in the kitchen and offered me a cup of tea.

I declined.

Then I spotted Justine, who was sitting at the kitchen table. She greeted me with the same wide and handsome smile as she had outside the newspaper office. She explained that after my magazine article had appeared she'd received calls from several prominent Caruthersville people, one of whom said she was related to Ralph Clayton's wife. This woman had said she hoped I would return to Caruthersville. If I did, she told Justine, there was someone she knew who would have the courage to help me get in to see my grandmother. "Without touching off the alarms," Justine added.

Justine looked at Denise and then she looked at me. Denise was smiling. "You know some people at the nursing home, don't you, Denise?"

Denise nodded. She looked at me. Then she picked up the telephone, dialed a number, and spoke quietly into the receiver. "Hello, Melissa?* Listen, can you tell me what room Miss Ocie is in? Room 206? You remember that article in the news magazine? Well, I have Miss Ocie's grandson here now, and he says it's important that he meet her before she dies. She's not dying any time soon?" Denise chuckled. "I need you to make sure that there are no supervisors in that area, because I'm going to bring him by now. We'll be there in twenty minutes."

In Denise's car, where we all piled in, I felt a strong elation. If it hadn't happened that Justine Clark saw me in the newspaper office that day, I might never have had this opportunity.

Justine remarked that she knew a woman who had known my mother when they were schoolgirls.

"You know," said Justine, "these people are so proud of their little town, they need to know that they can keep everything carefully under their thumb. They are so screened off from the decent things they can do for one another, it is just wrong. This is one crazy little town."

The nursing home was located in an open field next to a baseball diamond. The three of us walked to the visitors' entrance and were met by a nurse, who greeted Justine and Denise. She smiled at me and pointed toward Ocieola's room.

The room was dark as I walked in. Denise and Justine waited in the hall, chatting with their friend. The curtains were drawn against the afternoon light. There were two elderly people in their beds, but I couldn't recognize either of them. I looked at one and then the other, until Denise came in and said, "That's Miss Ocie there."

Ocieola was half asleep, with her legs drawn up almost to her chest. I was sure that this pose, common to someone in a coma, meant I was already too late. I looked around, and on the wall opposite her bed I saw pictures of her white relatives. There was Raebeth's daughter, Kay, with her husband and her three sons. There was a picture of Raebeth, Betty Lou, and my mother—who was the most beautiful of the three—taken, it appeared, when they were in their late teens. There was a picture of Ocieola's mother, the Indian-looking Nancy Barnette, who had married an Irishman named

Hinchy. There were pictures of Betty Lou's husband and their children. There were even pictures of the children of Raebeth's dead son. There, in full display, were all the white ones I had never known. The brown ones were all missing: me, my brothers, my father—there were no pictures of any of us.

There was, of course, no great surprise to me in this. It seemed as if time had stopped for Ocieola when my mother was still a young woman, even before she'd gone away to Chicago and before she'd married my father. The adult LaVerne had simply dropped out of Ocieola's universe, along with any other odd or unpleasant details of her frontier woman's life.

Curled up on the bed, Ocieola seemed so small, so fragile, that I couldn't help but feel a great tenderness toward her. The hospital bed seemed to swallow her. There was a thick smell of age and fatigue in the room. Ocieola was eighty-six years old. Next to the bed was a wheelchair.

I called Ocieola's name. She didn't move. I called her again. She stirred, half awake. She blinked her eyes hard. I called her name once more, and she awoke with a start. With great effort, she got up on one elbow. She was wearing a white shift.

"Ocieola?"

"Who's that?"

She seemed startled. I had a strong impulse to leave. This was a mistake. What if the things Raebeth had said were true, that a visit from me might damage her health? Maybe she would be so startled by my visit that it would make her ill.

"It's me, your grandson Scott."

"Who?"

"You remember me? Your grandson." Somehow I didn't feel comfortable enough to take a seat.

She blinked her eyes. For a full thirty seconds there was no response. I was sure then that the cause was lost and that the reports of her advanced senility were true. She would never remember me. I turned to go.

Suddenly Ocieola sat up.

"What are *you* doing here?" she demanded. She cleared her voice and spat into a pan.

"I'm here to see you," I said. "Finally. It's taken some doing."

"*You* aren't supposed to be here," she said. Her voice was getting stronger. It had a distinct steely edge now. Maybe, I thought, she was merely being curt. "*Who let you in?*"

"It's good to see you, Ocie. It's been a long time."

Ocieola sat up straight. She blinked her eyes.

"What do you want, Scott?" she asked.

"I came here to see you."

"Yes, I guess I knew you would."

I lied and said that she was looking well.

She said she wasn't. "I'm old," she said.

"What?" I asked. Her speech had become slurred.

"I'm old."

I said I'd noticed that there was a picture on the wall of LaVerne as a girl, but no pictures of me, my children, my wife, my father, or my brothers.

"Yeah," said Ocieola. "She was a pretty girl. A very pretty girl. I miss her."

I stood over Ocieola and looked at her hands. They were exactly like my mother's: small but strong, with stocky peasant's fingers. My mother had supported a family with those hands, and Ocieola had fed her family by chopping cotton with hers. I had always been amazed that my mother could produce such wonderful artwork and clothing designs with hands as unshapely, almost blunt, as hers. Even my mother had called them unsightly. But now they seemed beautiful. As I looked at Ocieola, I was amazed to see that my mother had also inherited her small nose. I realized then that this was probably what my mother would look like in her late years, and I felt that in some way I'd been given the gift of seeing into the future by looking at my past. In twenty years maybe I would look something like this myself, though I nourished the hope that my African and Native American blood would weigh more heavily in my favor.

"She looks a lot like you," I said.

Ocieola paused. "Thank you," she said.

"LaVerne loves you very much."

"I know she does. I love her, too."

"I know you do. She says you write her letters."

"I haven't heard from her in a long time. But I have a painting of hers she sent me without a letter. She didn't write a word. She sent a painting in an envelope."

"Did you understand the painting?"

"Pardon me?" Her words were becoming more slurred. This visit was tiring her out.

"Do you understand the painting she sent you?"

"No. Not really."

My mother's recent paintings tended to be abstract.

"I mean, it was beautiful, that painting," Ocieola said, "but I didn't understand it. You know, her and her brother, Huddie, used to paint along the banks of the Missouri River."

"She used to tell me about that when I was a child. She raised me on stories of how she and Huddie would disappear and paint for hours on the levee. She still has some of those paintings.

"I think it always hurt my mother that you abandoned her after she married my father."

"Pardon?" Ocieola's tone changed to the challenging I don't want to hear this tone my mother always used when she was feeling argumentative or cross.

"I think it hurt her badly that her family rejected her after she married my father." I could not bring myself to say that this drama of rejection and grievance was still going on. I was here to try to rewrite the script at last, so that I could get on with my own life, could forget the rage and pain and bitterness that had always been a poor substitute for the love I'd wanted to feel but could not.

"It was just one of those things," Ocieola said indifferently.

"I guess it was," I said. "It's important for you to know, though, that it's not too late for us to be here for each other, while there's still time left."

Suddenly Ocieola started. "What's that?" she asked, pointing at me.

She was distracted and hadn't heard, or had chosen not to hear, what I had just said.

"It's a camera," I said. "I was going to take some pictures of you."

"I'm not sure I would photograph well," she said, a hint of vanity in her voice. I laughed. I said I would love to take her picture, that it would be good to have a photograph to show my children.

"Well, you can have a picture."

"But I have to get you outside to do that."

"I can't do that," she said. She sounded afraid, wounded almost, that I should ask to be seen with her in full daylight.

"I can't go outside."

"Why not?"

"I just can't. I don't feel like it."

I tried cajolery. "You feel you can't? I'd love to have a picture of you. It's a little dark in here."

"Turn on the light," she said.

"Can I ask the nurse to wheel you outside where there's enough light?"

"No, I can't go outside."

I stopped pressing her and asked if I could sit down. She agreed, and I thanked her, rather too formally.

"I'm sick, Scott," Ocie said. "I have to lie down."

"I'm sorry," I said. "Go ahead. You can lie down if you want to. I'll put the covers over you."

That wasn't what she meant. She was inviting me to leave. She remained sitting upright. "That's all right," she said.

"If I send you a picture, will you put it up?"

"Yeah. You know, there's a lot of my family that I don't have pictures of."

She pointed to one of the pictures. "That's Kay."

Kay was pretty. I remembered then how deeply disappointed my mother had always been that Kay had followed her mother's lead and dropped out of touch.

I told her about my two children and about my wife. Ocieola said she had seen pictures of them.

It was time to go. "I love you, Ocie. It was very good to see you." Much better, I wanted to add, than I had expected. "Is there anything I could get you?"

The nurse came in. She asked Ocieola if she wanted the light turned on, and without waiting for an answer she turned it on.

Ocieola snapped, "What did you do that for?" The nurse apologized and left.

"Why were we out of touch for so long, and why didn't you let me come to see you earlier?"

"Scott, you know how it is. That's the way it's always been."

I was suddenly very weary. There was nothing else to say.

"You have to go now. I have to go to bed."

She paused for a moment. "You're a fine-looking boy," she said. "Tell LaVerne I love her. Tell her to write to me."

Just then the same nurse swept in again. She told Ocie it was time to go outside. "*I don't feel like it,*" said Ocie. The nurse told her not to get so upset. Ocieola turned out her night-light and lay down. I told her I was sorry we'd waited so long but I was glad we'd finally met.

"Okay," she said. "Good-bye."

"Good-bye," I said.

"Tell LaVerne I love her," she repeated.

I kissed her and left the room, feeling that I had somehow closed a chapter of grievances. I was surprised that the feelings of anger and shame and sorrow could drop off as suddenly as they did. But somehow, as I walked back out into the hot Caruthersville afternoon, I felt more free than I ever had in my life. I had put so much of the weight of racial blame on Ocieola, when it didn't truly belong on her shoulders alone. We were all guilty and all innocent in my family. By assuming some of that blame for things unsaid and undone, I felt I had cleared the way to live a more honest life, without fear or shame.

I had started this journey in part because I was concerned about the effect racial divisions might have on my children. I underestimated their power. I underestimated my own strength and the strength of Ocieola. Now, I felt I owed much to her power. I had discovered from her that I didn't need my hate so much. I could let it drop from me, like sand off the back of a dump truck. I needed to close the old wounds so that I wouldn't teach my children misguided racial lessons, which would only slow them down in a changing world. In the end, the religion of race diminishes each of us and makes us too small to contribute to the greater good. The part I had never acknowledged in my parents' story was that both my father's family and my mother's family had equally strong claims to dignity.

I wanted my children to know that, too. By seeing Ocieola and Clarence, I felt I had something more to offer them, and had also added something to myself. The trip had made me look more deeply into what the people there had contributed to my life. My mother's people were strong, but they had used their strength to limit themselves. My father's people were strong, but they hadn't realized how their dreams of equality were imperiled by the virus of race hate.

Thinking of these things, I felt it would be better, this time, to let Raebeth alone. I didn't want her to think that I was pressing her to change her feelings about the past and the future, if they were her crutch. In the months that followed, I called Raebeth and Ocieola regularly, merely to see if they were in good health. Clarence's death made their lives seem more precious.

I began sending cards to Ocieola each Christmas, each New Year's, each spring, when the fields around Caruthersville show the first faint shades of green. She held on to life in that nursing home until 1993. And, though I did not see her again, I didn't need to: I had already said my good-byes. Ocieola was a strong, determined woman. But I think she let her fear of the world crowd out her choices. Maybe she wasn't strong enough. I don't think she was as strong as Katherine, my father's mother. I wished they had known each other. Maybe Katherine could have taught Ocieola how not to give up so easily. Maybe Ocieola could have taught Katherine to let go a little more.

In my mind, both my parents' families belong to a tradition of pioneers. I think of them all this way now: as people who crossed boundaries. And I think of the inward boundaries I have crossed in following them. Going to Caruthersville, I knew, was an attempt at making a world that had always frightened me seem a little safer by seeing it on its own terms. Going there, I felt that my interior landscape had changed. I felt I had pushed back a river and found fertile ground where I could allow my own dignity to take root. I vowed to nourish this altered landscape simply and bravely, as a pioneer might on looking at this land for the first time. It was a blessing that comes from claiming one's family for the first time, and the measure of freedom I had been seeking all my life.

Permissions